Annekatrin Meißner, Suleika Bort, Erinch Sahan (eds.)
Doughnut Economics for Regenerative Business Design

New Economies | 5

Editorial

Our current economic systems are not geared towards the satisfaction of needs and the care for our environment and our fellow human beings, but solely towards growth and profit. The consequences of this are a constant reproduction of social inequalities along the axes of class, *race* and gender as well as the isolation of individuals and the destruction of nature.

The **New Economy** book series provides explanations for these multiple crises of our time and opens up possibilities for a sustainable, solidarity-based economy. It provides an editorial space for heterodox empirical research, paving the way for pluralistic, interdisciplinary and self-reflexive economics.

Annekatrin Meißner works as a postdoctoral researcher and managing director of the Institute of Applied Ethics in Business and Education at the University of Passau, Germany. There, she also graduated in intercultural and business studies with a focus on the Ibero-Romance cultural region and completed a PhD in social philosophy and business ethics. In her teaching and research, she concentrates on the ethical foundations of sustainable transformation within business and the economy, and on broader questions of business ethics and global responsibility.

Suleika Bort holds the Chair of International Management and Social Entrepreneurship at the University of Passau, Germany. She graduated in business administration and holds a PhD from Mannheim University. Her research is placed at the intersection of international management, sustainability and social entrepreneurship.

Erinch Sahan is the associate director for Investment at the Joseph Rowntree Foundation. Until 2025 he was the business and enterprise lead at Doughnut Economics Action Lab. Previously, Erinch served as the CEO of the World Fair Trade Organization, taught sustainability at various universities, and was in leadership roles at Oxfam, the Australian Government and Procter & Gamble. He has served on several boards, including the Social Enterprise World Forum and Finance Innovation Lab.

Annekatrin Meißner, Suleika Bort, Erinch Sahan (eds.)

Doughnut Economics for Regenerative Business Design

Case Studies and Critical Reflections

[transcript]

We would like to thank the Dr Hans-Karl Fischer Foundation for its financial support of the Institute of Applied Ethics in Business and Education at the University of Passau, which contributed in a significant manner to realise this book project. The open-access publication of this book was funded by the Open Access Publishing Fund of the Library of the University of Passau.

Bibliographic information published by the Deutsche Nationalbibliothek

The Deutsche Nationalbibliothek lists this publication in the Deutsche Nationalbibliografie; detailed bibliographic data are available online at https://dnb.dnb.de

2026 © Annekatrin Meißner, Suleika Bort, Erinch Sahan (eds.)
transcript Verlag | Hermannstraße 26 | D-33602 Bielefeld | live@transcript-verlag.de

Cover design: Maria Arndt
Cover illustration: created with Canva, provided by Doughnut Economics Action Lab
Printing: Majuskel Medienproduktion GmbH, Wetzlar
Print-ISBN: 978-3-8376-7652-5 | PDF-ISBN: 978-3-8394-7652-9
ISSN of series: 2942-1489 | eISSN of series: 2942-1497

Contents

Doughnut Economics for Regenerative and Distributive Business Design

Annekatrin Meißner, Suleika Bort, Erinch Sahan

In this chapter, we introduce the concept of Doughnut Economics and explain its relevance, its forward-looking nature, and why we consider this concept to be at the core of a regenerative and distributive business design. We explore the question of corporate responsibility in reshaping economic structures, drawing on Iris Marion Young's (2006) understanding of global responsibility. The underlying assumption of this book is that changing unjust economic structures requires both an outer organisational transformation, i.e. changes beyond the borders of an organisation and an inner organisational transformation, i.e., changes in the design within the organisation, which are interconnected and cannot be viewed in isolation. We then discuss how organisations[1] can transform with the help of a regenerative and distributive business design. Finally, we present the underlying methodology for the selection of the case studies and the structure of the book.

Introducing the Concept of Doughnut Economics

Climate change, biodiversity loss and growing societal inequalities are only some of the pressing issues of the 21st century that defy simple answers. In 2025, Earth Overshoot Day fell on July 24th, indicating that, on a global scale, humanity is consuming nature 1.8x faster than our planet's ecosystems can regenerate (Global Footprint Network 2025). One way of explaining the overshoot is due to the fact that humanity consumes resources faster than the speed at which these resources can be replenished. Such excessive use undermines the security of essential resources. The effects of ecological overexploitation are visible in phenomena such as deforestation, soil degradation, biodiversity loss, and the accumulation of carbon dioxide in the atmosphere, which contribute to more frequent extreme weather events and a

---

[1] Our main focus in the book lies on for-profit companies but we also address not-for-profit organisations. Thus, we will use the term organisations to include them both.

decline in food production. Some of these effects are already in place and cannot be reversed.

Lewis Akenji, member of the Club of Rome and of the board of the Global Footprint Network, states:

> "Overshoot will end. The question is how: by design or by disaster. A planned transition gives us better security than ceding to the whims of a planet thrown off balance by overshoot" (Club of Rome 2025).

The concept of planetary boundaries, developed by Johan Rockström and colleagues in 2015 and revised in 2019 and 2023, highlights that as of 2023, six out of nine planetary boundaries have already been crossed (Climate Change, Biosphere Integrity, Biogeochemical Flows, Land-System Change, Freshwater Change, Novel Entities) (Rockström et al. 2009, Richardson et al. 2023). The planetary boundaries framework is based on Earth system science and identifies nine processes crucial for the stability and resilience of the Earth system as a whole. The further these boundaries are exceeded, the more uncertain the continued stable functioning of the Earth's systems becomes. Organisations and the economic system in which they operate, influence the Earth's system in major ways. Against this backdrop, a transformation in how we conduct economic activities is imperative because it is a matter of human survival.

Recently, various approaches, such as the circular economy, regenerative business, the Economy for the Common Good approach, the wellbeing economy, post-growth, degrowth, systems thinking and many others, have emerged as potential alternatives to address the shortcomings of the current economic system. Inspired by and in addition to many of these approaches, economist Kate Raworth introduced the concept of the Doughnut Economy in 2012. The Doughnut Economy takes up the idea of planetary boundaries (Rockström et al. 2009) as an environmental ceiling and combines it with a social foundation comprising 12 social dimensions that are derived from the social priorities specified in the United Nations Sustainable Development Goals (SDGs), such as gender equality, health and education (Raworth 2017: 295). On a global level, none of the 12 social priorities has so far been achieved.

The Doughnut consists of two concentric rings: a social foundation to ensure that no one is left falling short of life's essentials, and an ecological ceiling to ensure that humanity does not collectively overshoot the planetary boundaries that protect Earth's life-supporting systems. Between these two sets of boundaries lies a doughnut-shaped space that is both ecologically safe and socially just: a space in which humanity can thrive.

Currently, humanity's economic activity is causing an overshoot on at least six of the nine planetary boundaries, resulting in a shortfall on life's essentials for many millions of people around the world. The current Doughnut portrait of humanity demonstrates the crises that our economies have generated (Figure 1).

Figure 1: Current global status of shortfall and overshoot in the Doughnut of social and plane-tary boundaries

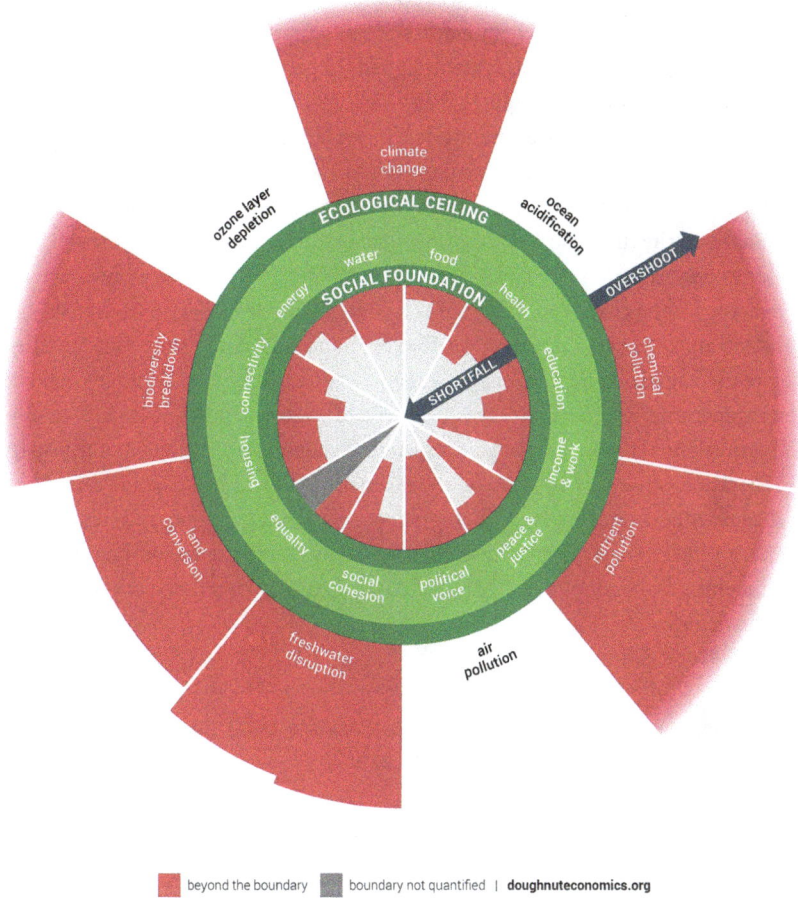

Source: Fanning/Raworth 2025: 49.

To reverse the overshoot of planetary boundaries and the shortfall in life's essen-tials that our economies are generating, it has become clear that we need to rethink the economy. To help support this, Doughnut Economics emerged based on seven ways of thinking and doing economics that differ significantly from conventional economics: (1) Change the Goals – from GDP to the Doughnut, (2) See the Big Picture – from self-contained market to embedded economy, (3) Nurture Human Nature – from rational economic man to social adaptable humans, (4) Get Savvy with Systems – from mechanical equilibrium to dynamic complexity, (5) Design to Distribute – from 'growth will even it up again' to distributive by design, (6) Create to Regenerate

– from 'growth will clean it up again' to regenerative by design, (7) Be Agnostic about Growth – from growth-addicted to growth-agnostic (Raworth 2017).

In the context of our book, we will elaborate in greater detail on the 'design to distribute' and 'create to regenerate' areas of Doughnut Economics, focusing on applying this to the way businesses are designed. In particular, we want to clarify our understanding of these two approaches – first in a macroeconomic context as regenerative and distributive economic design, and then in an organisational context as regenerative and distributive business design, always considering that both perspectives are interconnected and enable each other (Raworth 2017: 229).

Based on the dictionary of ecology (Schaefer 2012), the term regeneration concerning ecosystems has two meanings: Firstly, it highlights the ability of ecosystems to recover from a change in structure and function caused by extreme factors – to function after the cessation of a disturbance and to restore the state that prevailed before the negative influence/impact (regeneration capacity). An example would be the regeneration of a lake after the discharge of wastewater has ceased. Secondly, the term signifies the repair of an ecosystem through interventions that utilise its regeneration capacity. For example, the regeneration areas in a drained raised bog (Schaefer 2012: 242). However, the overshoot of our planetary boundaries and the damage to our ecosystems is not caused by a single extreme factor, but rather by the inherent design of our economy, which externalises costs onto ecosystems and human beings.

As Raworth points out,

> "Economics, it turns out, is not a matter of discovering laws: it is essentially a question of design" (Raworth 2017: 211).

We follow Wahl's (2022) definition of design, which he understands in a very broad sense as "human intentionality expressed through interactions and relationships" (Wahl 2022: 124). For example, our economic system is designed to perform a certain function based on a set of intentions and this design in turn defines and shapes the interactions and relationships between the users of that particular medium of exchange (Wahl 2022: 124). So, "design expresses *and* creates culture" (Wahl 2022: 124). This means that design is something that is socially created and it follows a worldview, and a worldview follows design (Wahl 2022: 131). Consequently, to transform our economies so that they become ecologically regenerative and socially distributive, redesigning is an essential way to change the worldview and understanding of economics and business practice.

The concept of a regenerative economic design represents the opposite of the degenerative linear economy design we all know, which follows the idea of taking resources and making products or services that are then used often only for a very short time. In other words, the take-make-use-lose model. Consider for example the fast fashion industry, which generates ever-growing amounts of waste, leading to the pollution of oceans, water and air around the planet.

A **'regenerative' economic design** refers to a design based on "a commitment to the life processes inherent in ecological design" (Wahl 2022: 12) and aligns with the living world, which thrives by continually recycling life's building blocks such as carbon, oxygen, water, nitrogen and phosphorus. It enables the natural cycles, which were broken by industrial activity, to be revitalised and to flow again (Raworth 2017: 212). In other words, it works with and within the cycles of the living world.

Figure 2: The Butterfly Economy: Regenerative by Design

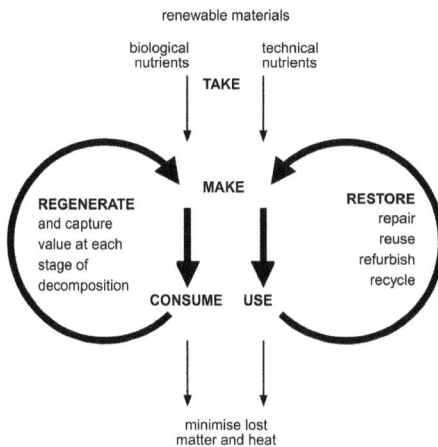

Source: Raworth 2017: 220.

Such a circular economy – or butterfly economy, as Raworth terms it – is regenerative by design based on cradle-to-cradle thinking (Braungart et al. 2007). The concept of 'Cradle-to-Cradle' entails the use of renewable energy and eradicates waste by design grounded on the principle "waste equals food". The butterfly emerges on the basis of two renewable materials which are differentiated, and which constitute the two wings of the butterfly (Figure 2): On one wing, biological nutrients, such as plants, animals or soil, become the source of production and are never 'used up' as they regenerate and capture value at each stage of decomposition. "The key to using them endlessly is to: ensure that they are harvested no faster than nature regenerates them" (Raworth 2017: 221). On the other wing of the butterfly, technical nutrients – such as plastics, synthetics and metals, which do not naturally decompose – are designed to be restored through repair, reuse, refurbishment and (as a last resort) recycling (Raworth 2017: 222). But it is also important to acknowledge that currently, no industrial loop can recapture and reuse 100% of its materials. Nevertheless, in a "regenerative economy, that material throughflow is transformed into *round-flow*" (Raworth 2017: 223), minimising the loss of matter and heat.

> The concept of **distributive economic design** refers to the idea of redesigning our economy as a distributive network of flows that can alter the distribution of income, wealth, time, opportunity and power in a way that helps to bring everyone above the Doughnut's social foundation and reduce inequalities. While the current divisive design of finance, business and trade tends to concentrate value and opportunity in the hands of a few, distributive design shares opportunity and value with all who co-create it (Sahan/van Winden 2022: 7). It is no longer about waiting for economic growth to reduce inequality but about designing diverse and distributive networks based on the principles of nature's thriving networks. Nature's design, based on a balanced system of efficiency and resilience, shows that networks are excellent structures for reliably distributing resources throughout a whole system (Raworth 2017: 175).

"Efficiency occurs when a system streamlines and simplifies its resource flow to achieve its aims, say by channelling resources directly between the larger nodes. Resilience, however, depends upon diversity and redundancy in the network, which means that here are ample alternative connections and options in times of shock of change. Too much efficiency makes a system vulnerable (as global financial regulators realised too late in 2008) while too much resilience makes it stagnant: vitality and robustness lie in balance between the two" (Raworth 2017: 175).

Doughnut economics points all actors towards efforts to redesign businesses embedded in these ideas of regenerative and distributive economic design. In particular, it focuses on the transformations in business design that can enable and unlock ambitious social and ecological action. While the responsibility for driving this transformation is broad and sometimes unspecified, it is particularly important for stakeholders who possess the most agency to drive such changes in design.

Corporate Responsibility for Changing Unjust Global Economic Structures

To discuss the question of how and why organisations bear responsibility for restructuring the frameworks of our economic system, we will refer to Iris Marion Young's social connection model of responsibility (Young 2006). In her work, Young points out that the current understanding of causal responsibility and the liability model are limited regarding questions of accountability in the context of global economic structures. A central critique of the liability model is its inability to capture indirect interactions. This poses a significant challenge, particularly for issues of global justice, as the increasing entanglement of economic processes, such as those seen in global supply chains, makes the direct causal attribution of responsibility more difficult. There are numerous situations in which no clear perpetrator can be identified for the suffering or difficulties others face. This subsequently leads to two tendencies: an increasing diffusion of responsibility, whereby responsibility is shifted onto others, or an overwhelming sense of responsibility when everyone is held accountable for everything (Young 2006).

Young addresses this deficiency with her concept of responsibility rooted in social connectedness and the accompanying understanding of global shared responsibility. She aims to bridge the gaps in responsibility attribution for consequences arising from structural injustices, such as exploitative working conditions in global supply chains or environmental pollution. According to Young, structural injustice exists

> "when social processes put large categories of persons under a systematic threat of domination or deprivation of the means to develop and exercise their capacities, at the same time as these processes enable others to dominate or have a wide range of opportunities for developing and exercising their capacities" (Young 2006: 114).

Exploitative relations within global supply chains, according to Young, are expressions of structural injustice, characterised by the fact that they result from the actions of numerous individuals and institutions pursuing their own goals and interests within existing institutional rules and accepted norms.

Young speaks of a **shared prospective responsibility** that addresses all stakeholders, which does not imply that everyone bears equal responsibility. Rather, as Young elucidates, this responsibility is determined by four criteria: *power, privileged position, interest,* and *collective ability.* The criterion of power relates to varying degrees of potential and actual possibility, such as access to resources and the ability to influence processes and their outcomes. Actors occupying a relatively privileged position within these structures bear greater moral responsibility for organised corrective efforts "because they are able to adapt to changed circumstances without suffering serious deprivation" (Young 2006: 128).

The underlying assumption of this book is that changing unjust economic structures needs both an outer organisational transformation, i.e. changes beyond the borders of an organisation and an inner organisational transformation, i.e. changes in the design within the organisation, which are interconnected and cannot be viewed in isolation. In the following, we outline how organisations can transform their business design.

Regenerative and Distributive Business Design Based on Doughnut Economics

What does this all mean for organisations?

Applied to organisations, a **regenerative business** is one whose core business helps to reconnect nature's cycles and that embraces biosphere stewardship and gives back to living systems as much as it can. "Because only generous design can bring us back below the Doughnut's ecological ceiling" (Raworth 2017: 218). To create generous designs, the approach of biomimicry can be taken as inspiration. Biomimicry, initiated by Janine Benyus, takes nature as our model, measure and mentor in a quest to learn and mimic life's cyclical processes – for example, by constructing buildings whose biomimetic living walls would sequester carbon dioxide, release oxygen, and filter the surrounding air (Raworth 2017: 218f, 227).

A shift in mindset is needed which asks, "How many diverse benefits can we layer into the design?" instead of "How much financial value can we extract from this?" (Raworth 2017: 227). As Raworth points out, there might be some overlap between the two ambitions, but if business is only interested in that overlap, regenerative design will fall short of its potential (Raworth 2017: 228). In fact, in many cases – and especially in challenging, competitive situations and under resource constraints – we see that the R (Regenerative) always comes after the P (Profit).

While a regenerative business focuses on ecological aspects, **a distributive business** is created to distribute financial wealth and other value sources, including income, knowledge, time, and power, in an equitable way (Raworth 2017). For example, here, Raworth highlights the importance of the open-source circular economy, which is based on the principles of modularity, open standards, open source and open data (Raworth 2017: 230). One of the central questions of design is "Who owns the labour?" For enterprises to be inherently distributive of the value they create, the two design principles of rooted membership and stakeholder finance are key and can flip the dominant ownership model as Kelly points out (Kelly 2012: 18). "From not-for-profits to community interest companies, the bottom-up experiment in redesign is giving rise to a network of enterprise alternatives" (Raworth 2017: 191). This allows organisations to contribute to the transformation from a divisive design to a distributive one.

Regenerative and distributive business design includes a wide range of innovative practices. With our case studies, we focus on the deep design of business which encompasses its purpose, networks, governance, ownership and financing, and shapes its strategic decisions and operational impacts, and ultimately determines whether or not businesses can transform to become part of a regenerative and distributive future (Sahan et al. 2022). The five design traits Purpose, Governance, Networks, Ownership and Finance were identified by the author and theorist Marjorie Kelly (Kelly 2012) and are central for shaping inner organisational transformation.

In applying this framework alongside Doughnut Economics, the question becomes: how do we move away from a design of the world of business that has resulted in a degenerative and divisive economy to one that is regenerative and distributive? And to do so, the question at the heart of the design of business must move from "how much value can we extract through this enterprise?" and instead become "how many benefits can we generate through this enterprise?". Figure 3 outlines the five design traits that helps to transform the design of business.

Figure 3: The Five Design Traits to Transform the Deep Design of Business

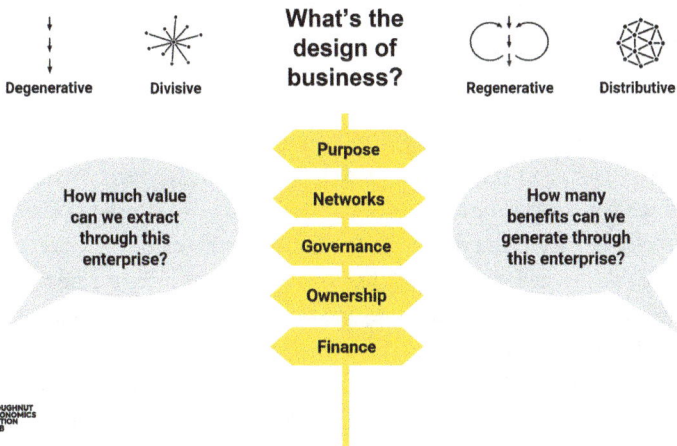

Source: Doughnut Economics Action Lab 2024: 40.

Purpose

A company's purpose describes why it exists and guides its activities. During the 20th century and into the 21st, the purpose of businesses has centred on maximising profits and satisfying shareholder interests. In regenerative and distributive businesses, however, purpose focuses on a higher goal that aligns with the ecological and social needs of the planet. Rather than being confined to a formal statement, a company's purpose is manifested through its actions, culture, products, and services. For instance, a company pursuing the purpose of contributing to human health and nutrition could provide products and engage in activities focused on nutritious and affordable food. To maintain long-term strategic commitment to its purpose, an organisation must embed it into its other deep design traits.

Network

The Network design trait refers to the relations of the organisations to their internal and external stakeholders. These stakeholders include employees, communities, competitors, supply chain partners, governments, customers and others. In conventional organisations, these networks are typically operations-driven, focusing primarily on efficiency, cost-effectiveness and the minimisation of risks. However, in a regenerative and distributive business design, the organisation's purpose fundamentally shapes these network relationships. For example, organisations with a regenerative and distributive business design prioritise long-term partnerships with suppliers over short-term transactions, incorporating fair and stable pricing agreements and codes of conduct. Similarly, to transform degenerative and divisive industry standards, regenerative and distributive businesses often collaborate with NGOs, competitors, and the government to amplify their impact.

Governance

Corporate governance is generally understood as the system of rules, processes, and practices by which companies are directed and controlled (Cadbury 2000). It encompasses three key aspects: the composition of the board of directors, the distribution of shareholders' rights, and the methods of information disclosure. Today's company boards are often dominated by shareholder interests, prioritising their interests in decision-making. In contrast, regenerative and distributive businesses adopt a more inclusive approach to governance, balancing the interests of diverse stakeholders, including shareholders, employees, customers, suppliers and the broader community. Multi-stakeholder boards, which represent a broad range of interests, and diversity in gender, nationality, and age, are key mechanisms for addressing trade-offs between ecological, social, and financial goals. Additionally, granting voting rights to NGOs or trusts and foundations that are purpose-focused can serve as mission-lock mechanisms that protect the company's purpose against external pressures and narrow commercial interests.

Ownership

Business owners typically hold the authority to determine the organisation's purpose and strategic direction. They also hold the rights to the profits that are generated. Traditionally, ownership is concentrated among founders, senior executives or external investors, whose individual motivations heavily influence the organisation's strategy. While some owners may align their businesses with broader societal or ecological goals, conventional ownership structures often prioritise short-term financial returns. Moreover, these conventional ownership forms frequently concentrate decision-making power in the hands of those not directly involved in operating the business or those who may not prioritise the organisation's social or ecological purpose. In response, alternative ownership models have emerged to balance power among various stakeholders and align governance with purpose. These alternative ownership models include businesses owned by foundations, trusts, members (cooperatives), employees and communities – and a myriad of hybrid models that have emerged. For instance, models such as steward-ownership, community ownership, platform cooperatives and employee-ownership trusts are spreading. Each model has distinct implications for how businesses operate and their capacity to align with broader societal and ecological goals.

Finance

A business's financing structure, as well as the expectations associated with specific financial mechanisms shapes its ability to become regenerative and distributive. Traditional sources of finance such as debt (borrowing) and equity (issuing shares) often hold firms back from effectively balancing profit with social and ecological impact. The pursuit of high, rapid financial returns can conflict with commitments to long-term investments in social and ecological goals. For example, developing a sustainable supply chain may seem costly in the short term, making it undesirable under conventional financing models, but it can provide significant long-term benefits, embedding resilience into the business. Alternative forms of finance can be a more suitable option for regenerative and distributive businesses, since they consider longer time horizons, implement new liquidity mechanisms, and shift investor expectations. For instance, crowdfunding enables a broader base of individual investors to support ventures with regenerative and distributive goals that may not receive backing from traditional financial sources. There is a host of alternative financing models for start-ups and early-stage businesses that may be a better fit than pursuing venture capital financing, such as revenue-based finance, impact-linked financing, and convertible grants, to name a few (Patton Power 2021). When organisations pursue purpose-aligned finance, they can retain control over decision-making while offering investors a fair return on investment.

Methodology and Structure of the Case Study Workbook

The case studies in this book were selected based on the following three criteria: (1) ecologically regenerative and/or socially distributive purpose orientation, (2) particularly innovative practice in one of the design traits, (3) based or active in German-speaking countries. The first criterion was the most important one, as it highlights the difference between regenerative and distributive organisations and those that give precedence to profit maximisation above all else. With our case studies, we aim to show that the prioritisation of a regenerative and distributive purpose can be combined with profit generation – but not with a preference for profit maximisation. The particularly innovative practice, as the second criterion, is of high importance as the examples show how inner organisational structural change in the design traits contributes to achieving the regenerative and distributive purpose of the organisation. The third criterion is based on the research gap in German-speaking countries on this specific topic.

With every organisation, between one and three expert interviews were conducted by the author following the paradigm of qualitative empirical research methodology. To enhance the validity of the findings, additional sources such as company websites, podcasts, impact reports, and media articles were also analysed. The interviews were carried out based on a standardised questionnaire, which was individually adapted to the respective organisation and the corresponding design trait. The interviews were then transcribed, coded and analysed using qualitative data analysis methods.

All case studies follow the same structure: Under each case study, there is a list of the organisation's regenerative and distributive purpose, the design traits it showcases and the innovative practice that it follows within a design trait, followed by the key facts about each organisation. Then there is an introductory section explaining the regenerative and distributive purpose, business model and objectives, and important additional information about the organisation's founding and history. The next section gives insights into the innovative practice of the specific design trait. Afterwards follow two sections on how the innovative design enables regenerative and distributive dynamics, and another section on the challenges arising from designing the specific design trait around the innovative practice. Given the degree of interactions and overlap between the design traits, the next section of the case studies explores these connections with other design traits. This section is followed by recommendations for organisations seeking to adapt their design traits based on the presented case. To conclude each case study, the final section highlights how the organisation with its innovative design trait contributes to inspiring economic re-design beyond the business.

The first three case studies on the purpose design trait follow a slightly different structure than those written on other design traits, as the focus is on clarifying how a regenerative and distributive purpose is embedded across the overall design of the organisation. This is also relevant for the other case studies as they were all selected by the criterion of following a regenerative and/or distributive purpose.

We acknowledge that there is potentially a large number of other firms that are also deploying regenerative and distributive business designs that we did not in-clude. The innovation and interest in this topic are spreading fast, and developments are encouraging. Nevertheless, we believe that all companies and organisations that we cover have a unique and inspiring approach to designing a regenerative and/or distributive business that could serve as an inspiration and provide insights for other businesses.

References

Braungart, M., McDonough, W., & Bollinger, A. (2007): Cradle-to-cradle design: Creating healthy emissions – a strategy for eco-effective product and system de-sign. *Journal of Cleaner Production*, 15 (13–14), 1337–1348, https://doi.org/10.1016/j.jclepro.2006.08.003.

Cadbury, S. A. (2000): The corporate governance agenda. *Corporate Governance: An In-ternational Review*, 8(1), 7–15.

Club of Rome (2025): Earth Overshoot Day 2024 falls on August 1st, https://www.club ofrome.org/impact-hubs/climate-emergency/earth-overshoot-day/, [Accessed 14 March 2025].

Doughnut Economics Action Lab (DEAL) (2024): Doughnut Design for Business. DEAL's guide to redesigning businesses through Doughnut Economics – Core workshop, Version 1.2 (March 2024), https://doughnuteconomics.org/tools/dou ghnut-design-for-business-core-tool#attachments, [Accessed 22 April 2025].

Fanning, A. L, Raworth, K. (2025): Doughnut of Social and Planetary Boundaries monitors a world out of balance, Nature 646 (8083): 47–56, https://doi.org/10.1038/s41586-025-09385-1.

Global Footprint Network (2025): Earth Overshoot Day 2025 falls on July 24th. Cor-recting Humanity's largest market failure, https://overshoot.footprintnetwork.org/newsroom/press-release-2025-english/, [Accessed 16 September 2025].

Holmes Jr, R. M., Waldman, D. A., Siegel, D. S., & Pepe, J. A. (2022): Declining trust in capitalism: Managerial, research, and public policy implications. *Academy of Management Perspectives*, 36(4), 984–1006.

Kelly, M. (2012): Owning Our Future: The Emerging Ownership Revolution. San Francisco.

Laloux, F. (2015): Reinventing Organizations. Munich.

Patton Power, A. (2021): Adventure Finance: How to Create a Funding Journey That Blends Profit and Purpose. Springer Books, Switzerland.

Raworth, K. (2017): Doughnut Economics: Seven Ways to Think Like a 21st-Century Economist. Random House Business Books.

Richardson, K., Steffen, W., Luch W., et al. (2023): Earth beyond six of nine planetary boundaries. *Science Advances*, 9(37), https://www.science.org/doi/10.1126/sciadv.adh2458.

Rockström, J., Steffen, W., Noone, K., & Persson, A. (2009): A safe operating space for humanity. *Nature*, 461(7263), 472–475, https://doi.org/10.1038/461472a.

Sahan, E., Ruiz, C. S., Raworth, K., van Winden, W., & van den Buuse, D. (2022): What Doughnut Economics means for business: Creating enterprises that are regenerative and distributive by design. Working Paper *Doughnut Economics Action Lab*, Amsterdam University of Applied Sciences.

Schaefer, M. (2012): Regeneration. In: Wörterbuch der Ökologie, (5th revised and expanded edition), Heidelberg, S. 42.

Wahl, D. C. (2022): Designing Regenerative Cultures. Axminster.

Young, I. M. (2006): Responsibility and global justice: A social connection model, *Social Philosophy and Policy*, 23(1), 102–130, https://doi.org/10.1017/S02650525060 60043.

Purpose Design

Case Study: WEtell

Nelly Rahimy

Purpose: Regenerative and Distributive Mobile Communications
Design Trait: Purpose

Key Facts

WEtell is Germany's first sustainable mobile communications provider, committed not only to minimising CO_2 emissions but also to generating its own green energy through photovoltaic systems. The company upholds the values of ecological sustainability, social fairness and data protection.

> **Seat:** Freiburg
> **Established:** 2019
> **Founders:** Nico Tucher, Alma Spribille, Andreas Schmucker, Benjamin Thaidigsman
> **Ownership:** Verantwortungseigentum (Steward Ownership)
> **Legal Form:** Limited Liability Company
> **Employees:** 26
> **Webpage:** https://www.WEtell.de/

Purpose, Business Model & Objectives

> Purpose: "Regenerative and Distributive Mobile Communications"

In 2018, Alma Spribille, Nico Tucher, Andreas Schmucker and Benjamin Thaidigsman decided they could no longer wait for the sustainability transition to occur without them. With sustainable infrastructure emerging in various sectors such as energy, smartphones, food, clothing, and transport, they sought a yet-untouched area where they could make a significant impact. They identified a glaring gap in sustainable mobile communications, with likes, phone calls, and photos contributing as much CO_2 emissions as domestic air travel.

> **Did you know that...**
> The mobile communications industry causes as much CO_2 emissions as Germany's domestic air travel? (WEtell 2025)

By 2019, *WEtell* was officially founded, with the aim of revolutionising mobile communications in Germany. By launching its company with a crowdfunding campaign, WEtell quickly sold 1,200 vouchers for mobile phone tariffs. Within three months, *WEtell* had installed 1,000 solar panels, producing more than enough energy for its 17,000 customers.

Insights into the Purpose of Regenerative and Distributive Mobile Telecommunication

WEtell's DNA is firmly anchored in sustainability. The company's goal extends beyond reducing its environmental footprint— it aims to reshape the mobile communications landscape. This includes not only CO_2 emission reduction and compensation but also defending customer privacy and promoting transparency and fairness in the market.

In essence, *WEtell's* mission boils down to sustainability:

> "We don't do sustainability to sell mobile services. We offer mobile services to promote sustainability." – Nico Tucher, Co-Founder

The founders' work reflects a regenerative philosophy that acknowledges the responsibility businesses have towards the ecosystems they operate within, both environmentally and socially. Nico Tucher describes his personal motivation in the following way:

> "If you're truly serious about purpose, it's not just about sustainability. At its core, I believe it's about something deeper—like love and connection to this planet. That's what people feel when they go out into nature — a sense of connection, like they're part of the bigger picture. If I can feel and sense that, then I won't destroy this planet. Instead, I'll do everything in my power to keep it functional, whatever kind of organism it is."

Specifically, the firm has identified four areas that define its purpose: climate action and the interrelated areas of fairness, transparency and data protection.

Figure 1: WEtell Purpose and Steward-Ownership

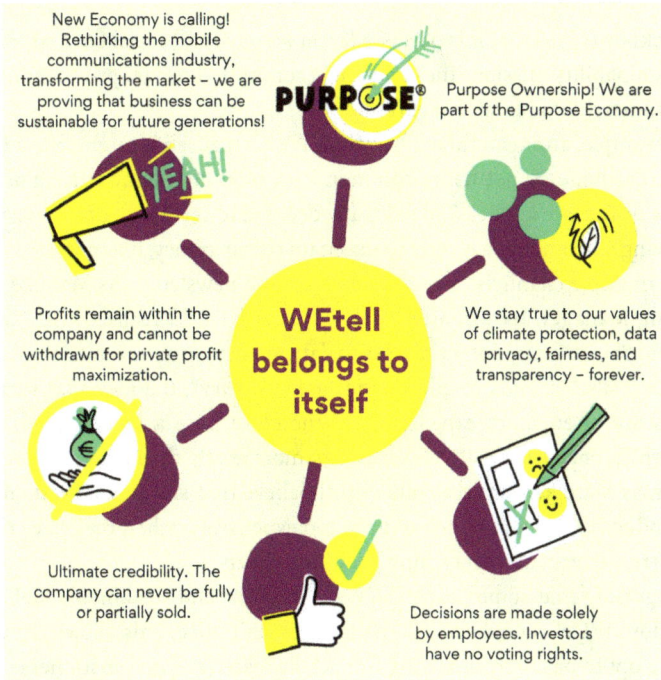

Source: Modified design based on WEtell 2025.

Climate Action

WEtell's philosophy asserts that simply reducing its environmental footprint is not enough: it must be regenerative, positively contributing to the rebuilding of natural ecosystems. This commitment is reflected in three key approaches: (1) avoiding carbon emissions wherever possible, (2) offsetting all emissions generated by the operation of the mobile network infrastructure—despite it not being owned by *WEtell*—through biochar projects, and (3) investing in the expansion of renewable energy sources. *WEtell* supports the transition to clean energy by producing its own electricity through self-built photovoltaic systems, generating more energy than its operations require and feeding the surplus back into the national grid.

> "We install so much photovoltaics that more electricity is fed into the German grid than all these mobile communications with all the masts and so on need for anyone." – Nico Tucher

Fairness, Data Protection and Transparency

WEtell acknowledges that it is part of a larger system, and social fairness is integral to its sustainability mission. The company is committed to data privacy and ensures that customers' data remains secure.

For example, after careful deliberation, *WEtell* realised it might face a competitive disadvantage by not using common data tracking methods such as Google Analytics or Facebook Pixel. The company decided to test these data analysis tools for studying customer behaviour. To maintain transparency, it announced this trial through multiple channels, including its blog and newsletter. As Mareike Kühnel, Marketing Manager, recalls, after the trial period *WEtell* realised that "the value gained didn't justify any potential risks to data privacy, so we reversed the decision".

Fairness also extends to addressing "green luxury", the idea that sustainable products are often more expensive and therefore pose a luxury good. *WEtell*'s tariffs, which encapsulate all its values, are more costly than comparable options. However, as Mareike Kühnel points out, "I believe that sustainable and, above all, fairly produced services are not actually too expensive; rather, they have the price they are truly worth, and everything else is too cheap."

Recognising that some people cannot afford fair and sustainable mobile communication, *WEtell* launched the "FAIRstärker" initiative. This allows regular customers to opt to pay more, enabling financially disadvantaged customers to access services at reduced rates.

WEtell's value of fairness also extends to its relationships with customers. The company promises fair and respectful service – no computers, no waiting line. This is in line with its loving and respectful relationships throughout. As Nico Tucher recalls,

> "I was at a trade fair recently, and a woman came up to me—she must have been in her early 50s. She wanted to know what we do, so I explained and mentioned some technical details. Then I talked about our service, and I said, 'When you call us, within 10 to 15 seconds, a real person picks up the phone and takes your issue seriously.' The woman started tearing up. She said in today's digital world, everything is optimised for processes, but no one really takes you seriously as a human when you call a customer hotline."

Impact Measurement

From the outset, *WEtell* has been deeply invested in measuring and communicating its impact. The company has completed its second Economy of the Common Good

Balance Sheet, achieving an above-average score of 547 points[1], which reflects its commitment to transparency and social responsibility. This score serves as a tangible metric that highlights *WEtell*'s efforts to operate in line with the principles of the Economy of the Common Good.

> "Of course, we have a lot of KPIs, especially in marketing, where a lot is about how many sales came in or how many people visited our homepage. So, there are these classic things where you can simply check if what we're doing is resonating. Personally, I also think, well, we've now done the second Common Good Balance Sheet, and I was involved in both, as I helped write the report. For me, that was a really beautiful way to see what we have achieved." – Mareike Kühnel

WEtell also closely monitors other key performance indicators, including its energy production and consumption. The company tracks the amount of energy it produces from renewable sources and ensures that its mobile telecommunication services are powered by green energy. In addition, *WEtell* keeps detailed records of how many FAIRstärkers they have been able to engage.

How the Purpose of Regenerative and Distributive Mobile Telecommunication is Embedded across the Design of the Business

Ownership Design

Early on, *WEtell* questioned how to safeguard its purpose as the company grew and faced potential profit-driven temptations. Its solution was the steward-ownership model. It did not take long for *WEtell* to embrace this model, integrating it into its business structure to ensure long-term purpose alignment.

As a steward-owned company, *WEtell* operates with three distinct types of shares.

- **A-shares (majority shares):** Owned by those actively working at the company, these shares ensure that only insiders who understand the business make critical decisions.
- **B-Shares:** Hold veto rights for decisions affecting the company's fundamental purpose such as selling the company. In *WEtell*'s case, 1% of the voting rights (B-Shares) are held by the Purpose Foundation.

---

1   A maximum of 1,000 Common Good points can be achieved. Minus points are awarded for practices that are detrimental to the Common Good, which can amount to a maximum of minus 3,600 points. On average, companies have scored 300 points in 2017 (Felber/Hagelberg 2017).

- **C-Shares:** Granted to founders to compensate for their initial risk and investment. These shares do not influence decision-making and eventually become void after payout, returning to *WEtell* GmbH.

By anchoring its purpose through steward-ownership, *WEtell* ensures that it always prioritises sustainable mobile phone networks. As profits are reinvested into the company instead of given to shareholders, *WEtell* has the freedom to allocate its finances toward its purpose. For example, 3.9% of its expenditure is dedicated to building photovoltaic stations or carbon capture projects. Moreover, removing the pressure to maximise profit enables *WEtell* to choose its partners based on sustainability criteria rather than profit potential.

Furthermore, the steward-ownership model prevents power from being concentrated with external shareholders or investors. Instead, decision-making power remains with active members of the company. *WEtell* supports decentralised decision-making, giving employees a direct role in shaping the company's future. The founding team, alongside employees, actively participates in governance, reinforcing a culture of transparency and shared responsibility.

Governance Design

The governance of *WEtell* is structured to ensure active involvement in the company. Decision-making power is distributed among *WEtell*'s steward-owners, who hold equal voting shares. Currently, these voting shares are divided among four individuals: the founders Alma Spribille, Andreas Schmucker, and Nico Tucher, as well as Ian Davidson, *WEtell*'s brand lead, who played a key role in building the company's identity. All four hold equal voting rights and share strategic responsibility.

The number of voting shares is not fixed. Additional members could be included in the future, or the group could be reduced. Initially, the founders determined the composition of this circle, as their strategic roles naturally aligned with governance responsibilities. However, *WEtell* aims to develop a process that would allow other employees to take part in governance decisions over time.

Operationally, *WEtell* functions with flat hierarchies and a trust-based culture, where open communication is encouraged. Employees are actively involved in decision-making processes and can voice their opinions freely without fear of repercussion. For instance, *WEtell* implements the SCRUM method for regular strategy and values alignment meetings, and employees even participate in financial planning discussions. This collective approach fosters a sense of shared ownership and purpose.

The company's ownership structure, free from external influences, allows the founding team to delegate decision-making authority to the most relevant experts within *WEtell*. For example, the service team independently sets its own priorities and strategies for smaller projects, consulting the founders primarily for support.

Decision-making at *WEtell* is deeply collaborative. While most decisions are made within smaller working units, key decisions are often discussed with the entire team. The goal is to find solutions that everyone can accept. For major decisions, the team votes with veto rights, and if no consensus is reached, they apply the principle of minimal resistance to find a solution that the majority agrees with.

> "Our business practice is that we don't vote on the vast majority of things but aim to find a solution that everyone can live with. [...] It's very rare for there to be any kind of contentious votes." – Nico Tucher

Network Design

Awareness of environmental issues like climate change and CO_2 emissions is crucial for consumers to make informed decisions when choosing a mobile network provider like *WEtell*. However, many people are unaware that their choice impacts more than just price and data availability: it also affects privacy, CO_2 emissions, and working conditions. To bridge this knowledge gap, *WEtell* places its network at the core of its mission.

WEtell not only educates its customers and partners but also engages the broader public. In 2022, the team participated in 14 podcast interviews, designed workshops around sustainable phones, and took part in Fridays for Future protests. The company also created a network around the protests on Lüzerath, where activists opposed the demolition of the village for coal mining expansion, to raise awareness for climate action. Its presence in the sustainability space is extensive and few podcasts on the topic have not featured *WEtell*. Beyond public engagement, they also focus on educating policymakers, and actively lobby for climate protection measures.

> "That's why *WEtell* is also active in this area. For example, through its work on the board of the German Sustainable Economy Association or Alma Spribille's involvement in the SME Advisory Board of the Ministry of Economic Affairs and Climate Action. In this way, we push decisions towards sustainability and contribute our ideas and expertise to the process." — Nico Tucher

Trust

A key aspect of embedding purpose into organisational design is establishing trust, especially in a climate where public scepticism towards sustainability claims runs high. Many startups with initially strong sustainability credentials have experienced backlash after scaling or exiting, leading to growing public doubt about whether companies can remain true to their values over time.

Nico Tucher recalls a customer conversation that highlighted this issue: while he was explaining *WEtell*'s mission and his commitment to never selling the company, the customer responded with a sceptical laugh. 'I believe you now. But what will it be like in five years' time? You can't say for sure yourself what it will be like then, then you want to scale. And the scaling point is often the point at which you leave this path, the values."

To address this scepticism, *WEtell* combines measurable impact with a purpose-focused legal form that is explicitly designed to protect its core mission. While the company rigorously measures and communicates its impact through technical data, it also acknowledges that most people neither have the time nor the expertise to analyse these complexities. This is where *WEtell*'s purpose becomes a powerful differentiator: it builds an emotional connection that bridges the gap between hard facts and human trust.

> "But most people are not primarily technically minded and, above all, they are not experts in the field. This means that what we actually need to achieve is to precisely convey these emotions. Trust." – Nico Tucher

Culture

WEtell's corporate culture is a key driver of its success. The purpose-driven mindset and flat hierarchies foster a sense of empowerment and engagement among employees. Many team members joined *WEtell* after experiencing a disconnect between their personal values and previous work environments. At *WEtell*, they discovered a place where they could not only align their sense of purpose with their work but also actively contribute to shaping the company's culture. This alignment leads to high levels of personal fulfilment, as one employee noted:

> "I came from a company that wasn't very value-driven. And I just really wanted [...] to go somewhere where I could do meaningful work. And I never would have thought of working for a mobile network provider." – Mareike Kühnel

Transparency is central to *WEtell*'s culture. The entire team is regularly updated on and involved in the company's financial situation, strategic direction, and future scenarios. This openness ensures that all employees understand the state of the company, can voice concerns, and gain insights into the long-term vision, reinforcing their trust and commitment to *WEtell*'s purpose.

Challenges Arising from Designing Purpose around Regenerative and Distributive Mobile Communications

Protecting *WEtell*'s Values

Even with purpose embedded in its legal and financial structure, *WEtell* is not immune to difficult decisions. As the company grows, it continually faces moments where its commitment to its values must be carefully balanced against the pressures and opportunities that come with scaling. Inevitably, trade-offs arise that require *WEtell* to make deliberate choices about its priorities.

Example: Discount System for Customers

A typical example involves balancing trade-offs between growth and *WEtell*'s commitment to fairness for all customers. On one occasion, a major client requested 500 SIM cards and expected a significant discount in return. This demand sparked an internal debate: *WEtell*'s principles of fairness and transparency clashed with the customer's expectations. The issue was not merely about the financial decision; it was about maintaining trustworthiness. Offering a discount to one large customer could compromise the company's promise of treating all customers equally, undermining the trust it had worked so hard to build. To uphold its values, *WEtell* introduced a transparent and fair discount system for customers who purchase large quantities of SIM cards. While quietly providing a bespoke and negotiated discount would have been easier and more commercially effective, the company chose transparency and reinforced its values while also adapting to commercial realities.

Example: Introducing a Transparent Wage System

A powerful example of *WEtell*'s collaborative culture is the recent introduction of a transparent wage system in October 2023. The decision arose from the recognition that the existing system no longer reflected market realities, particularly for specialised skills. The founders invited a team of employees to co-create a new, fairer wage model. This group, which represented different parts of the company, worked through various options and gathered feedback from the entire staff to ensure the solution would be both competitive and transparent.

The process was not just technical but emotional. Discussing wages openly revealed how deeply money and fairness are connected, even for those who primarily view work through a values-driven lens. Mareike Kühnel reflected on this, noting that "it was kind of an emotional moment to realise, oh, something actually did happen, and it's totally crazy because you don't really want to tie emotions to money. You want to focus on the idealistic existence."

Ultimately, the team proposed three models, and after collective discussion and a company-wide vote in which every employee had the right to veto, a new system was accepted unanimously. It is grounded in three guiding principles: recognizing the level of responsibility each role entails, ensuring salaries remain competitive with the market, and maintaining a fair balance by capping the highest salary at twice the lowest. In addition, the system includes the FAIRteiler, a flexible budget that allows employees to temporarily or permanently top up their salary to accommodate personal needs, such as caring for relatives or covering unexpected expenses.

Measurement of Societal Impact

While quantitative metrics like energy usage, CO_2 compensation or the number of FAIRstärkers are relatively easy to track, other areas of impact, especially those related to public influence, are more challenging to quantify.

A good example is the recent appointment of Alma Spribille to the executive board of an influential mobile telecommunications association. Through this role, Alma Spribille has the opportunity to actively promote sustainability in the mobile telecommunications industry and shape policies that could lead to more sustainable practices across the sector. However, the true impact of these activities is difficult to measure concretely. Political influence and long-term advocacy efforts, while vital for systemic change, often do not lend themselves to immediate or easily measurable outcomes.

Recommendations for Adopting a Regenerative and Distributive Purpose Design

Ensure Financial Independence
When seeking external funding, avoid becoming dependent on investors by retaining full decision-making power. Instead of granting voting rights to investors, opt for alternative financing models such as crowdfunding or crowdinvesting, which align better with long-term sustainability goals.

Embed Regenerative and Distributive Design from the Start
Integrating sustainability and the common good into your business model early on makes implementation significantly easier. A proactive approach ensures that regenerative and distributive considerations become a natural part of operations rather than an afterthought. Using Economy of the Common Good accounting can further support internal evaluation and highlight areas for development.

Engage Your Team in the Process
Employees are more committed to sustainability when they are actively involved in shaping initiatives rather than simply following imposed measures. Encouraging team participation fosters accountability and innovation, as more people contribute to identifying areas for improvement.

Inspiring Redesign Beyond the Business

WEtell sees itself as part of a broader movement toward a more sustainable and fair economic system, which aligns with the principles of the Doughnut Economy. While promoting fairness and transparency as its social responsibility, the company also focuses on regeneration on the ecological level by producing its own green energy. *WEtell*'s approach is about inspiring others to adopt similar values, with the ultimate goal of transforming the industry and contributing to a more equitable economy. As Mareike Kühnel recalls *WEtell*'s founders saying: "If we go bankrupt because everyone else is working as sustainably and fairly as we do, then we've reached our goal. And then we'll just find another branch and keep going."

References

Interview

with Nico Tucher, Co-founder & CEO (22/07/2024, 00:45h).
with Mareike Kühnel, Marketing Manager (17/10/2024, 00:48h).

Homepage

WEtell (2025): https://www.WEtell.de, [Accessed 2 April 2025].

Other Sources

Felber, C., & Hagelberg, G. (2017): The Economy for Common Good. A Workable, Transformative Ethics-Based Alternative, https://thenextsystem.org/sites/defa ult/files/2017-08/FelberHagelberg.pdf, [Accessed 2 April 2025].
WEtell (2023): Gemeinwohlbilanz (Economy of the Common Good Report), https:// www.wetell.de/media/filer_public/59/c5/59c59720-2831-4ab2-a4d7-7ce07a891f 15/2023_wetell_gemeinwohl-bilanz.pdf, [Accessed 2 April 2025].

Case Study: Wildplastic

Nelly Rahimy

Purpose: "Ridding the World of Wild Plastic Waste"
Design Trait: Purpose

Key Facts

Wildplastic is a limited liability company that is steward owned. Its goal is to reintegrate "wild plastic" (see info box) into the recycling system. The company cooperates with local NGOs and communities to collect plastic from the environment, which is then recycled into trash bags and, more recently, also packaging materials. *Wildplastic* operates under a steward-ownership model, which ensures that its mission remains at the core of its operations.

Seat: Hamburg
Established: 2019
Founders: Katrin Oeding, Christian Sigmund, Dieter Gottschalk, Fridtjof Detzner, Holger Ernst, Nadia Boegli, Jascha Mähler
Ownership: Verantwortungseigentum (Steward Ownership)
Legal form: Limited Liability Company
Employees: 17
Webpage: https://Wildplastic.com/

Purpose, Business Model & Objectives

Purpose: "Ridding the World of Wild Plastic Waste"

What happens when seven passionate people with different backgrounds travel the world? They return to Germany united by a shared mission: combat plastic waste.

In 2017, Fridtjof Detzner and Holger Ernst were traveling through Asia, while Christian Sigmund and Katrin Oeding explored Africa and South America. During their journeys, they encountered plastic waste everywhere—on beaches, in forests, deserts, and oceans. These experiences awakened a sense of responsibility within them. Upon their return, the founders had come to recognise plastic not only as an environmental hazard but also as a valuable, untapped resource that sparked their drive to act.

What is wild plastic?
"Wild plastic" refers to plastic waste that exists outside of formal recycling systems. It can be found in landfills, natural environments, and on streets. Unlike "ocean plastic," which describes plastic that has already entered marine ecosystems, wild plastic refers to waste at an earlier stage—before it reaches the water (Wildplastic, 2024).

Although the founders were initially scattered across Germany, they shared a singular problem: the global plastic crisis. What did it take to turn their idea into reality? Mainly, a network and expertise.

Through mutual connections, they teamed up with Nadia Boegli, Jascha Mähler, and Dieter Gottschalk. Each of them brought their unique background not only in business but in plastic, design, recycling and sustainability. In 2018, the team started with their initial idea: to produce a stylish trash bag and finance clean-ups with it. Over time, this idea evolved to its current business model.

The founders started gathering more like-minded people around them such as plastic–collecting organisations, investors and customers. Together, the seven founders created an entirely new value chain to get wild plastic back into the cycle. They source wild plastic from regions like Indonesia, Egypt, and South America.

In line with its motto, "trash to trash", *Wildplastic* launched its first product line with trash bags made from wild plastic. Now, the company aims to extend its reach and make an even greater impact with additional products such as delivery bags or toilet paper.

Insights into the Purpose of Eliminating Wild Plastic

From the start, *Wildplastic*'s founders were committed to creating a company that prioritised purpose over profit maximisation. Their goal was to create a profitable business on the one hand, and, more importantly, to make a lasting environmental and social impact on the other hand.

Understanding the Problem: A Plastic Crisis

Since the 1950s, plastic production and consumption have skyrocketed. Today, over 6.3 billion tons of plastic exist as waste globally, and an additional 400 million tons are produced each year. Despite the high recyclability and lightweight properties of plastic, only 10% of it is recycled, while 70% ends up in the environment. This vast quantity of unmanaged waste has severe consequences for both ecosystems and communities.

> "In short, 70 to 80 percent of the plastics produced globally are in the environment. This is a huge problem today. [...] the industry is producing more than ever, and we are saying that if we still produce plastics, then please use recycled and reused plastics. That's not happening at all today and that's our mission, to close the loops." — Christian Sigmund, CEO and Co-Founder

Wildplastic's aim is to transform the entire plastic system, from how society handles plastic waste to the policies that govern it. To achieve this aim, it actively participates in lobbying for plastic-positive legislation, advocating for policies that promote the use of recycled materials and discourage single-use plastics. By forming partnerships across industries and sectors, it fosters collaboration to drive widespread change.

To ensure its purpose remains at the heart of everything it does, *Wildplastic* has adopted a steward-ownership model. This model locks in the company's mission by legally prioritising purpose over profit and prevents any form of exit strategy that could compromise its long-term vision. In essence, *Wildplastic* has rendered itself a company that will only continue to exist as long as its mission is relevant.

> "Drastically speaking, when we've solved the problem and all the plastic has been cleaned up and returned to the cycle, there's no reason why we should continue operating the company." — Christian Sigmund

This mission highlights a departure from the traditional start-up focus on scaling and exiting. Under the steward-ownership model, *Wildplastic* is designed to prioritise its purpose above all else, ensuring long-term commitment to its core purpose, regardless of external pressures.

Dual Mission: Environmental and Social Impact

Wildplastic's mission goes beyond cleaning up plastic waste. The company aims to fundamentally transform the lifecycle of plastic and the way society perceives it. By turning environmental waste into useful products like trash bags and packaging, the company seeks to close the loop on plastic use and prevent it from re-entering ecosystems.

This purpose is deeply embedded in *Wildplastic*'s operations, influencing decisions at every level, from partnerships to product development.

While *Wildplastic*'s focus lies on recovering, recycling and reusing wild plastic, its purpose also has vital social dimensions. *Wildplastic* works closely with informal waste collectors, particularly in low-income countries where waste collection infrastructure is lacking.

> "The social aspect is that we must not forget that two billion people currently live without waste collection and at the same time there are informal collection organisations in these often low-income countries, which represent an informal waste collection system and which deserve all the support in the world. But they are currently marginalised, extremely underpaid and often discriminated against." – Christian Sigmund

By partnering with these communities, *Wildplastic* is not only cleaning the environment but also providing fair wages, dignified work and social empowerment to the people involved in collecting plastic waste.

How the Purpose of Eliminating Wild Plastic is Embedded across the Design of the Business

Finance and Ownership Design

Wildplastic sought financing models that aligned with its values, finding support through purpose-driven investors like Purpose Ventures e.G. Together, they developed a steward-ownership model that reflects its purpose. According to the golden share model, the Purpose Foundation holds 1% of the voting shares. While this might seem like a small percentage, it holds significant power: the golden share grants veto rights over any decisions that could divert the company from its purpose. This structure prevents profit-driven shifts and ensures the company remains mission-aligned.

Rather than pursuing exponential growth, investors expect sustainable, steady growth with fair returns over a 10-year horizon. The goal is to operate profitably, grow sustainably, and honour the trust investors placed in them.

The financial structure directly influences ownership and decision-making within the company. The founders see themselves as stewards of *Wildplastic*, with no planned or possible exit. Once they step down, decision-making power will pass to other active employees, ensuring the company remains true to its mission.

In terms of returns and equity distribution, *Wildplastic*'s financing rounds reflect different risk profiles, which are tied to varying multiples that determine investors' claims on returns. These multiples represent the potential return on investment (ROI) based on the stage at which investors provided funding. Earlier investors, who assumed more risk, are entitled to higher returns. In total, *Wildplastic* completed three financing rounds:

- Initial funding round: 5.3X multiple
- First investment round: 4.5X multiple
- Second investment round: 3X multiple

This means that if investors participated in the initial funding round with 10.000€, they could expect up to 53.000€ in returns. Once the total value is distributed to investors, *Wildplastic* can recall the shares and regain control of ownership.

> "This ensures there will be no mission drift for profit-driven reasons—so we don't start producing new plastic just because it's cheaper. At the same time, it guarantees that purpose and intent always remain at the core of our actions." – Christian Sigmund

Network Design

When the idea of *Wildplastic* began to form, no infrastructure existed to collect and process wild plastic at the scale the founders envisioned. Determined to make a difference, they set out to establish entirely new supply chains and networks, partnering with local NGOs and communities around the world.

> "The collection organisations need a partner to take the material off their hands and pay money for it. But that only happens if it can be processed at high quality. This is what's missing. No collection organisation has big brands knocking on their door asking for their waste, because there are still ten difficult steps in between. These collection organisations are the heart of our company. These are the people who do the important work on the ground—collecting, sorting, and ensuring that plastic finds its way back into the cycle."– Christian Sigmund

Wildplastic's first partnership was with *Plastic Bank*, an international organisation that empowers communities in countries in the global south to collect plastic waste in exchange for financial rewards. Volunteers from this organisation helped gather the first ton of plastic, enabling the creation of prototypes. This partnership allowed *Wildplastic* to not only access raw materials but also provide economic benefits to local communities.

Overview of countries where *Wildplastic* sources (Wildplastic, 2025)
Egypt: 12 tons
Ghana: 13.86 tons
Haiti: 137.69 tons
India: 199.88 tons
Indonesia: 42.62 tons
Liberia: 7.3 tons
Nigeria: 50.46 tons
Thailand: 127.25 tons

Today, *Wildplastic* collaborates with over 50 NGOs and community-based organisations to remove wild plastic from beaches, forests, and other ecosystems. Its operations span several regions, including Indonesia, Ghana, and Egypt. The partners are local fishing families, collecting organisations and waste aggregators. These organisations act as essential partners, ensuring that wild plastic is gathered sustainably and reintegrated into recycling streams.

In addition to global efforts, *Wildplastic* also formed new collaborations in Germany to meet its purpose. While trash bags were an important first step in combating pollution, the company identified the B2B-sector as a crucial next step. With thousands of packages being delivered every day around the world and the entire hygiene sector needing ecologic solutions, they can now proudly count companies like Otto, Hermes, and Goldeimer as partners. For example, in 2021, they launched the "Ottobag", a delivery bag made from at least 80% wild plastic. These partnerships signal a broader commitment to sustainability and set the foundation for scaling *Wildplastic*'s impact. By building global networks and collaborating with NGOs, waste collectors, and industry partners, *Wildplastic* seeks to expand its reach and multiply its impact.

"We don't claim that our solution will solve everything, but we want to set a great example."– Christian Sigmund

Impact-Focused Governance

Yes, profitability and fair wages are essential at *Wildplastic*, but the company's governance framework prioritises environmental and social impact as the ultimate measure of success.

"We measure success in impact instead of profits." – Christian Sigmund

To formalise this approach, *Wildplastic* incorporated impact assessment tools within its governance structure. Namely, *Wildplastic* conducted a Life Cycle Assessment

(LCA) comparing the environmental footprint of new plastic, recycled plastic, and wild plastic. The LCA revealed that *Wildplastic* bags emit between 32% and 55% fewer greenhouse gases than virgin Low-Density Polyethylene bags. For instance, the *Wildplastic* parcel bag alone reduces emissions by 55%, while WILDBAGs show reductions of 32% to 44%, depending on size. The assessment also demonstrated significant reductions in fossil energy consumption, water usage, and resource depletion.

In further alignment with its governance model, *Wildplastic* publishes an annual impact report alongside its financial report. In this report, the business tracks key metrics such as tons of plastic recovered, plastic provided to recyclers, and plastic cleaned up from the environment. These impact-focused metrics are its primary performance targets, shifting the company's focus from profits to environmental and social benefits.

Figure 1: Wildplastic's Impact Quantified

706.078 KG
WILD PLASTIC RECOVERED

1.406.022 KG
CO2 EMISSIONS SAVED

10.704 DAYS
WITH BETTER WORKING CONDITIONS

Source: Wildplastic 2024.

To enhance stakeholder engagement and ensure transparency across the value chain, *Wildplastic* launched the Wildtracker, a tool that allows customers to trace their *Wildplastic* products back to their origin. This transparency strengthens the connection between the product and its environmental benefits.

"No, we haven't defined any other KPIs, because in the *Wildplastic* business model, the KPIs are actually already a separate package. It's simple, we promise every tonne of plastic saved cleans up x square metres of the environment, saves ozone, O2 and ensures Z working days, better working conditions and so on. And it was possible for us to define even more KPIs, but if *WILDPLASTIC* is successful, then we are also successful in terms of impact." – Christian Sigmund

Challenges Arising from Designing Purpose around Eliminating Wild Plastic

Establishing Reliable Supply Chains

Especially during the first three years of *Wildplastic*'s journey, the supply chains posed the greatest challenge. Not only building supply chains from scratch but also dealing with country-specific challenges: For instance, sorting plastic is complicated by high levels of plastic pollution, while in Egypt, regulations on exports create additional hurdles. Most notably, *Wildplastic*'s collaborations with Haitian NGOs have been halted due to political instability.

Balancing Purpose with Practical Realities

Another ongoing challenge for *Wildplastic* has been balancing its mission with technical and operational limitations. Is it better to use 100% wild plastic or to compromise on the percentage to meet technical requirements?

One guiding principle in these situations is the company's desire to shift industry mindsets and make an impact. Sometimes, this requires innovation; other times, it requires adaptation and collaboration.

> "For example, with toilet paper, we can't technically use 100% wild plastic because it doesn't have the necessary mechanical properties. There's a very narrow corridor of requirements in the industry regarding tear resistance and usability, and there's little willingness to engage in discussions around this."- Christian Sigmund

Sales Strategy: Tackling the Cost of Sustainable Solutions

Another challenge for *Wildplastic* is creating enough sales. While it generates significant social and ecologic impact with its trash bags, sustainable solutions are often more expensive than their conventional alternatives. Social enterprises, in particular, struggle with scaling up sales operations, making it harder to compete with cheaper, less sustainable products. To address this, *Wildplastic* is exploring bonus models to incentivise its sales teams. As Christian Sigmund emphasises: "we also want to have a competitive ambition [...] we actually want even more impact, even more impact actually means even more deals". And rightly so, because what could be more important than getting *Wildplastic* products out there and thus spreading its mission?

Aligning Mission with Stakeholder Expectations

With its mission set from the beginning, *Wildplastic* has been eager to set the appropriate structures from the beginning, too. This involved effectively communicating its purpose and impact to avoid accusations of greenwashing. One of its initial steps was to set measurable targets for assessing impact. As Christian Sigmund explains:

> "In other words, at the beginning there was a life cycle assessment, a living wage inspection and a very robust process, so to speak, in which we repeatedly looked at the impact. But that was over-engineered in the sense that we didn't have any deals at the time."

Hence, spending resources on in-depth impact assessments from the beginning was a risk they were willing to take. However, this might be unavoidable for purpose-driven firms that want to counter any possible accusations of greenwashing.

Another example of managing stakeholder expectations was the organisational structure. *Wildplastic* wanted to create flat hierarchies and a fair and efficient working environment for employees. However, they soon realised that this over-engineering slowed decision-making processes, as not everyone needed to be involved in every decision.

Fighting against Industry Standards

One of the supporting missions that come with combating plastic waste is also to educate and support change in existing practices and policies. *Wildplastic* is active and participates in politics and lobbying. However, what they face are old, powerful and loud industry giants that are profiting from the status quo:

> "You also have to imagine that the oil and gas lobby (...) I think in the last 50 years they have somehow made a profit of 50 trillion euros, not just a profit, but a profit of 3 billion euros every day. And they can spend so much money on lobbying that this opponent simply seems almost overpowering right now, and yet it's complete madness, soberly considered, that this is still allowed at all." – Christian Sigmund

In this context, *Wildplastic*'s mission to transform the industry becomes even more critical. They aim to challenge these entrenched standards and advocate for sustainable practices, even when faced with formidable opposition.

Recommendations for Adopting a Regenerative and Distributive Purpose Design

Craft a bold, future-focused vision that aligns with your values and long-term aspirations. This vision does not need to be realised overnight, but should serve as a compass, guiding your decisions and actions through this transformative era.

Build strategic partnerships for greater impact. Collaboration is key to driving meaningful change. Partner with businesses, communities, and organisations that share your mission to amplify your efforts and create systemic impact. By working together, you can accelerate progress, share knowledge, and drive innovation.

Address the social and environmental dimensions of your challenge. Consider the broader implications of the issue you are tackling. For us, this meant recognising that plastic pollution disproportionately harms vulnerable communities and ecosystems. By embracing regenerative solutions—such as investing in recycled materials, circular systems, and innovative alternatives—we were able to generate a ripple effect that benefits both people and the planet.

Inspiring Redesign Beyond the Business

Wildplastic contributes to the transformation of the economic system by challenging the traditional profit-driven model with a purpose-driven, sustainable approach. By integrating environmental and social impact directly into its business design, *Wildplastic* promotes a circular economy, where waste is not just minimised but actively turned into valuable resources. Its steward-ownership structure, focus on transparency through tools like the *Wildtracker*, and commitment to sustainable growth over profit maximisation offer a blueprint for businesses to balance profitability with ecological responsibility. This shift helps to redefine success, not in terms of financial gain alone, but in creating positive, long-lasting environmental and social change.

References

Interview

with Christian Sigmund, CEO and Co-Founder (09/06/2024, 00:45h).

Homepage

Wildplastic (2024): https://wildplastic.com/pages/mission, [Accessed 5 March 2025].
Wildplastic (2025): https://wildplastic.com/pages/wildtracker, [Accessed 5 March 2025].

Other Sources

Planet A Ventures (2022): Life-cycle-assessment Wildplastic, https://drive.googl e.com/file/d/1N5P6m1G16gemQfvrPLqusXcr4M-rx6iX/view, [Accessed 11 April 2025].
Purpose Stiftung (2024): Wildplastic Case study, https://purpose-economy.org/con tent/uploads/purpose-WILDPLASTICcase-study.pdf, [Accessed 11 April 2025].

Case Study: WoodenValley

Nelly Rahimy

Purpose: Regenerative Construction: "To shape our living space jointly and consistently in a climate-positive way."
Design Trait: Purpose

Key Facts

WoodenValley aims to transform the construction industry toward regeneration. Through research, consulting, and education, the company promotes Cradle-to-Cradle principles that can enable sustainable building practices.

Seat: Stuttgart
Established: 2021
Founders: Kamila Pasko, Robert Böker, Christian Ritz
Ownership: Verantwortungseigentum (Steward Ownership)
Legal form: Not-for-profit Limited Liability Company (gGmbH)
Employees: 13
Webpage: https://woodenvalley.de/

Purpose, Business Model & Objectives

Purpose: Regenerative Construction: "To shape our living space jointly and consistently in a climate-positive way."

WoodenValley was founded with a clear and ambitious goal: to make construction regenerative. The founders were driven by the industry's significant ecological challenges: high emissions, excessive energy consumption, and waste generation. Inspired by the Cradle-to-Cradle concept, they set themselves the purpose of advancing regenerative construction.

Figure 1: Environmental Impact of the Construction Industry in Germany [1, 2, 3]

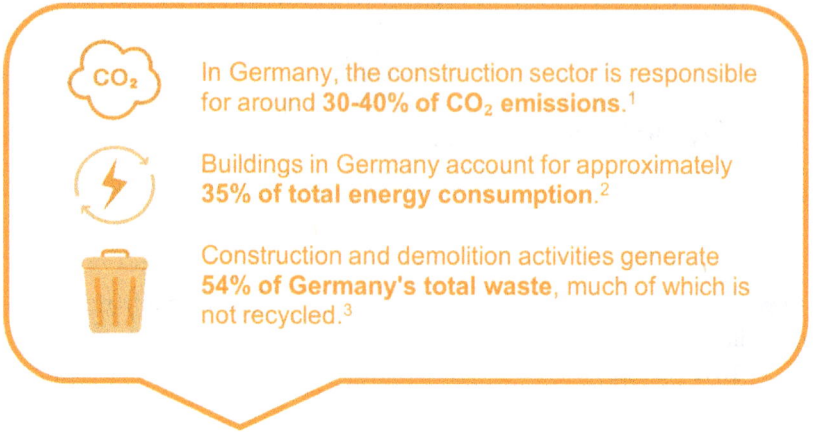

In Germany, the construction sector is responsible for around **30-40% of CO₂ emissions**.[1]

Buildings in Germany account for approximately **35% of total energy consumption**.[2]

Construction and demolition activities generate **54% of Germany's total waste**, much of which is not recycled.[3]

Source: Own Representation.

Cradle-to-Cradle (C2C)

"The goal is not to minimize the cradle-to-grave flow of materials, but to generate cyclical, cradle-to-cradle "metabolisms" that enable materials to maintain their status as resources and accumulate intelligence over time (upcycling). This inherently generates a synergistic relationship between ecological and economic systems—a positive recoupling of the relationship between economy and ecology" (Braungart et al. 2007).

The idea to bring the Cradle-to-Cradle concept into construction, or: *WoodenValley*, emerged during a high-school reunion between Robert Böker and Kamila Pasko. However, their initial search for investors was met with disappointment, as most were more interested in maximising their personal return on investment than promoting sustainability. As Robert Böker recalls,

"We attended an impact investing event at the end of 2022, and there was a programme focused on sustainability. It was quite interesting to observe how the investor network interpreted that concept. In reality, it turned out to be traditional thought patterns—just painted green."

---

1   Statistisches Bundesamt (2024).
2   Umweltbundesamt (2019).
3   Destatis (2021).

Eventually, Christian Ritz joined Kamila Pasko and Robert Böker on their mission: first as a business angel who shared their vision and later formally as a co-founder. Together, they divided *WoodenValley*'s activities. While Kamila Pasko focuses on raising awareness and promoting regenerative practices through education, Robert Böker oversees digital tools and processes that enhance sustainability in construction and Christian Ritz consults clients in adopting regenerative approaches within the construction industry. The business model generates revenue from research and consulting services to fund educational initiatives.

> "We have a business area for research and a business area for practical projects, where we do things for companies in exchange for money. So, the goal is to generate enough from the non-commercial and commercial operations to keep research and education running. What emerges from research and education is then funnelled back into practical projects to test its viability. The learnings from these projects are then fed back into research and education, creating a continuous cycle."– Robert Böker

Insights into the Purpose of Regenerative Construction

For *WoodenValley*, regenerative construction goes beyond carbon neutrality. It involves creating climate-positive solutions by not only minimising emissions but actively contributing to environmental regeneration. The company pursues this purpose through three interconnected pillars.

Three Pillars of Purpose

As *WoodenValley* grew, the founders identified three interconnected areas crucial for achieving their purpose: knowledge dissemination, research, and implementation through projects. These areas were formalised into the three pillars of their purpose-driven model: Consulting, Research, and Education. Together, these pillars underpin *WoodenValley*'s business while advancing its purpose of sustainability transformation in construction.

a) **Research:** *WoodenValley* collaborates with academic institutions, industry partners, and students to research sustainable construction techniques. One of its core innovations is life-cycle-optimised Building Information Modelling (BIM), which evaluates buildings based on circular economy principles. In this research project, *WoodenValley* demonstrated that the life cycles of different building options can be calculated at the earliest stages of the construction process. This calculation allows for precise, data-driven statements about which option generates lower CO_2 emissions or consumes fewer resources, which enables more informed decision-making.

"When you, as a building assembly, have access to these calculations, you have a much better foundation for decision-making than if you just decide by rule of thumb." – Christian Ritz

Additionally, they leverage machine learning and artificial intelligence to develop methods for documenting the CO_2 positivity of buildings. This research supports the issuance of emissions certificates and provides a much-needed tangible measure of environmental impact.

b) **Consulting**: *WoodenValley* helps companies with climate protection, circular construction, economic viability analysis, and CO_2 calculations. By quantifying the benefits of circular construction, they create a stronger financial argument for sustainable methods. Still, *WoodenValley* remains committed to its purpose, even if, in some cases, this means turning down clients who do not align:

"There are just a few no-gos. And those are the things we want to address now, especially if someone deliberately positions themselves completely differently in the market. I just mentioned this at [Company X], even though we have no direct connection to them. But it's one of those corporations that pretends to be something it's not, while essentially continuing to cement business practices worldwide, especially around water, in a way that is no longer acceptable. And with someone like that, we don't want to collaborate." – Christian Ritz

c) **Education**: Education is the third cornerstone of *WoodenValley*'s purpose, with the focus on two audiences:

- Young people: introducing sustainability concepts and fostering environmental awareness. Specifically, *WoodenValley* works towards integrating the Cradle-to-Cradle Concept into the school syllabus. As Kamila Pasko points out,

"Essentially, the goal is to integrate the concept of Cradle to Cradle into the curriculum [...] in the sense of education for sustainable development. And the integration of this specific topic [...] is meant to ensure that children ultimately develop [...] future competencies like problem-solving ori-entation, critical thinking, creativity, and self-determination."

- Professionals: providing practical insights into circular construction and material lifecycles. The increasing demand for educational programs underscores its foresight in addressing a critical gap in industry knowledge.

Education Flagship: W∞d.ii

WoodenValley's most recent contribution to its educational activities is its initiative, w∞d.ii. The project, a mobile real-world lab in the form of a tiny house, is designed to showcase and test circular construction principles. Built according to Cradle-to-Cradle standards, w∞d.ii is a space for education, innovation, and collaboration and aligns with *WoodenValley*'s broader purpose:

"To create an adaptable learning space where our future and life as part of the biosphere are at the centre. To design education for regeneration and invite individuals to take action with self-efficacy."

Figure 2: WoodenValley's W∞d.ii: Future Mobile and Educational Space

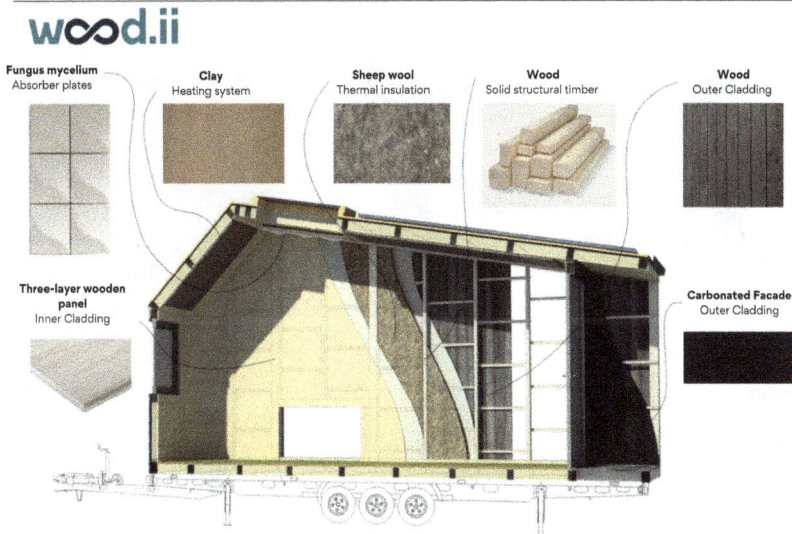

Source: WoodenValley 2024.

The project serves multiple audiences:

- Architecture and planning professionals engage with circular technologies.
- Young learners are introduced to sustainability through hands-on experiences.

The structure itself exemplifies regenerative construction. Features include:

- **Integrated solar panels**, placed within walls to reduce resource usage.
- A **plant-based water treatment system** that purifies water for reuse in the facility.
- **Circular and bio-based** materials showcased as part of the building's design.

Founders' Perspectives on *WoodenValley*'s Purpose

Notably, despite their shared vision, each founder articulates *WoodenValley*'s purpose uniquely, which reflects the depth of their engagement with the company's purpose.

> "We have taken it upon ourselves to implement and establish a circular economy in the construction industry, and we have intertwined that with promoting education and research in this field." – Robert Böker
>
> "Our purpose is enabling people to shape their living spaces in a self-determined, climate-positive way." – Kamila Pasko
>
> "Our purpose is about showing others how the circular economy works. That's one part of it. That's why this early phase in the education sector is also about using w∞d.ii for this purpose. The second part is to radically change existing business processes and workflows, in other words, to be disruptive. Basically, WoodenValley aims to show how it is now possible to achieve alignment between the requester of a building, i.e. the client, through to the architect, engineers, suppliers, contractors and so on – and in terms of ecology, the circular economy and sustainability." – Christian Ritz

How the Purpose of Regenerative Construction is Embedded across the Design of the Business

Finance Design

While access to financing is a persistent problem, *WoodenValley* does have access to some noteworthy funding opportunities. Its not-for-profit status and focus on a purpose-driven model have opened doors that would have otherwise been inaccessible to profit-driven companies. One such opportunity lies in accessing public funding, particularly for research projects:

"Because we have the additional topics of education and research, it makes it much easier for us to present ourselves as a non-university research institute for funding projects, educational projects, grants, etc. This allows us to access entirely different funding sources and in a different way than purely economically-driven companies." – Robert Böker

When initial investor searches proved unfruitful, *WoodenValley*'s independence and commitment to its purpose led the founders to pursue creative solutions, such as acquiring government funding and launching crowdfunding campaigns.

"This independence and flexibility to find other ways was fantastic. It made us more creative rather than leaving us in despair because there wasn't anyone sitting there tapping their finger on the table and saying, 'You know, I want my 10% in three years.' Instead, it was stressful, but in a different way. It was stressful for us because we wanted to achieve good value, but we didn't have someone breathing down our necks to whom we owed money."– Kamila Pasko

Ownership Design

During its financing search, *WoodenValley* explored alternative financing and legal models, and decided to adopt the steward-ownership model. With guidance from the Purpose Foundation, they established *WoodenValley* as a not-for-profit company (gGmbH). This legal form binds its activities to its mission of climate protection, ensuring that profits will always be reinvested into its purpose.

"And then, out of sheer defiance, we added the non-profit status to it, and in doing so, we deprived ourselves of the possibility of distributing profits in that form. So, in the current setup we are in, it's virtually impossible to take money out of the company that is not reinvested into the company's purpose." – Robert Böker

WoodenValley's steward-owned legal structure enhances its credibility when forming partnerships. As it prioritises purpose over profit, its partners trust in *WoodenValley*'s commitment to climate positivity and neutrality. This dedication is particularly evident in the company's customer relationships. For instance, its very first municipal client chose *WoodenValley* over for-profit consultants, recognising its mission-driven approach. As Kamila Pasko explains:

"Yes, it's really always the same question—this authenticity. Maybe they didn't take us seriously at first because we were a startup, but they believed us. They saw our passion and purpose, that we were working for the cause and not for our own Porsche. That made a huge difference in getting our foot in the door. We haven't done an enormous number of projects in the past years, but I can count four or five where I believe this was the initial reason. They saw our non-profit angle and thought, 'That's interesting; they're coming at this from a completely different perspective.'"

This transparency and clear sense of purpose enable *WoodenValley* to build strong and reliable relationships with various stakeholders who share its sustainability goals.

Network Design

WoodenValley's not-for-profit status and steward-ownership assure partners that the company is not motivated by economic gain but by a desire to advance the sustainability agenda, which in turn encourages deeper collaboration. As Robert Böker points out:

"Networks are vital for our survival. So, without SDG 17, it's very difficult."

Sustainable Development Goal 17, focused on partnerships for the goals, under-scores the importance of collaborative networks in achieving sustainable develop-ment. *WoodenValley* embodies this spirit, relying on strong partnerships in three main areas to advance its objectives.

One example of the power of this network is its collaboration with GLS Bank, a leading financial institution in sustainable banking. *WoodenValley* secured a loan from GLS to fund its operations, and this partnership is rooted in shared values around climate protection. Both parties are driven by enthusiasm for promoting sustainability, with a mutual mindset that challenges can always be overcome through collaborative effort.

Other key partners in *WoodenValley's* network include the NGO Cradle-to-Cradle, architects and sustainable material producers, with whom they frequently engage at fairs and events. These connections not only enhance their industry knowledge but also reinforce their network of supporters and collaborators. For example, the w∞d.ii tiny learning space serves as both an educational tool and a platform to deepen ties with these stakeholders, showcasing regenerative construction methods in action.

Another network-related part of *WoodenValley's* success comes from its team, consisting of like-minded, enthusiastic individuals who volunteer, network, and work as employees. *WoodenValley's* purpose is so inspiring that the company has no trouble attracting talent. As Kamila Pasko recalls, "the very first employee joined us primarily because of our purpose and our connection to Cradle-to-Cradle". Accord-ingly, their job postings always receive a surplus of applications. In addition, many people in their broader community are eager to support *WoodenValley's* purpose through volunteering and networking.

This collaborative approach allows *WoodenValley* to initiate projects that challenge industry norms. As Robert Böker explains:

"Because we don't have that economic orientation, we are, more or less, a neutral Switzerland. And there are projects we've started or want to initiate that initially caused some raised eyebrows because it's not common practice. For example, let's say you have a great construction project in mind where you deliberately want to involve two or three architecture firms—one that specialises in timber construction and another that is a leader in sustainable materials. That's not typical. To put it mildly."

These unconventional collaborations pool expertise and resources, pushing the construction industry toward more innovative, sustainable practices.

Their innovative approach has already been applied successfully, financing projects like w∞d.ii, their mobile real-world lab for circular construction.

Challenges Arising from Designing Purpose around Regenerative Construction

WoodenValley's mission to revolutionise the construction industry with sustainable practices comes with its share of significant challenges. These obstacles stem from financial constraints, mindsets regarding sustainability, and the conservative nature of the construction industry, which collectively slow progress toward regenerative construction.

Financing:

One of *WoodenValley*'s most persistent challenges is funding. As a purpose-driven organisation prioritising long-term impact over short-term profits, *WoodenValley* has struggled to attract traditional investors. This challenge extends to customers, particularly companies, where financial concerns often outweigh environmental considerations.

A recent project exemplifies this difficulty. *WoodenValley* conducted a lifecycle analysis to evaluate two options for reworking an old building: renovation and reconstruction with sustainable, recyclable materials. Despite their analysis clearly pointing to one of these alternatives as the more sustainable, the client ultimately chose the more cost-effective yet more environmentally harmful alternative. As Kamila Pasko observed:

"But in the end, they chose the environmentally worse option due to cost reasons. If this had been a public project governed by laws requiring lifecycle analyses, they wouldn't have been allowed to make such a decision."

Mindset around Sustainability:

Another significant challenge *WoodenValley* faces is the subjective nature of sustainability itself. Sustainability is a broad and often loosely defined concept, which varies significantly across industries, companies, and individuals. This subjectivity makes it difficult to establish common ground or universal standards when promoting sustainable practices in the construction sector.

"The problem, I believe, is that sustainability is quite subjective. Everyone defines it a little differently for themselves. Unfortunately, there is no clear way to measure it. There's no baseline—where exactly is the starting point? What does zero to ten look like? What score should we give ourselves? Where do we actually stand? Unfortunately, that just doesn't work so well." – Robert Böker

This lack of consistent measurement tools complicates their efforts to push for more sustainable practices. The United Nations' Sustainable Development Goals (SDGs) provide a framework for setting sustainability targets, offering companies like *WoodenValley* a point of reference to map their contributions. Documenting how they address each SDG and who their target audience is can help create a clearer picture. However, even with these guidelines, it remains challenging to compare sustainability metrics across projects.

As setting key performance indicators and other targets is key for any organisation, the difficulty of setting effective sustainability targets in this industry poses a particular challenge for *WoodenValley*. While their competitors focus on commercial and financial targets, being a purpose-driven organisation means that *WoodenValley* must develop credible and effective sustainability targets to guide its work.

Industry Standards and Resistance to Change:

While other industries such as food and fashion have been comparatively quicker in integrating sustainability principles, the construction sector remains particularly conservative, posing a persistent challenge to *WoodenValley*'s mission of promoting circular and sustainable building practices. This resistance to change is deeply rooted, with many industry players hesitant to adopt new materials or methods, even when they promise long-term environmental benefits.

"The field of construction is relatively conservative, and many companies make very good money with the existing system. Over the years, many processes have been optimised for efficiency, and everything works very, very well. The challenge we face is raising awareness and shifting toward a different approach to construction." – Robert Böker

The tendering processes further compound the problem. Current tendering frameworks are not designed to accommodate sustainable innovations:

"The problem is that the entire tendering system is not prepared for these new topics. The whole process is designed to follow standard procedures and methods that have been in place for 100 years. These new approaches simply aren't included, and unfortunately, they can't really be represented within the current framework." – Robert Böker

For instance, regulations often require multiple offers for any material purchase, which makes it challenging to use specialised sustainable materials such as fungal insulation, as there may be only one producer on the market. This results in sustainability-friendly innovations being disqualified from bids simply because they fail to fit within the established procurement framework.

As collaboration across the industry is critical to achieving sustainability goals, the resistance to change and lack of industry standards mean that *WoodenValley* often operates as an isolated pioneer within a broader industry where most mainstream actors do not prioritise sustainability.

Recommendations for Adopting a Regenerative and Distributive Purpose Design

Define a purpose that addresses a meaningful societal challenge while remaining broad enough for all employees, founders, and stakeholders to identify with and contribute to. As Christian Ritz explains:

"Whenever we were present and had meaningful conversations, the question came up: 'I still don't fully understand what they actually do—what is it really about?' This is partly because we have such a broad range of offerings. When you have that, and especially when you have a core product—or something that truly represents the heart of what you do, something that's easy to grasp—then I believe that's already a strong advantage. My advice to everyone would be to focus on developing that core with real emphasis before expanding into too many additional facets."

Choose a legal structure that aligns with your purpose and protects it over time. Consider adopting models like social enterprise or steward-ownership to formalise the commitment to purpose-driven business operations.
Develop strategic partnerships with like-minded organisations, communities, and financial institutions. This can help amplify impact, access new resources, and scale up efforts.

Inspiring Redesign Beyond the Business

WoodenValley contributes to economic transformation by promoting regenerative, circular construction practices that move away from the traditional linear economy. Or as Christian Ritz puts it,

> "Disruption. It's about completely redefining existing business fields. Not just in terms of the materials we inevitably address in the construction industry, but also in terms of processes. I believe it's not our core purpose, but it is part of the consideration: how much growth is truly important and right?"

Through its use of *Cradle-to-Cradle* design principles, the company ensures that all materials are reused, creating no waste in the process. Its not-for-profit status reinforces its commitment to purpose over profit, channelling financial surpluses into research and education. By demonstrating the financial viability of sustainable construction through economic analyses, *WoodenValley* challenges conventional models and inspires a shift toward long-term, purpose-driven business approaches in the construction industry.

References

Interviews

Robert Böker, Co-Founder WoodenValley, Interview, (07/05/2024, 00:48h).
Kamila Pasko, Co-Founder WoodenValley, Interview (23/10/2024, 00:52h).
Christian Ritz, Business Angel and Co-Founder WoodenValley (12/12/2024, 00:45h).

Homepage

WoodenValley (2025): https://woodenvalley.de/, [Accessed 22 April 2025].
Wooden Valley (2025a): https://woodenvalley.de/woodii, [Accessed 22 April 2025].

Other Sources

Braungart, M., McDonough, W., & Bollinger, A. (2007): Cradle-to-cradle design: Creating healthy emissions – a strategy for eco-effective product and system design. *Journal of Cleaner Production*, 15 (13–14), 1337–1348. https://doi.org/10.1016/j.jclepro.2006.08.003.

Destatis (2021): Abfallaufkommen in Deutschland im Jahr 2019 weiter auf hohem Niveau, https://www.destatis.de/DE/Presse/Pressemitteilungen/2021/06/PD21_261_321.html, [Accessed 22 April 2025].

Statistisches Bundesamt (2024): Treibhausgasemissionen des deutschen Bauhauptgewerbes* in den Jahren 2000 bis 2022 (in 1.000 Tonnen CO_2-Äquivalent) [Graph], https://de.statista.com/statistik/daten/studie/476879/umfrage/treibhausgasemissionen-des-deutschen-bauhauptgewerbes/, [Accessed 21 October 2024].

Umweltbundesamt (2019): Energy efficiency of residential buildings on the rise, but at a slower rate, https://www.umweltbundesamt.de/en/press/pressinformation/energy-efficiency-of-residential-buildings-on-the, [Accessed 22 April 2025].

WoodenValley (2024): Photo – WoodenValley's w∞d.ii: future mobile and educational space.

Network Design

Case Study: On Purpose Berlin

Jannes Kormann[1]

Purpose: On Purpose develops people to take on the greatest challenge of our time: to transform our economy from profit to purpose
Design Trait: Network
Innovative Practice: Community-Centred Network Design

Key Facts

On Purpose is an international social enterprise that initiates change by training and developing leaders who transform and lead new types of organisations. Building a community of changemakers, they want to transform the economy from being profit-driven to purpose-driven.

> **Established:** 2009 (London), 2015 (Paris), 2016 (Berlin)
> **Location:** London, Great Britain; Paris, France; Berlin, Germany
> **Founder:** Tom Rippin
> **Ownership:** Limited Liability Company (GmbH) in Germany (wholly owned by a UK not-for-profit)
> **Legal Form:** Limited Liability Company in Germany (GmbH)
> **Employees:** 6 (2024)
> **Webpage:** https://onpurpose.org/en/

---

1   Transparency note: The author was himself a participating Associate of the *On Purpose* leadership programme and is therefore an active part of the *On Purpose* community.

Purpose, Business Model & Objectives

> Purpose: "*On Purpose* develops people to take on the greatest challenge of our time: to transform our economy from profit to purpose."

> "We believe in putting purpose before profit. We're a community that helps you find your work in the world: work that matters and work you care about. We believe that only by doing this will we have a chance of solving society's most difficult problems." – Tom Rippin, *On Purpose* Founder and CEO

On Purpose is an international social enterprise founded in 2009 in London and expanded to Paris in 2015 and Berlin in 2016.[2] Its mission is to transform the economy from being profit-driven to purpose-driven. The organisation is based on the belief that the current economy is human-made and can be redesigned to benefit both people and the planet. To accomplish this goal, *On Purpose* initiates change by training and developing leaders who transform and lead existing organisations towards an economy that puts the wellbeing of the people and society over profit.

The proposed transformation is primarily driven by its one-year Associate Programme, which is designed for high-potential early- to mid-career professionals. The programme combines leadership development with recruitment, connecting individuals with socio-ecological organisations or those organisations aspiring to become more sustainable. These organisations benefit from a large network and the Associates' skills, while the Associates gain experience working on new or ongoing projects with socio-ecological goals in areas such as strategy and business development. In short, *On Purpose* offers organisations and individuals an opportunity to experiment with and debate new approaches to leadership and work.

> "Using placement as a lever, to bring people into impact, to pass on knowledge, to empower them to do good for the rest of their lives." — Lukas Marzi, Co-Managing Director

The full-time programme (figure 1) pays people to participate and starts each year in April and October. It includes two six-month work placements, supported by coaching on professional and personal development, mentoring, and weekly training sessions. Training covers impact measurement, regenerative management and leadership, systemic thinking, and personal development. After completing the

---

2   In this article, *On Purpose* refers to the Berlin location and *On Purpose* International to all three locations.

programme, Associates become part of the *On Purpose* community (figure 2) as Fellows, continuing to benefit from and contribute to the community.

Figure 1: On Purpose – Associate Programme

Source: Own Representation based on *On Purpose* 2024.

Insights into the Community-Centred Network Design

> "We are building a community that is shaping the economy of tomorrow. A community of people who want to do things differently, supporting one another, and creating a more positive future." — Saskia Klug, Community Manager

Hence, community building and support are central to *On Purpose*'s mission. *On Purpose* strives to empower its community to prioritise purpose over profit, working within planetary boundaries and promoting wellbeing in the understanding of enabling everyone to lead a dignified life. *On Purpose*'s vision, consequently, closely aligns with the principles of the Doughnut Economy.

However, *On Purpose* is a small organisation. While its core team manages the community and supports Associates and partner organisations, *On Purpose* strongly depends on the perspectives, commitment, and initiatives of community members, making strong relationships with them central. This community functions in a decentralised way across a wide range of areas, from climate change mitigation through reforestation to redesigning education systems to better serve children. Community members include two main customer groups, which are partner organisations and Associates, as well as the broader community of Fellows, coaches, mentors, and trainers (figure 2).

Figure 2: On Purpose Community Member Groups

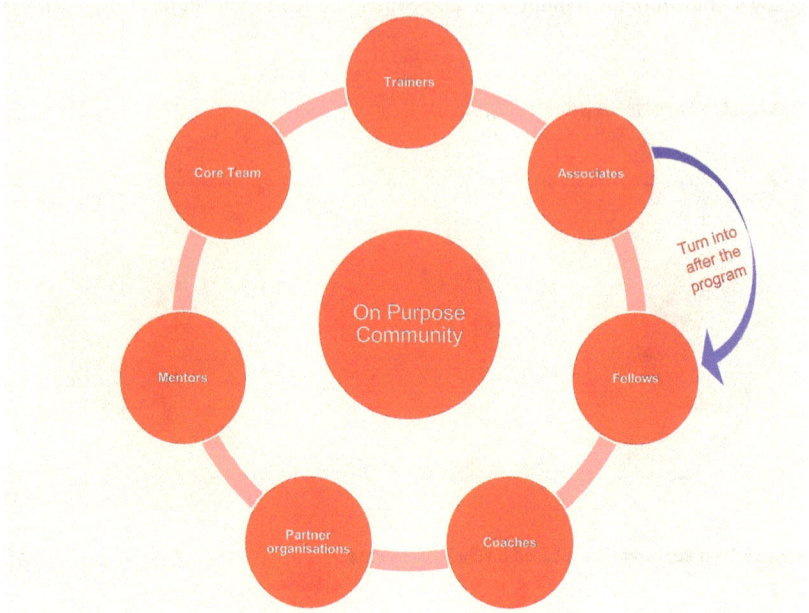

Source: Own representation, based on *On Purpose* 2024.

Partner Organisations

The organisations referred to as partner organisations come from various sectors and range in size, including both for-profit and not-for-profit entities, foundations, and social enterprises. Despite their diversity, they all seek to enhance their socioecological impact.

> "Customers? We see the participating organisations as partners and also call them partner organisations. We don't see it as a classic service relationship, even if money is paid. The money is paid for participating in the one year. This can be repeated, but the organisation remains a partner forever." — Lukas Marzi

On Purpose strives to meet diverse needs, even if the organisation is not actively involved in the current programme. For some, the recruitment service is especially valuable, and they appreciate the Associates' new perspectives, motivation, and impact, with satisfaction rates for the Associates in the 2022 cohorts being consistently high (9.2 and 9.0 out of 10, Impact report 2023). These organisations are not actively involved in the community, believing that the recruitment service is sufficient compensation for the financial investment. Despite strong relationships, interactions between *On Purpose* and these organisations are not highly formalised, with only two mandatory check-ins per year. Other organisations prefer to be more involved, leveraging the network for outreach or staff referrals to fully benefit from the community. The core idea is that engagement, such as attending events, is required to reap the greater rewards.

Associates

Associates form a second customer group. The programme is designed around their needs and expectations, fostering a strong relationship between *On Purpose* and them. Associates form close ties, supporting and challenging one another, learning, and sharing experiences within their cohort. Bonding the cohort *On Purpose* opens up the possibility to build deep relationships through a four-day induction at the beginning of the year, followed by a joint retreat.

On Purpose collects regular feedback from Associates to assess their well-being and ensure the programme meets their expectations and its purpose of driving change. Feedback helps to adjust the training programme to fit each cohort's needs. The focus remains on the individual Associate, as Lukas Marzi said: "How are the Associates doing? How do they feel empowered by the programme?"

Community

The community serves as a "home for the leaders: a community that develops, challenges and sustains itself and others, to help bring about (a shift in our) economy" (Impact Report 2023). To achieve this and foster interaction, *On Purpose* regularly organises events that bring together current participants, Fellows, coaches, mentors, trainers, and partner organisations. Gatherings foster connections within the community and encourage sharing knowledge and expertise across industries. Regular events include summer and winter parties, content-related get-togethers, and many self-organised meetings and retreats. To integrate newcomers, the current cohort organises two events: one for all members of the community and another joint weekend with cohorts from Paris and London, strengthening bonds between international locations.

The wider community includes coaches, mentors, and trainers, many of whom are Fellows. These groups are passionate about the programme's purpose and maintain it by volunteering their time to support Associates. These groups benefit mostly from experimenting with new methods in workshops and interactions with Associates, as well as from the feedback they receive.

These relationships in the *On Purpose* community rest on at least two pillars: shared values and mutual learning and support.

Value-driven Relationships

Shared values guide both *On Purpose* and the entire community. Over time, common and codified values have emerged, reflecting interactions between members.

> "We have defined values as *On Purpose*, with the entire community, so that the values are also supported by the community. And it works!" — Saskia Klug

These community values include choosing optimism, learning together, stepping up, engaging our head and heart and acting with integrity. Besides these, Lukas Marzi mentioned values like empathy, loyalty, and the belief that a better future can be shaped. Cooperation is central as the community relies on individuals working together. *On Purpose* invites all members to act authentically, showing their whole selves rather than just their professional personas. The focus on human needs extends to working with organisations with different values, leading to more genuine, supportive relationships. As Lukas Marzi states, "Because of the relationship we have with our stakeholders (...) communication is on a completely different level than I see anywhere else."

Trust is a key feature in relationships, both with individuals and organisations. A leap in trust is extended to all members, with the assumption of positive intent. For example, the Associate selection process looks beyond CVs to understand individuals' motivations and alignment with *On Purpose*'s values. This leap in trust strengthens the network as the trust is repaid in numerous ways: Members contribute through feedback, ideas, and recommendations, taking on sales and business development tasks, and Fellows engage as trainers, coaches, or mentors.

In relationships with partner organisations, conflicts are resolved through dialogue rather than relying on signed contracts. Received feedback shows that *On Purpose* acts with integrity and is solution-oriented in difficult negotiations, which fosters long-term partnerships.

Learning Together and Mutual Support

Joint learning is a key element of the community. Friday workshops focus on topics such as financing, measuring impact, and leading change at an individual, organisational, and systemic level. The workshops inspire change and motivate individuals to pursue their purpose. Notably, 99% of Associates share the learning from these workshops with others (Impact report 2022).

Additionally, 98% of Associates remain committed to the impact sector and creating change after ending the programme (Impact report 2022), also due to the strong mutual support within the community. The community thrives on the notion of contributing to positive societal change, characterised by a cooperative attitude without expecting anything in return. Asking for help is encouraged, and members are glad to offer support or connect others with someone who can assist. Every interaction in the community strengthens collaboration. New members constantly introduce fresh viewpoints, which drives innovation and inspiration within the network. So, the cycle of giving and receiving trust enriches everyone.

"The idea in the network is that if everyone helps everyone, then everyone has been helped." — Lukas Marzi

How the Community-Centred Network Design Enables Regenerative and Distributive Dynamics

Purpose as the Starting Point

The potential of the *On Purpose* community starts with its purpose to develop people to take on the greatest challenge of our time: to transform our economy from profit to purpose. As founder Tom Rippin explains, "we believe in putting purpose before profit. We're a community that helps you find your work in the world: work that matters and work you care about." Purpose drives decisions and actions. The individual takes a step back and looks at what would be good for the community or society, independently of *On Purpose*. When selecting partner organisations, *On Purpose* remains flexible, sometimes adjusting fees to fulfil its purpose, making it possible to join the programme for smaller organisations, too. Similarly, Associates are chosen based on their potential to make an impact, even before enough partner organisations are secured. "We want to create the largest possible number of connections between Associates and organisations to fulfil our purpose, not to get rich. So, purpose before profit," says Lukas Marzi. This commitment to purpose underpins the whole organisation.

Continuous Improvement

On Purpose thrives, driven by a feedback culture and constant learning and improvement, to fulfil the potential of the community. While developing how to accelerate team and programme evolution, they learn what people need to be leaders and contribute to change and prioritise cultivating a growth mindset, for example, with the weekly check-ins, where individuals are asked about their highlights and challenges of the week to give them space to express themselves. The focus on learning ensures continued inspiration for the community and beyond. It keeps everyone accountable and helps to address previous areas of development.

Living and Vibrant Community

On Purpose is a dynamic organisation. One of its priorities is to evolve as a healthy organisation, overcoming traditional beliefs as about what defines success or effort. It draws inspiration both internally and from the wider sector. The connection to the sector helps drive ongoing development within *On Purpose*, aiming to lead transformation by continuously integrating new ideas. As a 'breathing system', they then allow internal changes to influence both the community and wider society. Moreover, with the programme offered and the community-centred network design, a continuous flow of new Associates and a constant further development of the community are created. Therefore, *On Purpose* also benefits from its expanding community in the socio-ecological sector, and it distributes the transformative purpose further.

Challenges Arising from Designing Network around a Community

Dependence on the Community

The value of *On Purpose* lies in its relationships and the exchange within its community. However, this reliance also presents challenges, as the business model is heavily dependent on voluntary engagement from its community. For major decisions, *On Purpose* involves the community, a process which, while generally beneficial, determines *On Purpose*'s actions. Lukas Marzi admits that the coaches, mentors and trainers could be more closely integrated, as previous efforts to engage them through regular meetups have seen limited attendance. While community building takes time, *On Purpose* is currently working on new ways to foster co-creation. Newly tried online and conference formats begin to make an impact.

Financial Pressure

On Purpose's greatest challenge mirrors that of the wider sustainability field. Organisations prioritising impact over profit struggle in the current economic system, which often disadvantages 'impact-focused' businesses that don't externalise costs. *On Purpose* operates independently as a limited company, funded by partner organisations. Thus, financial constraints in the sector inevitably affect it. The fundamental problem of the entire sector is that not enough money is spent on a good cause.

On Purpose repeatedly hears that the service offered should be free of charge to better fulfil its purpose, allowing it to match even more individuals. For *On Purpose*'s business, in turn, it is crucial not to be dependent on subsidies and to charge organisations for services. Part of the business is to show that companies like *On Purpose* can do good with the help of economic means.

Since the organisations are *On Purpose*'s only source of income, the financial burden is felt across the community. Many contribute pro bono or work for lower pay than in comparable roles. This results in financial pressure that can be seen in *On Purpose*'s personnel structure and salaries, which are not comparable to those in classic industries. Though the organisational culture and personal growth opportunities make *On Purpose* an attractive employer, salary increases are constrained.

Lukas Marzi mentioned that a healthy community cannot rely solely on voluntary work, but paid resources from the team are necessary. Therefore, compromises must be made. Lukas Marzi states: "Every day (...), we always have to weigh up what to do now, how to prioritise and which (...) ideas are off the table?" Associates contribute their time and receive a modest salary of €23,000 gross per year, but the non-monetary benefits—relationships and network access—are significant. Still, these added values can only offset the low pay to a certain extent and for a limited time.

Diversity of Programme Participants

The financial limitations also affect the diversity of participants, as less privileged groups may be unable to afford it. *On Purpose* has acknowledged its own biases and strives for greater diversity (Impact report 2023), and the paid programme seems to be more inclusive than other programmes where you have to pay to participate. However, diversity remains a challenge within the current financial framework.

Mental Challenges in Pursuit of Purpose

People in the general socio-ecological sector deal intensively with the crises of present times and exhaust themselves for a good cause. The drive to fulfil their purpose can also lead members of this community to overwork, with work and personal life often blurring and getting lost in the end. This can result in mental distress, a challenge *On Purpose* recognises and addresses through reflection and support within its community.

Balancing Expectations and Conflicts

Managing a broad community with varied stakeholders inevitably creates conflicts. *On Purpose*, as they must balance the varying needs and views not only of the Associates, invests significant energy in balancing interests. The human-centred approach still generates pressure and may also conflict with economically necessary interests. Tensions arise between Associates and organisations due to differences in culture, communication, or mental health concerns. *On Purpose* acts as a neutral mediator, focusing on understanding all sides and finding solutions. Yet, some conflicts require compromises that do not please all sides. Thus, *On Purpose* aims to set clear expectations for all parties early in the collaboration.

Preferences in the matching process can also lead to tensions, as both Associates and organisations can favour the same partners. The matching algorithm considers preferences but cannot always fulfil all requests, also relying on *On Purpose*'s experience. Over time, partnerships that were initially not preferred often prove successful.

On Purpose invests significant energy into shaping the Associate Programme because it aligns with its own purpose. Still, some organisations view *On Purpose* primarily as a recruitment agency, valuing the programme for its immediate benefits. However, they may not benefit from the long-term impact of Associates, as many move on after completing the programme. This results in a mismatch between what *On Purpose* offers (to society) and what organisations pay for.

Differing opinions also arise when selecting partner organisations—some Fellows believe only regenerative organisations should be included, while others are open to organisations still beginning their transformation. Such debates can create social pressure for *On Purpose* as the community closely watches and evaluates its decisions.

Overall, managing the community's expectations and diverse requirements is a priority. *On Purpose*'s approach is to behave transparently and make decisions aligned with its values, though balancing interests remains a time-consuming and challenging task.

Interactions with Other Design Traits

Ownership Design

On Purpose International operates as a not-for-profit company limited by guarantee[3] based in London, which wholly owns the Berlin entity and is one of two members of the Paris organisation (along with a Paris On Purpose Fellow). The constitution of *On Purpose* does not allow the distribution of profits to shareholders. *On Purpose* International is governed by a board comprising a Chair, a Fellow Representative from the Fellow Advisory Board, several more non-executive directors and the founder, Tom Rippin. Each board member has equal voting rights. Tom Rippin also serves as CEO, influencing the company since its inception.

---

3   A Company Limited by Guarantee (CLG) is a not-for-profit corporate structure in the UK, primarily used for not-for-profit purposes. It has no shareholders or capital; instead, members act as guarantors with a limited financial commitment, and while profits cannot be distributed to members, directors and employees can receive salaries.

While Berlin is a subsidiary of London, each location operates independently yet is increasingly growing closer together. As employees foster relationships, they are seeking to apply the lessons they teach on the programme to themselves and focus on becoming more than the sum of their parts. Lukas Marzi reflects this, stating, "we are characterised by the founder Tom. However, I refer to him as a colleague and not as the founder or boss, because it also feels very different when working together."

The ownership structure underscores the organisation's purpose. *On Purpose* is generally open to new ownership models such as steward-ownership, promoting trustful relationships from the outset.

Governance Design - Decision-Making Processes

The network trait is evident in *On Purpose*'s decision-making and new work approaches. Decisions are generally made equitably, but the process involves learning how "a team of volunteers and full-time staff can work together (…) rather than get in each other's way" (Impact Report 2023).

London does not make decisions for Berlin. Two city leads manage key decisions while consulting their teams. Decision-making is role-based, similar to the Associate collaboration process.

Various stakeholder groups are engaged differently in decisions. At the strategic level, Fellows participate through the Fellow Advisory Board, which comprises two Fellows from each city who invigorate the fellowship and support self-organisation. These six alumni agree that a member represents Fellows at the board, allowing them to influence the organisation's direction and voice community concerns.

Fellows and Associates are informed of decisions via Slack and participate in regular discussions about strategic matters such as organisational values and communication structures. However, some decisions, such as determining an individual's continuation in the programme, are made by *On Purpose* without community input. "If we were to involve the Associates, we would have a very strongly influenced decision and (…) that is not necessarily the best decision considering all voices and opinions" (Lukas Marzi).

Although the exchange with partner organisations is not as intensive as with Associates and Fellows, their feedback also influences the programme. Beyond that, they are informed about significant monetary changes, such as inflation-related salary increases.

Governance Design - New Work Methods

On Purpose's internal dynamics are shaped by its external environment and the community, necessitating the adoption of new approaches to create change. Consequently, *On Purpose* continuously refines its internal structures, testing new salary and reward systems (Impact report 2022), role-based decision-making, and self-organisation. *On Purpose* experiments with new ideas, consciously implementing or discarding them.

> "We benefit greatly from the relationship with the outside world, with our community, we experience things there that we do ourselves and take things into the team." — Lukas Marzi

Recommendations for Adopting a Community-Centred Network Design

In addition to the aforesaid leap of trust that goes hand in hand with a positive image of human beings, two other factors helped *On Purpose* to establish a community-centred network design:

Use Systems Thinking in Shaping Your Business Strategy

A core element of the Associate Programme is recognising the world as a complex system.

> "Systems theory is a different way of understanding the world: instead of analysing the world by separating things into ever-smaller parts, systems thinking recognises the importance of how parts are connected and attempts to understand the whole" (Impact Report 2022).

This understanding allows one to recognise how our current economy is functioning and how global risks are nested and reinforcing. This knowledge makes it easier to question previous beliefs and values and change the status quo.

Invest in Inner Work and Development to Realise the Full Potential of Your Employees

Another critical factor for *On Purpose* is inner work. The programme emphasises the need for personal development as a foundation for societal and business transformation. To lead, show empathy, and build trust, self-awareness and confidence are essential. This process involves recognising one's patterns, addressing personal issues, and unlearning past beliefs, creating a more reflective and responsive approach to others.

Inner work is also essential for navigating trade-offs and compromises amidst today's crises:

"Being healthy in an economy that has not yet transformed requires a constant balancing act between ambitious idealism and practical realism. We want to challenge ourselves to live with that tension" (Impact Report 2022).

On Purpose invests time with Associates and leaves space for relationship building, offering coaching, individual sessions, and collaborative approaches like check-ins, and sharing weekly highlights and challenges. Informal dialogue in various settings, including nature retreats, strengthens connections and fosters deeper conversations.

Though personal work happens individually, *On Purpose* provides inspiration for inner development, which is key to driving change in the community. This focus on inner work is validated by 94% of Associates committing to continuous self-development post-programme (Impact Report 2022).

Inspiring Redesign Beyond the Business

On Purpose influences the economic system at the organisational and individual levels, focusing primarily on the personal transformation of Associates. The programme's impact on individuals can be life-changing, with participants decentralising their learning to create wider change.

"Our programme aims to transform Associates so that they, in turn, can help lead the wider transformation we need – in the organisations within which they work and the economy as a whole" (Impact Report 2023).

The impact at the organisational level is more limited. Although *On Purpose* sets high standards for the needed transformation, these levers have not been actively addressed by the organisations. The programme's goal is long-term participation, not rapid organisational transformation. They prefer Associates to carry these standards back to their organisations rather than addressing them directly, which could strain relationships. In this regard, 99% of Associates bring their learning back to their workplaces (Impact Report 2023).

Additionally, most organisations are in the sustainability field, a niche within the economy, and further systemic change would require another programme or expanded participation.

The value of the *On Purpose* community can be summarised by the following quote:

"I truly believe that a network is more than the sum of its parts, then [...] the main driver for our healthy community is the warm, open, and authentic interaction with each other. [...] And in the end, it's just a great pleasure for us to be able to create this connection between people." — Lukas Marzi

References

Interview

with Lukas Marzi, Co-Managing Director in Berlin, Head of Network & Partnerships (05/09/2024, 01:09h).
with Saskia Klug, Community Manager in Berlin (18/09/2024, 00:25h).

Homepage

On Purpose (2024): https://onpurpose.org/de/, [Accessed 23 April 2025].

Other Sources:

Marzi, Lukas (2024): Die Bedeutung von Verbindungen – wie Netzwerke Impact generieren, https://sigu-plattform.de/die-bedeutung-von-verbindungen-wie-netzwerke-impact-generieren/, [Accessed 23 April 2025].
On Purpose (2022): Impact Report, https://new-media.onpurpose.org/documents/220407_On_Purpose_Impact_report.pdf, [Accessed 23 April 2025].
On Purpose (2023): Impact Report, https://onpurpose.org/en/our-stories/our-impact-purpose-impact-report-2023/, [Accessed 23 April 2025].

Case Study: Commown

Sarah Keil

Purpose: Transforming the electronics sector into a sustainable and responsible sector, by changing the structure from a sales model to a cooperative-based rental model enabling a 2–3 times longer life of the devices.
Design Trait: Network
Innovative Practice: Cooperative Network Design

Key Facts

Commown is a cooperative for sustainable electronics offering fair and sustainable modular smartphones, headphones, laptops and computers in the form of a rental model for their members.

> **Established:** 2018
> **Location:** Straßburg, France
> **Founder:** Élie Assémat
> **Ownership:** Not-for-profit Cooperative in France
> **Legal Form:** Société coopérative d'intérêt collectif (not-for-profit cooperative), Société anonyme (public limited company with variable capital)[1]
> **Employees:** 15 full-time, 15 apprentices (2025)
> **Members:** ~1000
> **Webpage:** https://commown.coop/de/

---

1   This legal form is specific to the French legal system and does not have a direct equivalent in other jurisdictions; therefore, the original French terms are maintained. Throughout the interview with *Commown*, emphasis was consistently placed on the cooperative aspect, which serves as the central point of reference for the entire case study.

Purpose, Business Model & Objectives

> *Commown* has set itself the goal of transforming the electronics sector into a sustainable and responsible sector, by changing the structure from a sales model to a cooperative-based rental model, enabling a 2–3 times longer life of the devices.

Today's electrical industry is characterised by poor working conditions in mines and production facilities, a highly negative environmental impact and inadequate recycling of old appliances. These challenges underline the need for changing how we produce, consume, and recycle electronic devices. To tackle these problems and challenges, *Commown* was founded in France in 2018 to make the electronic industry more sustainable. In addition to France, the main sales market is Germany, where a branch was opened in Berlin in 2021. *Commown* is unique in the electronic industry as the only co-operative dedicated to sustainable electronics.

Commown's business model consists of renting out electronic devices such as smartphones, laptops, and headphones instead of selling them, as conventional companies do. To this end, sustainable products that are repairable and more durable are selected, such as *Fairphone* or the computer brand *Why*. While the business models of other electronic device manufacturers often aim to ensure a new device is purchased as quickly as possible, *Commown*'s approach is entirely different. It is built on a rental model that incentivises all parts of the network to maximise the longevity of the devices. While other companies profit from replacing their products as quickly as possible, *Commown* is focused on keeping the equipment in operation for as long as possible. This leads to a shift in the focus within the business model of *Commown*. Robin Angelé[2], an employee at *Commown*, who was interviewed for this case study, emphasises the following:

> "And what we are trying to do with *Commown* is to show that with a different business model, namely with rental, the interest is completely different. It's the other way round, because we only rent out the appliances and then we have an interest in ensuring that those who use the appliances remain in operation for as long as possible."

Commown offers a comprehensive service for hardware and software in order to ensure the longevity and durability of the devices, and to ensure their software remains updated. With this approach, the company is challenging the electronic industry's

---

2   At the time of the interview, Robin Angelé was employed at *Commown*; however, he is no longer with the company.

status quo and aims to prove that positive contributions to society and the environment can be aligned with commercial success, benefiting companies, customers, and the planet alike.

Insights into the Cooperative Network Design

Instead of a traditional hierarchical corporate structure, that prevails in the technology and electronics industry, *Commown* relies on a cooperative network design which brings together a wide array of participants, going beyond typical customer-manufacturer relationships. It allows not only customers but also the manufacturers of the products, marketing partners, and even public institutions, such as cities, to become members, fostering a comprehensive and inclusive approach to sustainability and shared goals.

Shift from Customers to Members

The cooperative network design is characterised by a shift from traditional customers as end-users to customers as members and participants. This network structure incentivises members as well as the company itself to work together to maximise the lifespan of products.

Commown pursues an alternative business model compared to many other companies that use their approach to marketing, software, and hardware to encourage consumers to buy new products more quickly, which is known as planned obsolescence.

In terms of software, at *Commown* this means working with alternative operating systems that allow older devices to continue to be used safely and efficiently. In this way, new functions and security updates can be provided without replacing the hardware. In terms of hardware, this means working exclusively with modular devices that are characterised by durability and easy repairability. The modular design allows *Commown* to repair or replace individual components of the devices instead of selling products that become unusable after a short time and require the entire device to be replaced. This system makes a circular economy feasible. The appliances can be repaired, and spare parts can also be used to repair other appliances, which minimises resources and thus protects the environment. *Commown* also takes an innovative approach to pricing, which differs significantly from the strategy of other companies. It uses an innovative pricing model that encourages customers/members to keep the devices for as long as possible by decreasing prices with an ongoing rental period. Instead of incentivising their customers/members to make frequent new purchases, *Commown*'s customers are rewarded for long-term use of the products.

Figure 1: Designed for Repair: Extending Product Lifespan Through Repairability

Source: Commown 2024a.

Shift from Manufacturer to Members

Manufacturers are a key stakeholder group within *Commown*'s cooperative network. *Commown* collaborates with manufacturers who share the vision of a more sustainable electronics industry. These partners, as members of their network, are carefully selected for their commitment to sustainability, modularity, and high social standards within their operations. This cooperation emphasises choosing partners that prioritise longevity, reparability, and resource conservation at the centre of their product development. Robin Angelé explains:

> "Our role is really to work with the manufacturers that already exist on the market and that are sustainable and modular and that offer the best social conditions for employees."

Commown attaches great importance to developing long-term partnerships with its manufacturers which result in collaborations that are characterised by trust and transparency and are based on shared values and goals. By working closely with companies that are actively committed to fair and sustainable electronics, *Commown* creates a stable network that promotes the durability and reparability of products. The mutual exchange of expertise and values creates the basis for jointly advancing innovative solutions for a regenerative electronics industry. With reliable, like-minded manufacturers as network members, new ideas for the design of modular, repairable and durable electronic products can be developed and implemented.

Collaboration with Other Organisations

Commown's network extends beyond customers and manufacturers and includes a large number of organisational partnerships with like-minded actors that share a common purpose. The role within these networks depends on the organisation and its objectives. In some organisations, *Commown* acts as a co-founder and actively participates in the development of campaigns. In other organisations, the company acts only as a member and concentrates on supporting specific relevant projects.

For example, *Commown* is currently collaborating with *WEtell*, a sustainable telecommunications provider. Their joint campaign offers customers a discount on their monthly tariff when they rent a smartphone from *Commown* after purchasing a plan from *WEtell*. This partnership not only promotes the rental model but also enhances awareness of sustainability within the telecommunications sector. *Commown* also collaborates with *SEND*, the social entrepreneurship network in Germany that engages in various programs aimed at fostering social impact. At the Impact Fair in Frankfurt, they had a shared booth with *SEND* and other social enterprises to raise awareness about their innovative rental model. Furthermore, organisations like Cradle-to-Cradle host exhibitions in Berlin, where *Commown* participates by having a showroom for discussions about sustainability and innovation.

By collaborating with different organisations and engaging in various events, *Commown* contributes not only to the dissemination of their rental model approach but also contributes to a growing movement toward sustainability that encompasses the broader electronic sector.

How the Cooperative Network Design Enables Regenerative and Distributive Dynamics

Commown's cooperative network design generates multiple opportunities for achieving their ecologically regenerative and socially distributive purpose:

Mutually Beneficial Cooperative Network

The cooperative network and *Commown*'s clear rejection of planned obsolescence create a model that is beneficial for both *Commown* and its customers. As revenue is not based on frequent new purchases but on the long-term use of the devices, there is a common goal: to keep the devices in working order for as long as possible. Customers benefit from ongoing support, including a comprehensive service and repair package to ensure long-term, trouble-free operation. Customers can be sure that their equipment will always remain operational. To achieve this goal, *Commown* is committed to the regenerative use of resources: defective parts can simply be replaced and reused in other appliances, promoting an environmentally friendly circular economy. This approach reflects Raworth's concept of a regenerative economy, illustrated in Figure 1. This model, which is also known as the Butterfly Economy, consists of two interrelated cycles: a biological cycle that ensures resources regenerate naturally and a technical cycle that focuses on restoring and reusing materials rather than discarding them.

Figure 2: The Butterfly Economy: Regeneration by Design – the Example of Commown

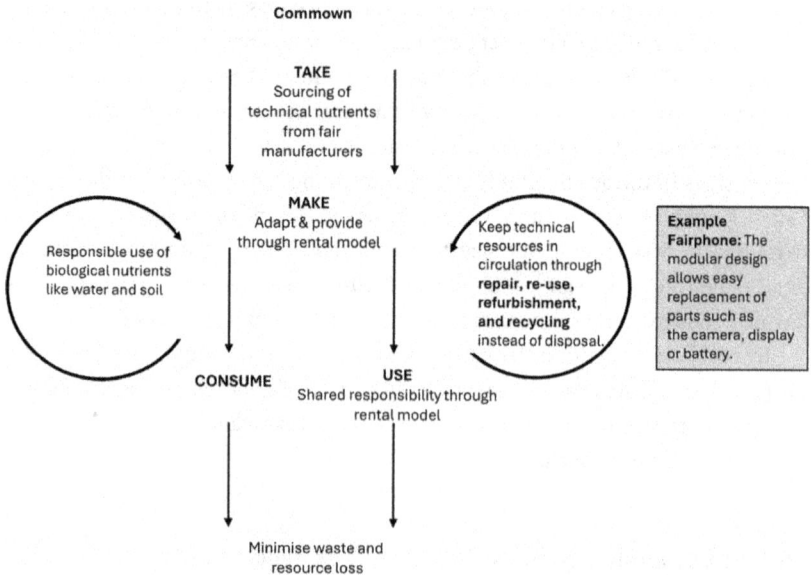

Source: Own representation based on Raworth 2017: 220.

Community Based on Mutual Trust

The eye-to-eye relationship creates a strong sense of community and deep trust among customers. A significant contribution to this is that *Commown* calls each of its new customers personally to provide detailed information about the business model and answer any questions. This direct contact not only promotes customer confidence but reinforces that they are part of a community. As Robin Angelé points out, this sense of community and trust is reflected in the behaviour of customers who, for example, "advertise for us on social networks, even though we sometimes don't ask for it. That comes from the sense of community the network creates."

Beyond personal relationships, *Commown*'s cooperative structure ensures that trust is embedded in its decision-making processes. Customers, who are also members of the cooperation, can actively participate in shaping the company's direction. At the General Assembly, members vote on important decisions and must approve the budget, which also includes possible price increases. In cases where prices could rise sharply, members therefore can use their vote and, if necessary, vote against such adjustments.

The trust-based network extends beyond customers to include manufacturers, who also influence the cooperative's direction through their involvement in the supervisory and executive board. Manufacturers can actively contribute their know-how and expertise and thus directly influence strategic decisions such as product range design and product development. This collaborative structure strengthens the relationship with stakeholders, as their expertise and concerns can flow directly into decision-making processes.

A prime example of this collaborative approach is *Fairphone*, a key member of the cooperative. By being elected to the executive board by the General Assembly, *Fairphone* exemplifies how direct involvement in ownership and decision-making structures facilitates mutual trust-based cooperation through a simplified exchange of information and direct feedback. Actions and activities can be better harmonised from both the operational and strategic levels, which increases the efficiency and effectiveness of the company in reaching its purpose. The cooperation also enables the targeted and coordinated implementation of joint projects, for example in marketing, which further strengthens brand perception and customer loyalty.

Moreover, by bringing all stakeholders together, *Commown* receives valuable, direct feedback from its members through the General Assemblies. In an industry dominated by large companies, the network structure of this cooperative model allows *Commown* to adapt its strategy and product range based on members' insights. At the same time, it turns members into advocates and ambassadors, building trust and support.

Dissemination of the Rental Model

A major advantage of the well-developed network structures is the extensive opportunity to actively integrate partner companies into the sustainable rental model and thus make the electronics industry more sustainable. An illustrative example of this is the cooperation with *Fairphone*. Originally, *Fairphone* sold its devices directly to *Commown*, which then rented them out to customers. However, this model has evolved over the years: *Fairphone* is now more involved in the system by renting devices directly to *Commown* instead of selling them. As a result, *Fairphone* receives a commission for each month in which the devices are rented. This close collaboration promotes a sustainable business model, as both *Fairphone* and *Commown* are strongly committed to keeping the devices as durable and functional as possible. Moreover, this partnership aligns with a regenerative purpose, as the sustainable practices adopted by *Commown* and *Fairphone* can be passed on through their cooperative network, potentially inspiring their partners to implement similar initiatives. By actively involving partners, *Commown* becomes a role model for sustainability, inspiring other sectors beyond the electronics industry to adopt and implement comparable sustainable practices.

Visibility – Raising Awareness

Collaboration with like-minded organisations in the electronics industry is a key element of *Commown*'s strategic development. This approach helps to increase awareness of the rental model, particularly in markets where *Commown* is not yet strongly represented. Through its diverse partnerships, *Commown* gains access to a larger audience and reaches numerous organisations to present the rental model and promote its dissemination. In this way, the cooperation helps to create a broader awareness of sustainable consumption alternatives and to publicise the advantages of the rental model in various electronic sectors. Furthermore, by bringing together the resources and expertise of various parties, common goals can be achieved, enabling the exchange of best practices and discussion of new industry developments. This enables *Commown* to stay one step ahead of others and to adapt its business model to the changing market requirements.

Challenges Arising from Designing Network around a Cooperative

Unfamiliarity of the Cooperative-based Rental Model

A major challenge for the company in achieving its purpose is that many people are unfamiliar with the rental-based business model. They are also unfamiliar with the way *Commown* has been designed to integrate various stakeholders into its enterprise design. According to Robin Angelé, "People are not so used to this model. So, you have to explain it."

People have questions about the rental conditions, the cooperative model and the aspect of sustainability. Regarding the rental model, customers are often unsure as to whether they can buy the appliances afterwards or must return them. The cooperative model also raises questions, partly because the rules and the handling differ from cooperative to cooperative. *Commown*'s task is to explain what exactly is so interesting about the model and how exactly it works with cooperative shares.

It is often necessary to explain the relationship between the rental and cooperative models. Many people do not realise that they can remain a member of the cooperative without renting an electrical appliance. Moreover, the *Commown* team needs to educate people about why this model is sustainable and what advantages it offers over other models.

Limited Choice of Suitable Manufacturers

One of the challenges that *Commown* faces is finding manufacturers on the market with whom they can work and who support the idea of the rental business model and the circular principles. As Robin Angelé emphasises, "Of course, we are limited in terms of the manufacturers that already exist."

Commown only rents out electronic products that are manufactured sustainably and fairly, such as *Fairphone*, Gerrard Street headphones or the Shiftphone. Although sustainability is also playing an increasingly important role in the electronics industry, the number of sustainable manufacturers is limited, partly due to the strong and dominant competition that focuses on mass production and fast exchanges of its products. This makes it difficult for *Commown* to expand and extend its range. The limited number of manufacturers prevents the company from expanding its product portfolio and thus attracting more customers.

Time and Value – Coherency Effort for Finding Suitable Partners

Further to the challenge of finding suitable partners, *Commown* attaches great importance to long-term partnerships with its manufacturers that are based on trust and reciprocal support. However, establishing and maintaining these partnerships can take a lot of time. Before the cooperation can even begin, *Commown* must already dedicate a great amount of time to see whether the values and standards match and whether a partnership is a good fit. Only if this is the case, can other aspects, such as different parts of working together or contract negotiations, be concluded. While these long-lasting partnerships are, of course, valuable, the lengthy process of establishing them slows *Commown* down in expanding its manufacturer network.

Interactions with Other Design Traits

Ownership Design

One of the greatest opportunities arising from the company's network structures lies in the cooperative's ownership structure. A cooperative exists for its members and anyone who wishes to become a member – whether as a customer, manufacturer or in another role – has the opportunity to acquire shares in the cooperative. This membership provides the right to participate in the general meeting of *Commown* and to have a say in decisions. Critically, regardless of the number of shares someone or an organisation owns, each member only has one vote. This means that the usual principle that the person who invests more also has more influence is deliberately not applied. Robin Angelé summarises the Ownership Design as follows:

> "What is different with us is that we are a cooperative. This means that customers can also become members by simply buying a share in a cooperative. They can even do this at the same time as renting a unit. And they have a say in the election at the general meeting, where important decisions are made."

Governance Design

Decision-making power is also carefully balanced in the general meeting. The voting rights are divided into four categories: 50% of the votes go to the executive board and employees, 20% are allocated to customers and communications partners, 15% to investors, and another 15% to manufacturers. Additionally, an advisory supervisory board provides insights and suggestions, stepping in when there are differing views on certain decisions. This cooperative model enables different stakeholders – from customers and partners to manufacturers – as well as their expertise and their opinions to be brought together to work together on the development of sustainable and profitable electronics. The direct involvement of customers and manufacturers in the ownership and decision-making structure improves the exchange of information and feedback. As Robin Angelé points out:

> "Our goal is actually to bring all these different stakeholders under the same table and see how we can make these electronics more sustainable for everyone."

Finance Design

Financially, the cooperative structure enables independence for *Commown*, as ownership remains within the cooperative, limiting the influence of external investors and shareholders compared to a traditional "one share, one vote" model. For instance, the legal framework of cooperative law in France mandates that at least 57.5% of *Commown*'s profits be reinvested into the cooperative. Moreover, dividend payouts are capped based at the average rate of obligations over the past three years plus two percentage points. These structures ensure that most profits are reinvested, and that long-term strategies and sustainable growth are prioritised over short-term profit maximisation. For start-ups that rely on traditional financing models and external investors, the pressure to maximise profits can grow rapidly, which can often lead to price increases or inadequate pay for employees. Even if it is more challenging for *Commown* to raise capital for the cooperative model, the company remains independent. The right to have a say within the cooperative means that internal pressure remains low, and decisions can be made in the interests of all members.

Recommendations for Adopting a Cooperative Network Design

Some success factors of *Commown* have already been mentioned throughout the case study. However, several additional factors are essential for the success of *Commown*:

Build Mutual Trust and Support

Building cooperative relationships at *Commown* is based on a strong relationship of trust within the network. By renting out electrical devices with the clear aim of maximising their lifespan, *Commown* puts care and sustainability at the heart of its business. This approach creates a foundation of trust that is essential for long-lasting partnerships. When challenges arise, *Commown*'s collaborative spirit supports all stakeholders and fosters a culture of cooperation that goes beyond individual transactions and contributes to the common goal of a sustainable, responsible society.

Develop Personal Relationship

At the beginning of every customer relationship, *Commown* attaches particular importance to close and personal contact. This intensive contact is important to create trust and a stable foundation for collaboration. Once the basis of the relationship has been established, the frequency of contact can be reduced without jeopardising the quality of the partnership. This approach creates a long-term connection based on mutual understanding and trust, offering flexibility and reliability to both sides.

Ensuring Manufacturer Availability

To ensure *Commown*'s long-term success, it is important to ensure that there are enough manufacturers and partners who share the company's values and ideas. Strengthening collaborations with like-minded producers is crucial, as a lack of suitable partners could limit the availability of sustainable devices and hinder the growth of the rental model. With a wider range of cooperation partners and a stronger presence on the market, customers' awareness and understanding grows – and with it the cooperative basis on which *Commown* is built.

Inspiring Redesign Beyond the Business

Commown is part of a bigger movement to transform the electronics industry towards sustainability. Through its cooperative network-based rental model that focuses on renting rather than selling electronic devices, the company is making a major contribution to transforming the economy and changing the way consumer goods are used and perceived.

The rental approach and the repair of the devices not only extend the life of the products but also reduce the consumption of resources as it takes away the necessity to constantly produce and dispose of electronic devices. This leads to a lower negative environmental impact and promotes awareness of 'non-consumption' by showing customers that the value of a product lies not in its ownership, but rather in its use and functionality. This perspective motivates consumers to appreciate the advantages of long-term use of a device instead of constantly upgrading to the newest model. The model also challenges the throwaway mentality. With the rental model, consumers realise that it is possible to own electronic devices for a long period of time. Consumers no longer need to buy a new device to keep up with the latest technology; regular updates and repairs keep devices state-of-the-art even after many years. By changing consumer habits in this way, *Commown* is making a significant contribution to more sustainable consumption.

Furthermore, *Commown* can be a role model for others in the industry. The company shows that even in a highly competitive industry, it is possible to pursue alternative business models, in their case, the circular economy that considers both regenerative and distributive aspects. This model not only promotes the fair distribution of resources and the regeneration of ecological systems but also allows *Commown* to operate in a financially profitable manner. *Commown* redefines how electronic devices are consumed and valued, encouraging a conscious use of technology. Through reuse, repair and recycling, the company actively contributes to avoiding waste and conserving natural resources. In this way, *Commown* inspires people and companies to rethink their responsibility for a sustainable future. As Robin Angelé summarises:

> "Our aim is really to show that it is possible to offer a business model that is profitable for companies, more sustainable and also interesting for customers."

References

Interview

with Robin Angelé, Employee in the area of international development at Commown at that time (30/04/2024, 01:16h).

Homepage

Commown (2024): Die Kooperative für nachhaltige Elektronik – Ökologische und modulare Smartphones, Kopfhörer, Laptops und Computer, https://commown.coop/de/ [Accessed 2 March 2024].
Commown (2024a): Presse Kit Commown, Fairphone 4.

Other Sources:

Raworth, Kate (2017): Doughnut Economics. Seven Ways to Think like a 21st-Century Economist, London.

Case Study: Sekem & Ebda

Sarah Keil

Purpose: "Sustainable development towards a future where every human being can unfold his individual potential; where mankind lives together in social forms reflecting human dignity; and where all economic activity is conducted in accordance with ecological and ethical principles."

Design Trait: Network

Innovative Practice: Economy of Love Based Network Design

Key Facts

SEKEM and EBDA

	SEKEM is a holistic development organisation focused on sustainable agriculture, education, and social initiatives based on biodynamic principles.	Egyptian Biodynamic Association (EBDA) supports Egyptian farmers in their transition to biodynamic agriculture.
Established:	1977	1994
Location:	Al Salam City, Egypt	Al Salam City, Egypt
Founder:	Dr. Ibrahim Abouleish	Dr. Ibrahim Abouleish
Ownership:	Holding	Association
Legal Form:	Egyptian Joint Stock Company	Association
Employees/ Members:	2.003 (2023)	103 (2024)
Homepage:	https://sekem.com/en/index/	https://ebda.earth/

SEKEM EUROPE

Supports *SEKEM*'s goal by processing *SEKEMS*'s products made from biodynamic ingredients.

Established: 2006
Location: Goslar
Founder: Dr. Ibrahim Abouleish
Ownership: Limited Liability Company (GmbH)
Legal Form: Limited Liability Company (GmbH)

Purpose, Business Model & Objectives

Purpose: "Sustainable development towards a future where every human being can unfold his individual potential; where mankind lives together in social forms reflecting human dignity; and where all economic activity is conducted in accordance with ecological and ethical principles."

Founded in 1977 by Dr. Ibrahim Abouleish, the *SEKEM* Initiative arose from a vision to transform the desert into fertile land. In pursuit of this idea, Dr. Ibrahim Abouleish dug the first wells on untouched desert soil near Cairo in 1977 to revitalise the soil with biodynamic agriculture.

Biodynamic agriculture
"Biodynamic farming is a holistic, ecological and ethical approach to farming and gardening that dates back to 1924 and evolved ever since. Going beyond the organic standard, through holistic management practices biodynamic farming focuses on reinforcing the interaction between soil, plants, animals, and humans in an environmentally friendly and regenerative way. In this way, the farm becomes a unique living organism in which each part nurtures the other: humans, plants, animals, and soil strive together" (Demeter 2025).

From this foundation grew a network of companies and educational institutions such as Heliopolis University, a vocational training centre, and a school with all levels of education. The Egyptian Biodynamic Agriculture Association (*EBDA*), founded by *SEKEM* in 1994, forms a central part of this network. The *EBDA* was established to support Egyptian farmers in transitioning from conventional to biodynamic agriculture, with the goal of promoting rural development and sustainability. This central task continues *SEKEM*'s commitment to fostering organic and biodynamic agriculture.

Although the *EBDA* operates independently, it is based on *SEKEM*'s core values and continues its vision in close collaboration with *SEKEM*. The *EBDA* plays a key role in *SEKEM*'s network, as it serves as an agricultural foundation, providing training, research, and advice to farmers across Egypt. It promotes sustainable practices aligned with *SEKEM*'s vision, focusing on the ecological principles of both organic and biodynamic agriculture. While organic farming emphasises ecological processes and biodiversity, biodynamic agriculture takes a broader holistic approach, viewing soil fertility, plant growth, and livestock care as an interconnected system. The collaboration lays the foundation for *SEKEM*'s closed value chain, ensures that the network's agricultural, social and educational initiatives are aligned, and puts the biodynamic principles that form the foundation of *SEKEM*'s holistic development approach into practice.

This interconnection can further be seen in the fact that the farmers who are under contract with *SEKEM* are accompanied and certified by the *EBDA*. Thus, the *EBDA* acts as a bridge between the farmers and *SEKEM*, ensuring that the farmers meet the high ecological standards that are essential for *SEKEM*'s mission and its products. The scale of this network is reflected in the significant trade volumes it facilitates, as *SEKEM*'s ecosystem connects numerous agricultural suppliers, processing units, and distribution channels that move large quantities of biodynamic products both locally and internationally, generating a net profit of EGP 40,266,243 in 2023. Moreover, *SEKEM* and the *EBDA* were jointly awarded a prize for sustainable business practices, recognising their commitment to regenerative agriculture and environmental stewardship in Egypt, further underlining their close cooperation.

SEKEM Europe, a subsidiary of *SEKEM* founded in 2005 and based in Germany, also plays a central role in this network. It serves both as a conduit for sustainable Egyptian products to Europe and as an ambassador for the values and initiatives promoted by *SEKEM* and the *EBDA*. In addition to economic activities, *SEKEM* has maintained close cultural ties with Germany for over 40 years. In collaboration with the support association *SEKEM* Friends Germany e.V., *SEKEM* conducts social and development-oriented projects to foster intercultural understanding between Egypt and Germany.

This interconnectedness between *SEKEM*, the *EBDA* and *SEKEM* Europe clearly shows that the work of the farmers and their sustainable farming methods are one of the core purposes of this network. Without the *EBDA* and its support for the farmers, the realisation of *SEKEM*'s vision would be less attainable. Likewise, *SEKEM* Europe implements this vision and ensures that ecological and social responsibility extends beyond Egypt.

Insights into the Economy of Love Based Network Design

The special feature and uniqueness of the network structures lie above all in the diversity of the stakeholders with whom the *EBDA* is in contact, as well as in the special nature of the relationship with the farmers. A key expression of these relationships is the Economy of Love Reporting Standard which was initiated by the *EBDA* and based on the values of *SEKEM*. The standard was adopted by *SEKEM* and all its members in all areas and is now intended to be spread globally. Justus Harm, Co-Executive Director of *EBDA*, who was interviewed for this case study, emphasises: "The standard is inspired by *SEKEM*, by the work that the *SEKEM* initiative has done."

The Standard encompasses four dimensions, which are considered and implemented in a holistic approach: Economic, ecological, social, and cultural. The economic dimension is about fair and transparent value creation and distribution to all stakeholders. For example, income from CO_2 credits is distributed equally among all farmers regardless of who has sold how many. Additionally, farmers practising biodynamic agriculture receive credits for innovative practices through the Economy of Love. The ecological dimension refers to the active regeneration of the world through biodynamic farming methods. For instance, by using compost, organic fertilisers and biodynamic preparations, as well as crop rotation, the soil is continuously vitalised and enriched with nutrients. In this way, *SEKEM* has managed to transform parts of the desert into fertile land. The social dimension focuses on fair working conditions that promote the well-being of employees and create better jobs. Employees are provided with health and social insurance, and various tools, such as the Roundtable, are used to engage in dialogue with employees, ensuring that their opinions and concerns are heard and integrated into decision-making processes. The cultural dimension focuses on collective development, promoting education, well-being, and creative collaboration within *SEKEM* and the wider community. This is fostered through educational institutions like the *SEKEM* School and Heliopolis University, alongside initiatives in music, theatre, arts, and research. Justus Harm states:

> "We believe that through a transparent economic system, responsible consumers and producers can actively protect nature and ensure that every person across the supply chain is fairly compensated and protected from exploitation."

Figure 1: The Four Dimensions of the Economy of Love

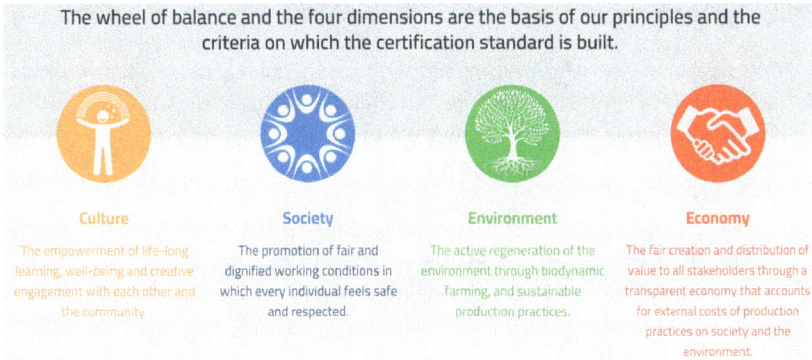

The wheel of balance and the four dimensions are the basis of our principles and the criteria on which the certification standard is built.

Culture	Society	Environment	Economy
The empowerment of life-long learning, well-being and creative engagement with each other and the community	The promotion of fair and dignified working conditions in which every individual feels safe and respected.	The active regeneration of the environment through biodynamic farming, and sustainable production practices.	The fair creation and distribution of value to all stakeholders through a transparent economy that accounts for external costs of production practices on society and the environment.

Source: Economy of Love, 2025.

Through the Economy of Love Standard, *SEKEM* and the *EBDA* enable farmers to transition from conventional to biodynamic, regenerative farming. This shift not only supports ecological sustainability but also drives community development, ensuring that farmers are rewarded for their work and that they contribute to the well-being of the broader society. To date, the initiative has supported over 10,000 farmers and converted more than 40,000 acres of land. Mohamed Seddik, an Egyptian farmer, aptly summarises the Economy of Love Standard with the following words:

"Economy of Love means that I understand your challenges and you understand mine, so that we can support each other with love and respect."

This holistic approach makes it possible to unite the values of *SEKEM* and *EBDA* in one standard and to spread the vision nationally and internationally among farmers and other companies. In this way, the values underpinning these relationships are now visible through the Standard.

Another integral element of *SEKEM*'s holistic approach are the CO_2 credits, known as "Whole System Credits". Land use change, primarily due to conventional agriculture, is a leading cause of biodiversity loss. However, biodiversity is one of the nine planetary boundaries and therefore essential for ecosystems and human life. To address this challenge, the *EBDA* actively supports farmers in transitioning to biodynamic farming, helping them implement sustainable agricultural practices. Through methods such as reforestation, composting, carbon storage in soil, and renewable energy use, farmers can bind more CO_2 while enhancing soil fertility and ecosystem health. Recognising the importance of this transition, the *EBDA* continuously works to provide the best possible support to individual farmers and farmers' associations. This includes a wide range of services, all aimed at helping the 16,368 farmers within the *EBDA* network meet the standards for organic and biodynamic certification. Justus Harm highlights the significance of this work:

> "We have been active for 30 years, supporting companies and farms that work biodynamically in Egypt with training, consultancy, learning materials, access to market, various farm inputs, etc., in order to prepare them for the organic and Demeter market, so to speak, and to support the marketing of the farmers' products."

Through the **Whole System Credits**, the *EBDA* acknowledges and rewards farmers for their dedication to biodynamic agriculture, ensuring that their efforts in regenerative farming and CO_2 reduction are both valued and financially supported. The credits measure CO_2 savings from biodynamic farming, allowing farmers to earn and sell credits on the CO_2 certificate market. According to *SEKEM*, this approach offers a valuable contribution to society. These credits acknowledge farmers' environmental efforts while promoting a comprehensive strategy that encompasses biodiversity, soil health, and sustainable land stewardship. Aligned with the core values of the Economy of Love – transparency and accountability across the value chain – this certification system helps ensure that every aspect of the process is both measurable and meaningful.

To ensure equality and to avoid disparities caused by uneven sales of individual certificates, the Whole System Credits of all participating farmers are pooled into a collective fund. The income from the sale of these certificates is then distributed fairly among all farmers. Additionally, a "solidarity buffer" is implemented, reserving 20% of each issued credit as a safeguard. This buffer mitigates risks for the entire farming community, covering losses if a farmer cannot continue cultivating sustainably the following year. These mechanisms enhance fairness, reduce risks, and foster resilience, reinforcing the holistic nature of the Economy of Love.

How the Economy of Love Based Network Design Enables Regenerative and Distributive Dynamics

Due to the Economy of Love Based Network Design the following potentials arise for achieving the regenerative and distributive purpose:

Deep Understanding and Trust

Transparency, a central criterion of the Economy of Love, serves as a foundation for fostering deep understanding and trust within the network. A key tool in achieving this is the Impact Trace Tool, which allows buyers to trace the entire value chain of a product by simply scanning a QR code. Consumers can see exactly who produced the products and what contributions the farmers make with their biodynamic cultivation. The tool further highlights externalised costs, such as environmental degradation or CO_2 emissions, making the real price of a product transparent and showing the wider influence of consumer choices on both society and the planet. By using the Impact Trace Tool, a link is also established between the various stakeholders within the value chain of a particular product. Justus Harm summarises the tool as follows:

> "The Impact Trace Tool connects the various stakeholders who are involved in the value chain, so to speak, in the value creation of a particular product, and mainly also familiarises end customers with what impact they actually have."

In addition, the purchase of Whole System Credits enhances this trust. Companies that purchase the credits receive a code that shows exactly which farmer they have purchased the certificate from. In this way, companies know exactly which farmers they are supporting and what direct impact they are having on the environment and local farming practices.

By enabling such transparency and connection, the Economy of Love promotes a shared understanding and trust among consumers, producers, and all other stakeholders, laying the groundwork for a more sustainable and responsible economy.

Holistic Sustainable Development

The Economy of Love network fosters a holistic approach that not only promotes farmers' transition to biodynamic agriculture, but also positively impacts their local communities by reducing water consumption, lowering CO_2 emissions and supporting sustainable land use. A central component of this holistic system is the distributive design of the Whole System Credits, which provide farmers with an additional source of income. This strengthens their economic stability and incentivises them to continue pursuing sustainable agricultural practices. The EBDA has now decided that, with this additional source of income, farmers are no longer allowed to sell their products at premium prices, which was previously necessary due to the higher production costs in organic farming. Instead, they must now offer their products at more affordable prices, ensuring that more people have access to healthy organic products. This creates a sustainable and balanced economic model that promotes long-term, equitable development.

Improvement of Biodynamic Agricultural Methods

The improvement of biodynamic agricultural methods is deeply rooted in a culture of collaboration and shared learning. This sense of togetherness is actively fostered through tools that connect farmers and stakeholders across the value chain. One such tool is the Participatory Guarantee System (PGS), a widely used approach across the organic movement and by organisations like the World Fair Trade Organisation as a credible alternative to third-party certification. This system not only ensures transparency but also integrates peer-to-peer support and assessment, allowing farmers to actively participate in verifying organic standards. However, despite its growing adoption, PGS is not yet officially recognised as a certification system in all countries. Even so, it provides a valuable platform where farmers can share their experiences, exchange knowledge, and collaboratively develop their practices, creating a supportive network of continuous learning and growth.

Roundtable meetings further exemplify this spirit of collaboration. These regular gatherings bring farmers, companies, and other stakeholders together to discuss challenges, brainstorm solutions, and co-create innovative approaches. Such discussions not only strengthen community bonds but also lead to advancements in biodynamic and regenerative farming methods.

The Impact Trace Tool adds another layer to this interconnected approach by linking stakeholders throughout the value chain. By scanning a QR code, buyers can trace a product's journey, understand farmers' contributions, and see the broader impact of their choices. This shared visibility strengthens accountability and cooperation among all involved.

Dissemination

The extensive network, which includes wide range of stakeholders, offers the opportunity to distribute the shared values and strategies of *SEKEM* and the *EBDA*. The dissemination of these takes place in a variety of ways. Particularly noteworthy is the cooperation with previously conventional associations that want to support their members in the transition to more sustainable business practices. Through this cooperation, knowledge can be passed on and existing structures can be changed. The Economy of Love approach has also inspired international interest, with *SEKEM*'s model now being adopted in several countries. Partnerships with countries such as India, Tunisia and Italy are helping local farmers adopt sustainable practices inspired by *SEKEM*'s model. These diverse and inclusive approaches foster intensive and collaborative partnerships, driving the development and implementation of more sustainable practices and further establishing the Economy of Love.

Challenges Arising from Designing Network around the Economy of Love

Sensitisation for Biodynamic Agriculture

One challenge is to educate and sensitise farmers to the values and principles of *SEKEM* and the *EBDA*. For many farmers, conventional farming has been the norm for generations. Consequently, they often remain unaware of the social and sustainable benefits arising from the principles of the *SEKEM* initiative and the Economy of Love. It is therefore necessary to inform farmers about the positive impact that organic and biodynamic farming methods can have on their businesses, economic existence, and the environment.

Measurement of the Whole Credit System

Implementing an effective Whole Credit System presents a challenge, as it requires a robust local governance structure supported by partners with expertise in accurate and reliable CO_2 storage calculation. However, a stable local governance structure is not always provided. In addition, local validation and verification bodies are essential to ensure compliance with the established standards. This complex and resource-intensive process demands both technical expertise and close cooperation among various stakeholders.

Intensive Information and Support

While close cooperation with farmers is vital for the initiative's success and expansion, it is also highly time-consuming and resource-intensive. Nearly 70 agricultural engineers at *SEKEM* work to support farmers in implementing and maintaining sustainable practices. This support involves regular visits, consultations, training sessions, and phone support, ensuring compliance with certification standards. Justus Harm emphasises:

> "So at the moment, I have 69 agricultural engineers, so to speak advisors, full-time employees in the association, who are spread throughout the country and whose main task is to advise the farmers, organise training and fulfil all the wishes that the farmers have."

Interactions with Other Design Traits

Governance Design

As its name implies, the *EBDA* is an association and therefore belongs to its members, the farmers. This structure gives the farmers a central role in the association's decision-making processes. Annually, members come together for a general assembly to vote on important matters and elect the board of directors. This elected board then takes over the management of the organisation as it appoints the executive director to run the operational side of the business.

Another feature of the *EBDA*'s associative structure is its interactive, flat governance system, which gives farmers a high degree of participation. As members of the association, farmers have voting rights, allowing them to actively contribute to decisions. Stakeholder meetings, for instance, always include farmers or their representatives, ensuring direct interaction with other members. This flat hierarchy promotes dialogue and direct interaction between members, empowering farmers to actively contribute their opinions and needs, thus playing a key role in shaping the association's development.

The *EBDA*'s participatory nature is further enhanced by the regular Roundtable discussions, which foster connections both among farmers and between farmers and companies. These meetings allow all parties to openly share their challenges, perspectives, and needs while working together to find solutions and offer mutual support. This approach fosters equitable cooperation that respects everyone's interests and builds sustainable, long-term partnerships.

Finance Design

The *EBDA*'s financial resources stem from several sources. In addition to income from the cooperation with Demeter and Demeter licenses, the new source of income from the Whole System Credits is particularly important. Approximately 15 percent of the revenue from the sale of these certificates goes directly to the association. These funds are used to cover the *EBDA*'s constantly growing costs for the recruitment of new consultants, the organisation of further training courses, the creation of learning materials and the further development of the certification processes. Membership fees from farmers constitute another source of income, although the *EBDA* keeps these low to minimise the financial burden on farmers. Overall, these various sources of income help the *EBDA* to expand its activities and continuously pursue its mission to promote biodynamic agriculture and sustainable practices.

Recommendations for Adopting an Economy of Love Based Network Design

Flexibility

A central element of the *EBDA* is its flexible cooperation with a diverse network of stakeholders. Their systemic approach means that they do not stick rigidly to fixed partners but instead dynamically assess who can help on the respective path. This flexibility enables the *EBDA* to constantly optimise cooperation and ensure that all parties involved receive the best possible support to achieve common goals. Justus Harm describes this flexibility as follows:

> "We always look at who can help us or who wants to help us along the way and who we can support on their individual path."

Continuous Improvement

SEKEM and the *EBDA* foster a culture of continuous improvement through their collaborative structure. Regular Roundtables and open communication among stakeholders provide a platform for exchanging knowledge, sharing experiences, and jointly developing innovative solutions.

Cultivating Togetherness

SEKEM promotes a strong sense of community by fostering education, cultural initiatives, and creative collaboration that benefit everyone involved by enabling collective growth and cultural development. This holistic approach strengthens connections within the organisation and the wider community, creating a shared foundation for sustainable progress.

Inspiring Redesign Beyond the Business

Systemic change is the focus of *SEKEM* and the *EBDA*'S mission. The aim is to fundamentally transform the agricultural sector and to further train and educate both consumers and farmers in rethinking agriculture and nutrition. Agriculture plays a particularly important role in this transformation because an estimated 23% of total anthropogenic greenhouse gas emissions (2007–2016) derive from Agriculture, Forestry and Other Land Use (AFOLU) (IPCC 2019: p.6). However, by transitioning to a regenerative-biodynamic agriculture, part of the problem can become part of the solution, as it can make a significant contribution to protecting the environment. Justus Harm emphasises:

> "If we change to regenerative-ecological agriculture, then agriculture is part of the solution and part of the system change."

Through the Economy of Love Standard and Whole System Credits, *EBDA* farmers are making substantial contributions to CO_2 sequestration in soil, water storage, and ecosystem strengthening in terms of biodiversity, resilience, and soil fertility. By switching to organic and biodynamic farming, they are strengthening essential ecosystem services, which in turn benefit both the local community and the farmers themselves.

Agriculture and related sectors employ a significant portion of the global workforce. Successfully transforming this sector sustainably and driving rapid change could lead to systemic change far beyond Egypt. The *EBDA* model is already being observed and replicated in other countries, where organisations seek to apply similar principles to enhance sustainability in their agricultural systems. Such a transformation would not only revolutionise agriculture but also fundamentally reshape our economy and way of life, fostering a more sustainable and just society.

For this change to take place, sustainable agriculture must emerge as a lucrative business that farmers perceive as financially attractive. This necessitates that the transition to sustainable farming practices offers not only ecological advantages but also tangible economic benefits to farmers. As sustainable farming demonstrates its financial viability, it will likely attract an increasing number of farmers to join the transition.

References

Interview

with Justus Harm, Co-Executive Director EBDA (2/06/2024, 1:00h).

Homepage

EBDA (2025): The Egyptian Biodynamic Association – Promoting Sustainable Agriculture since 1994, https://ebda.earth/, [Accessed 7 March 2024].
SEKEM (2025): Sustainable Development since 1977, https://sekem.com/en/index/, [Accessed 1 March 2024].

Other Sources

Demeter (2025): Biodynamic Approach and Principles, https://demeter.net/biodyn
amics/biodynamic-approach/, [Accessed 24 April 2025].

Economy of Love (2025): https://www.economyoflove.net/, [Accessed 5 March
2024].

IFOAM Organics International (2025): Participatory Guarantee Systems (PGS),
https://www.ifoam.bio/our-work/how/standards-certification/participatory-
guarantee-systems, [Accessed 17 February 2025].

IPCC (2019): Climate Change and Land – An IPCC Special Report on climate change,
desertification, land degradation, sustainable land management, food security,
and greenhouse gas fluxes in terrestrial ecosystems, https://www.ipcc.ch/site/
assets/uploads/2019/11/SRCCL-Full-Report-Compiled-191128.pdf, [Accessed 22
April 2025].

Case Study: Sonnentor

Sina Kehrwieder & Nelly Rahimy

Purpose: To create organic products that support people and nature
Design Trait: Network
Innovative Practice: Regionally Responsibility-Based Network Design

Key Facts

Sonnentor is a family-owned company specialising in 100% organic herbs, spices, and teas, built on fair partnerships with local and global producers. Based in Austria, it actively supports its structurally weaker home region by creating jobs, fostering economic resilience, and leading initiatives that prioritise organic farming, social equity, and environmental regeneration.

> **Founded:** 1988
> **Industry:** Organic food
> **Location:** Sprögnitz, Austria
> **Founded by:** Johannes Gutmann
> **Ownership:** Family-Owned
> **Legal form:** Limited Liability Company (GmbH)
> **Employees:** 544 (2022/2023)
> **Webpage:** https://www.sonnentor.com/de-at

Purpose, Business Model & Objectives

> Purpose: To create organic products that support people and nature

Founded in 1988, *Sonnentor* has grown into a well-recognised brand, closely associated with its founder, Johannes Gutmann and, more importantly, for its commitment to organic farming. Known for his signature red glasses and Lederhosen,

Gutmann had a clear vision from the outset: to sell only high-quality, organic, and sustainable food and to create impact in his home region, the Waldviertel in Austria. Initially a pioneer of the organic market, *Sonnentor* has grown into a global network with over 1000 agricultural partners, far beyond the three farming families who launched the journey.

> "The idea of Purpose was present from the very beginning and it has developed in various directions. Naturally, the situation is completely different now, with 360 employees in Austria, nationwide in Germany, 180 in the Czech Republic, and 1,000 farmers worldwide growing for us, compared to how it started—as a one-man business with three regional farming families." — Verena Königsberger, Corporate Communication Manager

Sonnentor as a company has evolved and grown, yet the core philosophy remains unchanged: a commitment to ethical partnerships and ecological responsibility.

> "These two aspects [regional ties and ecological conviction] are very, very deep in our DNA and are absolutely cross-cutting issues in our company. Every department is involved." — Florian Krautzer, CSR-Manager

To minimise its ecological footprint, *Sonnentor* has long been committed to clean energy transformation. For decades, the company has integrated renewable energy solutions, continuously eliminating fossil fuel dependency and accelerating its shift towards net neutrality. Key initiatives include:

- Purchasing 100% green energy since 1992
- Implementing a wood-chip heating system
- Expanding its photovoltaic system to maximise solar energy use

Thanks to these efforts, *Sonnentor*'s own emissions are now equivalent to those of just thirteen Austrian households per year. While significant progress has been made, the company remains dedicated to achieving long-term net-zero emissions. *Sonnentor* aims to eliminate all fossil GHG emissions from its own operations by 2030, while supporting projects and developments aimed at sequestering CO_2 from the atmosphere, such as building up humus within its supply chain or generating biochar from its waste stems in production.

Insights into the Regionally Responsibility-Based Network Design

One of *Sonnentor*'s most distinctive qualities is its deep and fair network of partnerships, which includes suppliers, employees, customers, and communities. Since 2011, *Sonnentor* has been part of the "Economy for the Common Good" movement and discloses its sustainable activities within its biennial Common Good Report. Specifically, the following areas are analysed: Dealing with suppliers, employees and customers, ownership and financial structures as well as the general social environment and the impact of the product. In 2023, the company scored 746 points (out of 1000), including 87.50% in the criteria supplier ethics.

Figure 1: Economy for the Common Good

Economy for the Common Good (ECG)

The Economy for the Common Good (ECG) is an economic model that prioritizes a good life for everyone on a healthy planet. Instead of focusing solely on profit, ECG businesses commit to values such as human dignity, solidarity, social justice, environmental sustainability, and transparency.

1. Common Good Balance Sheet
Businesses assess their contribution to society and sustainability using the Common Good Matrix.

2. ECG Label
Products receive a score, helping consumers make ethical choices.

3. Policy Support
Fairer taxation and incentives make ECG businesses more competitive.

Source: Economy for the Common Good 2025.

Suppliers

Strong supplier relationships are essential for *Sonnentor*, as they form the foundation of its business. From the very beginning, the brand has remained closely connected to its regional roots—not just as a commitment to local areas but also as a fundamental principle of how it engages with business partners. Whenever possible, *Sonnentor* sources all herbs and spices that can grow locally from Austria and neighbouring countries, reinforcing its dedication to regional agriculture in rural areas.

To ensure high-quality and sustainable sourcing, *Sonnentor* has strict requirements for its cultivation partners. Farmers must be certified organic producers under EU Organic Regulation, hold an organic certification for all herbs and spices they intend to grow, have expertise in matching crop selection to soil suitability and possess the necessary machinery for cultivation, processing, and harvesting, as well as drying facilities.

Beyond these requirements, *Sonnentor* ensures fairness in supplier relationships through three key practices: fair pricing, direct trade, and long-term partnerships.

Fair Prices

Sonnentor guarantees its suppliers fair prices, ensuring stability regardless of fluctuations in global market prices. For one, *Sonnentor* establishes cultivation and supply contracts that guarantee minimum prices above standard market rates.

Direct Trade

A key element of *Sonnentor*'s purpose is its commitment to direct trade, sourcing products directly from farmers or local partners, bypassing intermediaries whenever possible. While intermediaries can help connect small-scale producers to markets and reduce risk through diversification, direct trade gives *Sonnentor* the flexibility needed to sustain fair and stable prices across its international supply chain. This approach allows the company to pay stable, fair prices that provide producers a secure and long-term livelihood. Today, approximately 60% of *Sonnentor*'s herbs, spices, and coffee are sourced through direct trade.

> "It is very important to us that the values that we have stood for from the beginning – the ones that have made us successful – are also upheld internationally. We want to ensure that equality, trust, the strong gut feeling that we have built up are carried into our supply chain worldwide." — Florian Krautzer

Even when working beyond its immediate regional network, *Sonnentor* remains committed to respectful and fair supplier relationships.

Long-Term Partnerships

Sonnentor focuses on long-term partnerships that ensure stability for both the company and its suppliers. More than 60% of raw material partners have supplied *Sonnentor* for more than 5 years, while all three original local farmers still supply *Sonnentor*, some in second, some in the third generation, after 37 years. *Sonnentor* fosters partnerships with a long-term vision, offering mutual planning security and strengthening trust for future collaboration. It's about

> "taking a long-term approach, not just (...) setting rigid demands like, 'These are our conditions and if you can't fulfil them, you're out'. Instead, we say, 'Here's how we envision working together—can you do that? If not, why? Could you do it next year? Or the year after?' This mindset ensures planning security, allowing us to grow and evolve together." — Florian Krautzer

Regular on-site visits and advance financing that assists partners expand their production capacities are important tools in maintaining regionally responsible supplier relationships. For example, *Sonnentor* provided advance financing to one of its partners in Kosovo, enabling them to develop new, organic products and capabilities.

Employees

The regionally-based network design also includes its employees. As one of the largest employers in the rural, structurally weak Waldviertel region, *Sonnentor* plays a crucial role in providing stable jobs and strengthening the local economy and community.

> "We see ourselves as a strong regional employer in the Waldviertel. You might know the Waldviertel – a structurally somewhat weaker area where one might have to travel a bit further to get to work, as there aren't so many companies in the region. And we have always seen ourselves as a very strong employer; we have 320 employees right here at our location in the Waldviertel." — Verena Königsberger

With 320 employees at its headquarters and additional home-based workers, the company not only offers direct employment but also supports many farming families through seasonal and flexible work opportunities. For example, it supports rural farming families who may have seasonal work fluctuations by including them in the hand packing process.

> "There are approximately 60 or more men and women who work as freelance contractors from home. These are often farming families who take on more hand-packaging work in the winter when there is less fieldwork. We place a strong emphasis on continuing this practice. It may not always be the most economically efficient decision, as we could achieve a much higher output with machines." — Verena Königsberger

Unlike many traditional businesses, *Sonnentor* rejects rigid performance quotas and instead trusts its employees to work at their own pace. This pressure-free environment fosters a culture of respect and well-being, recognising that individual productivity may vary from day to day.

> "Unlike other companies, we don't have a set requirement for employees to produce a specific number of units per day. That simply doesn't exist here. Instead, we place a certain level of trust in our employees, trusting that the work will get done. Of course, some colleagues are faster than others—that's just how it is and always will be. But we don't apply pressure; we trust that our employees will do their best." — Verena Königsberger

Fig 2: Hand-Packaging at Sonnentor

Source: Sonnentor 2024.

Including Employees in the Purpose

Furthermore, *Sonnentor* ensures that employees are not just workers but active participants in the company's purpose. To foster engagement and inclusion, *Sonnentor* regularly shares updates on sustainability initiatives, company values, and business decisions through its internal magazine, social intranet, and mobile communication tools. This communication is a vital tool in bridging the classical gap between office and production workers.

> "We wanted to minimise this gap as much as possible, which is why implementing a mobile app was a must-have for us. This tool ensures that every employee can access information at the same time—if they choose to. We recently saw how valuable this was when we experienced severe flooding in our region two weeks ago. On a Sunday, I was able to quickly send out a message to all employees using a special push notification feature. The message popped up directly on the phones of those who had opted in, allowing us to instantly reach everyone—whether they were in production, administration, or our retail stores—even outside of regular working hours." — Verena Königsberger

Beyond traditional communication, *Sonnentor* gamifies engagement to encourage employees to interact with company values. For example, employees can participate in company-wide challenges, such as:

- **Health initiatives**, like the annual "Adios Zucker" (Goodbye Sugar) campaign, where employees receive training on healthy eating and take part in sugar-free cooking classes.
- **Inclusion in product development.** With an internal ideas and feedback box on the company's social intranet, employees can easily submit suggestions. Many new products also go through an internal testing phase, where employees can volunteer to try prototypes and provide feedback, as seen with the 3 Minze tea, which was tested by 15 employees.
- **Interactive quizzes on the Economy for the Common Good report.** Such quizzes about *Sonnentor's* sustainability goals foster a sense of shared purpose. This way, *Sonnentor* makes sure "that employees are also informed about its contents and that it's not just something we create for external purposes" (Verena Königsberger).
- **Sustainability competitions.** For example, the company conducted an upcycling challenge where employees repurposed packaging materials into new creations. The winning idea—gift wrap sewn from tea bag covers—was later showcased on social media, inspiring both employees and fans.

Work-Life Balance & Holistic Well-Being

The company offers a range of benefits, from sports classes and therapy services to free lunches, embodying its values (namely respect, recognition, and health) through a supportive work culture. These include:

- **Flexible work models**, including remote work options and a four-day workweek for much of the production team.
- **A company daycare centre**, "Sonnenscheinchen" (ray of sunshine), helping employees balance work and family life.
- **Free organic lunches** for all employees, with a focus on healthy, sustainable eating (two vegetarian/vegan days per week).

"We also take part in Veganuary, the international campaign promoting plant-based eating. The goal is to showcase vegan cooking and encourage employees to explore it. In general, we offer our employees a free organic lunch from Monday to Thursday in our organic restaurant. Everything served is, of course, organic—aligning with our company's values and commitment to sustainability."—(Verena Königsberger

- **Health & wellness initiatives**, such as free sports classes, therapy services, and regular health workshops. Each campaign revolves around a *Sonnentor*-specific theme, often featuring one of their in-house herbal experts. Employees can initiate and participate in herbal workshops, baking or cooking courses, all linked to sustainability—such as regional cooking, plant-based recipes, or waste reduction, like baking your own bread to avoid packaging waste.

Customers

Naturally, the customers are also crucial stakeholders for *Sonnentor*, both as buyers and as active participants in the purpose. Through social media engagement, the customer magazine FREUDE, and direct communication channels, the company fosters strong relationships that provide valuable insights into consumer needs. *Sonnentor* takes a deliberate approach to distribution, prioritising direct customer engagement over conventional supermarket sales. The company sells most of its products through:

- 17 franchise partners who uphold *Sonnentor*'s values
- Independent health food stores
- Online sales, allowing direct interaction with customers

By bypassing traditional grocery retail, *Sonnentor* maintains greater control over its prices rather than being pressured by large retailers' cost-cutting demands. Furthermore, the stores serve as educational spaces rather than just points of sale, ensuring customised customer advice, and strengthening its direct relationships with consumers. This direct sales model mirrors *Sonnentor*'s commitment to direct trade in sourcing—building transparent, trust-based relationships at every stage, from suppliers to end customers.

This customer-driven approach is reflected in product development:

- 50% of all new products are based on direct customer feedback and requests. For example, *Sonnentor*'s "Beste für Reste" (Best for Leftovers), a spice blend designed for leftover food, was co-created with its social media community. Fans participated in the process by voting on recipes, packaging designs, and even the product name.
- The *Sonnentor* community has even played a financial role, contributing capital via a crowdfunding campaign to support the company's internal energy transition.

Community Impact

Sonnentor's commitment to social and environmental responsibility extends beyond its own operations, actively supporting communities, sustainable agriculture, and democratic engagement. This way, *Sonnentor* fosters long-term positive change both locally and globally.

Sonnentor invests in social projects that align with its values, supporting health, organic farming, and regional empowerment. One such initiative in Uganda promotes the local production and distribution of clean, efficient cooking stoves, reducing indoor air pollution and improving health outcomes for families.

"There is less smoke indoors, meaning better health for the families. They also save time and money on fuel. Most importantly, these stoves are developed locally, made with local materials, and maintained by local businesses. It strengthens the region—and that's something in our DNA, so it's great to promote this elsewhere too." — Florian Krautzer

Sonnentor actively works to protect farmers from the risks of conventional agriculture. In Austria, *Sonnentor* and its farmers established an association that helps them insure against pesticide drift damage from neighbouring non-organic farms. This initiative functions as an alternative insurance model, allowing affected farmers to claim compensation for lost revenue without the bureaucratic hurdles of traditional insurance contracts. Additionally, the company collaborates with "Enkeltaugliches Österreich", an organisation advocating for large-scale organic agriculture, sustainable forestry, and biodiversity protection. This initiative also financially supports farmers impacted by external environmental damage, ensuring greater security within the organic farming network.

Additionally, *Sonnentor*'s founder has stepped back from daily operations to focus on advocacy and education, giving talks at universities, schools, and businesses on sustainable business practices and responsible entrepreneurship. Furthermore, he is particularly engaged in promoting democratic politics.

"Actually, it is important for us not to position ourselves along party-political lines. However, this political cause is still very important to us. We are currently participating in an initiative called 'Love Politics,' which is all about encouraging people to stand up for democracy and exercise their right to vote."—Verena Königsberger

How the Regionally Responsibility-Based Network Design Enables Regenerative and Distributive Dynamics

Increased Resilience

The responsibility-based network design creates reliable, long-term partnerships. These partnerships cannot be replicated easily, as the organisation of the relationship is inherently time-consuming and requires time to develop.

"This is the central credo, and long-term partnerships work when you treat each other fairly, when you create predictability, when you work together as equals, when you build trust and exchange ideas and visit each other" — Florian Krautzer

This long-term approach results in further benefits such as improved planning and mutual reliability. Especially during times of crisis, *Sonnentor* is able to rely on its networks to ensure its prosperity and security.

"Yes, during the pandemic, we were one of the few companies in our bubble, I would say, that was able to deliver without restrictions when you have such long-term partnerships and know each other well then you also go the extra mile. If you know that things will continue next year and the year after that then you simply help each other in a different way I think that makes us more resilient, yes. I can only speak for us now, but these good partnerships definitely helped us." — Florian Krautzer

This was particularly evident during the COVID-19 pandemic. When *Sonnentor's* field representatives in Germany were unable to perform their usual duties, they stepped in to assist local farming partners with fieldwork. In Austria, the company called on employees to help with the harvest when travel restrictions prevented seasonal workers from entering the country. Meanwhile, the company's Greek farming partner returned the favour by supporting *Sonnentor's* hand-packaging operations in Sprögnitz alongside his wife.

The company's commitment to strong relationships with its stakeholders is not only a moral imperative – it's also a key competitive advantage, yielding resilient connections that are especially valuable during challenging times.

Innovation

Innovations are not only the result of inputs within the company and the wishes expressed by customers. Innovation and new product development are made possible continuously and, above all, reliably by investing in partnerships. Customer requests may point to new market needs. Internal suggestions are taken seriously as well and have recently led to noticeable improvements in production by saving resources.

"It is absolutely encouraged for employees to contribute ideas—everyone can actively participate, and this is genuinely put into practice. Before we introduced our social intranet, we had a physical suggestion box in the company where employees could submit ideas. At first, it worked well, but over time, engagement declined. Now, with our social intranet, we have a dedicated Ideas & Feedback Box, making it much easier for employees to submit their suggestions via a simple form.

We regularly receive great ideas—not just from our retail stores but also from our production employees." — Verena Königsberger

Skilled Labour Selection Instead of Shortage

Sonnentor's sustainability efforts are a big part of the company's image and public presence, attracting like-minded people with similar values. The company receives numerous applications every year and therefore has no problem with a potential shortage of skilled labour. In addition, employees have a high commitment and a low fluctuation rate.

"*Sonnentor* is known for being a very sustainable company in the region and be-yond (...) and that also attracts a certain kind of people who want to work at *Son-nentor.*"—Florian Krautzer

The appreciative work culture contributes to this low fluctuation rate of 8,5% (in con-trast to around 14% within the industry).

Challenges Arising From Designing Networks Around Regional Responsibility

While *Sonnentor*'s regionally focused network offers many benefits, it also presents unique challenges. These arise from the pioneering nature of the company's early days, the intensive effort required to maintain supplier relationships, the scalabil-ity limits of such a hands-on approach, and the company's reliance on long-term partnerships.

Building and Maintaining Supplier Network

Creating and sustaining regionally anchored supply networks is no simple task. It requires significant upfront investment and long-term commitment. "Finding new raw materials or something is not easy because you can't just reach onto the shelf or call and say, 'I'll order x quantity then and then, there and there'" Florian Krautzer. Unlike conventional businesses that can source materials on demand, *Sonnentor* carefully chooses and empowers new suppliers before they can reliably deliver. Despite this additional effort, the high product quality that results makes it a worthwhile benefit that customers recognise and appreciate.

Company Growth and Scalability

As *Sonnentor* has grown, maintaining intensive supplier relationships has become more challenging. The company acknowledges that its hands-on, relationship-driven approach is not infinitely scalable, yet it remains committed to preserving its values. This involves balancing trade-offs such as in the case with hand packing. While the company has retained hand-packing in some cases, it admits that "not everything can be done by hand anymore. For our best-selling products, we simply cannot keep up with demand through manual work alone—we saw this clearly during the COVID-19 pandemic when demand surged" (Verena Königsberger).

This makes it a potential challenge, as the intensive relationships do not appear to be infinitely scalable. Nevertheless, the supply of the required volume of goods and products must be guaranteed at a consistently high level of quality. But even with increasing growth, "we want to stay the way we are" (Sonnentor 2025). Business activities should continue to be characterised by the values that have made *Sonnentor* so successful to date.

Greater Dependency on Partnerships

Because *Sonnentor* prioritises long-term supplier relationships, it does not have the same flexibility as businesses that can quickly switch to new suppliers if problems arise. Building new partnerships is time-consuming and labour-intensive, making it crucial to nurture and protect existing relationships. When problems arise, efforts are made to cooperate and communicate in a solution-oriented manner,

> "because it is more important for us to maintain and expand a partnership over time than to go looking for a new one now, also because I mentioned it before, it is simply extremely time-consuming and labour-intensive to build something like that." — Florian Krautzer

For example, *Sonnentor* has provided advance financing to key partners or sought out organisations in regions like Tanzania that can coordinate hundreds of farming families to ensure timely, high-quality deliveries.

Interactions with Other Design Traits

Finance Design

One important design trait interaction is with financing. *Sonnentor* places value in its high amount of equity (67%) and its financial independence. "For stockholders who are only after quick profits, there is no place here. We are owner-managed and in-dependent of external investors" (Sonnentor 2025). While *Sonnentor* generally avoids outside investors, it is not completely closed to external funding—but only from trusted sources.

> "If we do take external investments, they must come from people we absolutely trust—especially our fans and employees. We regularly offer opportunities for them to participate in our sustainable projects." — Florian Krautzer

In this vein, *Sonnentor* has tapped into crowd-based financing, allowing customers and supporters to contribute directly to sustainable projects. One key example is the "Crowd Sunding" project, which financed the construction of *Sonnentor*'s own photo-voltaic system through a discounted product voucher system. Supporters could pur-chase discounted vouchers for €400, which were allocated specifically for expanding the photovoltaic system. In return, participants received €500 in *Sonnentor* vouch-ers, distributed over five years, equating to a 5% annual return—surpassing typical bank interest rates. This carefully curated financial strategy ensures that *Sonnentor* remains aligned with its core values, safeguarding its ability to make ethical, long-term decisions rather than being driven by short-term financial pressures.

Recommendations for Adopting a Regionally Responsibility-Based Network Design

Authentic Commitment to Purpose

What has begun with Johannes Gutmann, continues to drive *Sonnentor* today: the company positions itself as both a brand and a business with purpose, attracting like-minded employees, customers, and partners through consistent media pres-ence and a compelling sustainability narrative. However, a shared purpose must be deeply ingrained in everyday business practices, instead of serving as a mere brand-ing tool. At *Sonnentor*, this authentic commitment is reflected in supplier partner-ships, employee relations, and social initiatives that directly align with its purpose. Everything ties back to the heart of the company.

Maintain Long-Term, Respectful Partnerships

To build a resilient, regionally-based network, it is essential to foster open com-munication and cooperation on equal footing. Prioritising mutual respect, fairness, and long-term commitment ensures that partnerships are not just transactional but genuinely sustainable.

Inspiring Redesign Beyond the Business

Sonnentor's business model stands as a direct counterpoint to the notion that conventional companies have no viable alternatives.

> "We show that it can be done." —Florian Krautzer

Sonnentor proves that economic success does not have to come at the expense of environmental and social responsibility. Instead, prioritising long-term supplier relationships, meaningful customer engagement, and active employee participation strengthens both the company and the broader community. While *Sonnentor* once operated without clear role models, it now strives to become one—demonstrating that distributive and regenerative business practices are not only possible but also beneficial. By leading by example, *Sonnentor* contributes to a fundamental shift in business thinking and a cross-industry transformation toward a more sustainable economic system.

References

Interviews

with Florian Krautzer, CSR Manager of *Sonnentor* (29/03/2023, 0:53h).
with Verena Königsberger, Corporate Communication Manager of *Sonnentor* (26/09/2024, 00:43h).

Homepage

Sonnentor (2025): https://www.sonnentor.com/de-at, [Accessed 10 April 2025].

Other Sources:

Economy for the Common Good (2025): https://www.econgood.org/what-is-ecg/ecg-in-a-nutshell, [Accessed 10 April 2025].

Case Study: Wildling Shoes

Sina Kehrwieder

Purpose: "We want to transfer the regenerative effect that our shoes have on our well-being to our entire business. To achieve this, we rely on partnership-based production, innovative materials from regenerative cultivation and the promotion of re-naturation projects" (Wildling Shoes 2025a).
Design Trait: Network
Innovative Practice: Re:generative Network Design

Key Facts

Wildling Shoes is a regenerative shoe producer that focuses on partnership-based production, innovative materials from regenerative cultivation like hemp and embraces the "restore, preserve, enhance" triad to translate the regenerative impact of their shoes to the entire way of doing business.

> **Founded:** 2015
> **Industry:** Fashion/Shoes
> **Location:** Engelskirchen, Germany
> **Founded by:** Anna and Ran Yona
> **Ownership:** family-owned by Anna and Ran Yona, and a friendly associate partner
> **Legal Form:** Limited Liability Company (GmbH)
> **Employees:** 202 (2025)
> **Webpage:** https://www.wildling.shoes/en

Purpose, Business Model & Objectives

Purpose: "We want to transfer the regenerative effect that our shoes have on our well-being to our entire business. To achieve this, we rely on partnership-based production, innovative materials from regenerative cultivation and the promotion of renaturation projects."

In 2015, Ran and Anna Yona were looking for adequate footwear for their children. When they couldn't find what they were looking for, they decided to create it themselves, founding *Wildling Shoes* in the process. The company designs minimalist footwear for children and adults with soles that are as light and flexible as possible, so as not to hinder the foot's natural range of motion. *Wildling Shoes* have been developed to support the body's natural musculoskeletal functions, helping to correct misalignments and promote overall health and well-being.

Wildling Shoes aims to transfer the principle of regeneration to all parts of their value chain, doing business based on the understanding of regeneration as "giving back more than you take" — Anna Yona

Therefore, they strive to create as many benefits as possible for their stakeholders and the general society, in order to restore, preserve and enhance (Wildling Shoes, 2025b).

Through innovative product design and the use of new regenerative materials such as Washi Paper or dog wool, which otherwise would be discarded as waste, *Wildling Shoes* promotes circular production. The company actively strives to optimise processes within a circular economy, emphasising the transformative power of regional supply chains that amplify positive impact along the value chain. For example, to minimise production waste, *Wildling Shoes* reuses fabric stocks from previous models to create new products called "Refoxed Models". Moreover, to promote recycling, some designs are composed of only three elements – fleece, thread and sole – making them easier to disassemble and recycle at the end of their life cycle.

The added value *Wildling Shoes* generates extends well beyond the company itself. Since 2022, the company has been a certified member of the B Corporation network. In 2023, it co-founded the Unlearn Business Lab, a platform designed to foster exchange and collaboration in pursuit of a circular, regenerative economy.

B Corporations:

According to B Lab, a certified B Corporation™, or B Corp, pursues the vision of a better economic system in which businesses benefit people, communities, and the planet. It prioritises long-term investments over short-term profits and measures its success through the positive impact it creates (B Lab 2025).

Insights into the Re:generative Network Design

Wildling Shoes' re:generative network design is an innovative practice aimed at building relationships across its value chain. It is characterised by several core aspects:

A Broad Understanding of Stakeholders, Including Nature

At the heart of *Wildling Shoes'* re:generative network design lies the inclusion of a broad range of stakeholders in the company's interactions and decision-making processes. This expansive understanding explicitly extends to

> "nature, which comes into contact with us in any way or with which we come into contact, for example when fibres are grown and when we use chemicals, if we cannot recycle a product afterwards and so on, then of course this is also a very important stakeholder."—Anna Yona

Anna Yona points out that it is increasingly difficult, and ultimately artificial, to separate ourselves as human beings from the environment, as we are all inherently interconnected.

Partner Selection Based on Shared Values and Personal Connection

For *Wildling Shoes,* long-term partnerships are essential for achieving their regenerative purpose. The company deliberately avoids the term "suppliers", instead referring to "partners"—organisations and businesses with whom they collaborate closely. Rather than relying primarily on labels or certifications, which smaller partners often cannot afford, *Wildling Shoes* places greater importance on mutual insight and authentic alignment. The partner selection is based on the criteria of transparency, trust, personal connection and shared regenerative and distributive values. Especially transparency through open exchange and understanding of a partner's way of working and underlying values builds the foundation for a trusting relationship. As Anna Yona explains, the first test is always "Can we come round? Can we have a look?" – a question that reflects their commitment to personal connection and shared values. If these elements are not present, *Wildling Shoes* will not enter a partnership, even if doing so would make economic sense. This shared value base also includes a mutual willingness to improve, for example, by working together to enhance working conditions, as Anna Yona further explains:

> "So now, for example, at the production sites in Portugal, to say, okay, the basic atmosphere is right, the interaction with each other is right, the pay is right and now we can just look together, can we organise the workplaces even better or are there still safety facilities where we can have an influence or not? That's always really important to us."

Building Long-Term Partnerships for Developing Regenerative Materials in Regional Supply Chains

Wildling Shoes actively supports the development of regenerative materials by cultivating long-term partnerships with producers working within local supply chains. These collaborations aim to strengthen ecological resilience and promote circular economy practices. One example is *Wildling Shoes'* partnership with **Nordwolle**, a northern German wool producer that sources wool from the endangered Pomeranian sheep. Once on the brink of extinction, this breed had been sidelined in conventional wool production due to its coarser wool, which cannot be dyed in vibrant colours and is considered less marketable than Merino wool. As a result, Pomeranian wool was often treated as waste. However, this sheep breed is exceptionally well adapted to the rainy conditions of northern Germany: its dense, long fibres provide excellent water resistance. By using this wool in its shoes, Wildling not only repurposes a previously discarded material but also supports biodiversity and landscape conservation. Through this long-term partnership with Nordwolle, *Wildling Shoes* helps ensure the survival of the breed while also repurposing previously discarded wool for shoe production, making a valuable contribution to circular economy practices.

A second key partnership that *Wildling Shoes* maintains is with **VirgoCoop**, a French cooperative striving to transform the textile industry by establishing local and ethical supply chains for European hemp. Once widely cultivated, hemp textiles in Europe were largely replaced by cotton. Yet it is highly adaptable to different climates, requires significantly less water than cotton, and presents a more sustainable alternative for textile production. Through its partnership with VirgoCoop, Wildling contributes to revitalising this ecologically sound crop within European production networks.

Figure 1: European Hemp for Local Textile Production

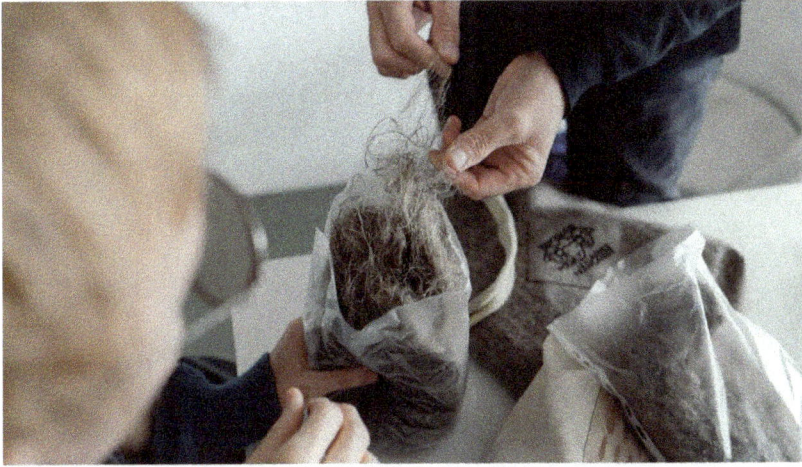

Source: Wildling Shoes 2025f.

Nevertheless, traditional cultivation and processing techniques for hemp, along with the necessary infrastructure such as factories, have largely disappeared. As a result, both the knowledge and the corresponding value chains must be re-established from the ground up. *Wildling Shoes* considers itself an active partner in this revival, working closely with VirgoCoop to rebuild a regional and fair value chain for hemp in Europe, particularly for textile and footwear production. The cooperation goes beyond sourcing: *Wildling Shoes* not only purchases fabrics from VirgoCoop's weaving mill but is also financially invested in the cooperative. In 2022, *Wildling Shoes* became a co-shareholder of VirgoCoop, enabling the cooperative to invest in production facilities for hemp processing. This deep level of collaboration reflects a new kind of relationship, what *Wildling Shoes* refers to as "regenerative collective", where partners work hand-in-hand to co-create resilient, equitable, and future-oriented production systems.

Temporary Partnerships as a Platform for Raising Awareness for Shared Values

Temporary partnerships at *Wildling Shoes* often take the form of limited-edition products—collaboratively designed shoes that serve as platforms for raising awareness and celebrating shared values. An example of this strategy is the "Nkwo x *Wildling*" collaboration, curated by Beatrace Oola, the initiator of Fashion Africa Now. Nkwo is an African sustainable fashion brand dedicated to reducing textile waste by creating its own fabric from repurposed textile remnants. The name of the collaboratively designed shoe, **ONU**, means **"together"** and symbolises this new, equitable approach to cooperation. As Anna Yona explains:

> "With NKWO, the Onu shoe, it was very much about systemic racism, about colonial relationships, about how we can truly take the first steps towards doing things differently—both in the way we collaborate and in how we make things like innovation and creativity visible. It's about ensuring that it's not just a case of taking something and selling it as one's own, but rather fostering a different kind of cooperation".

Initiating a Broader Regenerative Network

As one of the co-founders of the Unlearn Business Lab, *Wildling Shoes* seeks to engage with a broader network of social entrepreneurs, individuals, and progressive businesses to transform economic system design towards greater circularity (UBL 2025). This transformation is supported through the creation of a community space that fosters dialogue and exchange, as well as the development of new formats and collaborative concepts aimed at enabling systemic change.

How the Re:generative Network Design Enables Regenerative and Distributive Dynamics

Wildling Shoes' specific re:generative network design enables both regenerative and distributive dynamics in multiple areas of the business:

Direct Distribution Channels Provide Quality Service

One key example is the company's focus on direct sales, primarily through its website and three curated showrooms in Germany (Cologne, Berlin and Engelskirchen). This direct-to-customer approach allows *Wildling Shoes* to maintain strong relationships with its customers, offering a level of service and connection that competitors relying on intermediaries often cannot match. This approach also enables *Wildling Shoes* to offer services such as product repairs through its dedicated Repair Centre. Smaller repairs (such as fixing eyelets) are carried out onsite in Engelskirchen, whereas more complex repairs are carried out by a partner in Portugal.

> "Four to six people are involved in a repair at *Wildling*: The Customer Service team receives the repair request and initiates further processing, one person carries out the repair, and the logistics team registers the returned pair (and, of course, sends it back once the work is done). And none of this would be possible without the IT department, which manages the entire process" (Wildling Shoes 2024).

Figure 2: Repair Centre

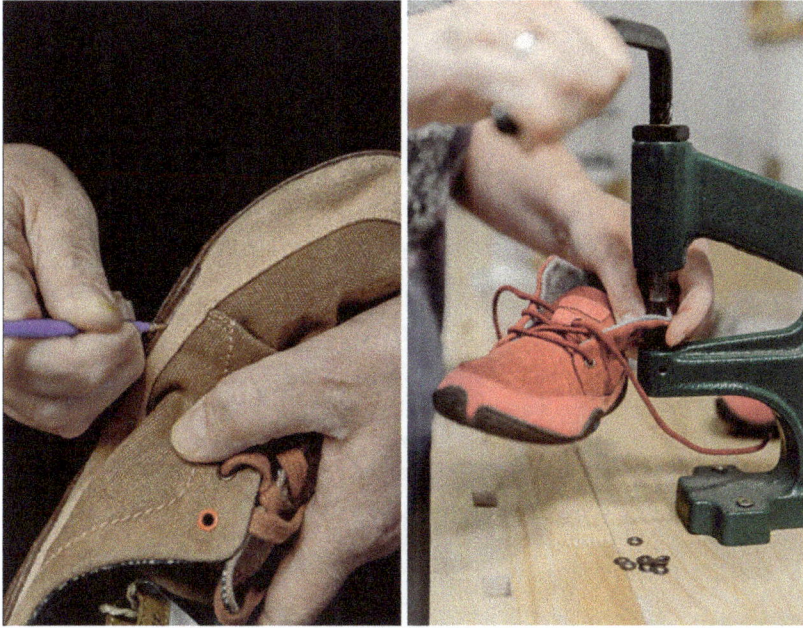

Source: Kaufmann 2022.

Wildling Shoes' direct distribution channels make this service possible in the first place, while also conserving resources and reducing waste.

Efficient Use of Resources and a Loyal Community

Wildling Shoes promotes efficient resource use by repurposing materials from previous production cycles. Rather than disposing of surplus stock, these materials are reused under the label "Refoxed" or offered at reduced prices as B-stock. This strategy reduces production-related waste and is warmly embraced by *Wildling Shoes'* customer community.

The company also uses drop marketing strategies (announcing a launch date on social media to create excitement for new products). Customers' purchasing behaviour then serves as a real-time feedback mechanism, guiding production volumes and helping to prevent overproduction and minimise storage space. This approach depends on a strong, interactive relationship with *Wildling Shoes'* online community. Creating unique stories for each product enhances emotional attachment and sets it apart from mass-produced alternatives.

Since the company was founded, *Wildling Shoes* has been supported by a highly engaged customer base. For example, in *Wildling Shoes'* Facebook group, enthusiastic fans of the brand swap or resell their used shoes, prolonging the lifespan of the products even further. The group was initially created during the company's crowdfunding phase, when the first products were offered as a bundle of several shoes, and buyers pooled together online to share the packages. The group has since grown to over 19,000 members. This engagement is actively encouraged by *Wildling Shoes*. It aligns with the company's goal of maximising the efficiency and sustainability of material use, while minimising waste. Crowdfunding remains a cornerstone of Wildling's founding narrative and its close-knit, value-driven community.

> "Yes, I believe it was a very meaningful decision both in terms of brand development and product innovation. It allowed us to engage in a highly effective exchange right from the start and quickly adapt to the actual needs of the market and our customers. It was also about bringing the product to market together creating a strong sense of identification among those who supported us. Naturally, this fosters a deeper connection to the company." — Anna Yona

A Loyal Customer Community as a Base of a Resilient Company

Wildling Shoes' re:generative network design contributes to the company's resilience by preserving its sensitivity to external shifts and heightening its awareness of the need to change, ultimately enabling greater adaptability over time.

What may seem like a bonus in stable times becomes essential during economic downturns. Strong, robust networks of deeply engaged customers and long-term partnerships with suppliers offer a powerful competitive advantage that cannot easily be replicated. As Anna Yona puts it,

> "a network is also a source of security", which is especially important if the going ever gets tough. She further adds: "Where you have strong partnerships and work together as equals, you can of course talk to each other in a completely different way, even in times of crisis. And in some way, we can find out each other's needs."

Creative Freedom and Leeway

The necessity of finding new ways to enable the use and processing of regenerative materials in circular and regional supply chains fosters greater creativity and ingenuity in developing innovative solutions (such as using yarn made from dog fur or materials like washi tape). For example, minimising material usage in the final shoe led to a distinctive product, while the search for a waterproof regenerative material resulted in the partnership with Nordwolle and the creative co-development on how to use this specific type of wool for shoes. This flexibility is rooted in the company's original intent to disrupt the status quo, strive for continuous improvement, and develop new pathways.

Being less constrained by traditional investors or standardised industry processes provides greater freedom to explore unconventional approaches. Financial independence is, therefore, crucial to enabling these decisions to be made freely.

> "Also, in the sense of [a more creative pricing model]: How can we offer different price points? For example, can we make B-grade goods available? That way, we don't have to dispose of them on the one hand, and on the other hand, we can offer a better price." — Anna Yona

Pursuing Knowledge as a Shared Public Resource

Ideally, re:generative network design enables regenerative and distributive dynamics across industries. Anna Yona (2023) highlights the need to explore ways to

> "join forces with other brands, for example, to support such resource systems and suppliers from different directions? How can we collaborate with food manufacturers on the one hand, who also need agricultural land, and on the other hand, precisely, with other fashion companies?"

Wildling Shoes actively promotes the establishment of European supply chains and the use of regional materials wherever possible, while also recognising that efficient resource management requires cross-industry collaboration to drive sustainable change. However, this proves challenging, as different collaboration partners often pursue different goals and priorities. To overcome this challenge, emerging knowledge must be treated as a common good, ensuring that society as a whole, and not just individual companies, benefits.

Reciprocity plays a key role, as reciprocal relationships within the network provide mutual benefits. For example, partners gain access to wider audiences and exchange valuable information. In the long term, the goal is to move closer to achieving broader circularity within the economy. "We want to take steps forward on the path to circularity. We want [a] circular shoe as our goal" (Anna Yona).

Challenges Arising from Designing Networks around Re:generation

However, the re:generative network design also brings specific challenges that *Wildling Shoes* has had and continues to face:

Trade-Off Between Customers' Product Expectations and Available Re:generative Solutions

The case study reveals that *Wildling Shoes* must navigate a constant balancing act between customer expectations regarding product characteristics and the regenerative values the company upholds. For example, customers typically expect a "super durable, totally waterproof and at the same time sustainably produced product" (Anna Yona).

Yet research into re:generative materials and processes that deliver all these characteristics simultaneously is still at an early stage. In contrast, conventional chemical solutions, such as Teflon, have benefited from decades of research and development. Teflon belongs to a group of synthetic chemicals known as PFAS, often called "forever chemicals" because they do not break down in the environment and accumulate over time. PFAS are harmful to both human health and the environment (EEA 2025). For these very reasons, *Wildling Shoes* deliberately does not use such chemicals, even though they would easily meet customer expectations for waterproofing. Instead, the company has to find ways to meet customer needs within the boundaries of its regenerative values. Similar challenges arise when it comes to issues such as which colour they want to use for their shoes.

Trade-Off Between Customers' Price Expectations and the Real Costs of Regenerative Circular Products

Wildling Shoes would like to offer their shoes at a much more affordable price to meet customer demands. However, the company's commitment to fair partnerships, ensuring living wages, and its use of regenerative materials lead to significantly higher production costs under the current economic conditions.

While these reasons are valid and aligned with *Wildling Shoes'* purpose, the resulting higher prices remain a barrier for customers with lower incomes. *Wildling Shoes* is attempting to address this challenge by extending the lifespan of its products through services such as repairs and by introducing a more flexible pricing policy in selected areas, such as offering discounted seconds.

Requirement of Time for Compromises and the Development of Alternative Strategies

As explained, the differing expectations between customers regarding product features and prices, and *Wildling Shoes'* values, require significant time to find compromises and develop alternative ways to fulfil customer expectations while staying true to their principles. According to Anna Yona, compromises are inevitable in some areas. The complexity and, in some cases, simple incompatibility of these demands require a considerable amount of additional energy and resources. This discrepancy between the performance of different (non-)sustainable materials is partly rooted in outdated incentive structures (e.g. insufficient support in the area of materials research). Flawed incentives in research, especially those overlooking sustainability, intensify competition with conventional products in terms of price and performance. As a result, companies such as *Wildling Shoes* often face conflicts of interest and difficult trade-off decisions. A strong ethical foundation, while admirable, can therefore complicate decision-making, occasionally turning the very values that guide the business into limiting factors for operational flexibility.

Flat Hierarchies Depend on High Competencies in Self-Responsibility and Empowerment of Employees

Wildling Shoes is organised in flat hierarchies, which necessitate a strong focus on internal capability and competency development. A less hierarchical structure demands a high degree of individual self-responsibility, requiring that employees be appropriately empowered before they can operate effectively within this framework. This experience prompted *Wildling Shoes* to concentrate on internal processes, with the aim of better understanding and refining its organisational structures.

Today, the company operates approximately 15 teams, each comprising up to eight members, in order to maintain efficient workflows. Flat hierarchies are supported by the implementation of team leads, whose roles become particularly significant during periods of dynamic growth: they consolidate information, set priorities, and manage open positions. However, leadership at *Wildling Shoes* is conceived as a service function rather than a position of authority.

Interactions with Other Design Traits

Governance Design

The importance of regenerative structures and working conditions runs through the entire company: *Wilding Shoes* fosters a holistic approach to its general work culture, placing particular emphasis on New Work concepts such as promoting remote work and enabling meaningful work. Collaboration instead of competition is emphasised across all areas of the company.

Great importance is attached to the compatibility of work, leisure time and family life. The focus is always on creating genuine value, whether this is through providing greater flexibility and leisure time for employees, offering high-quality and health-promoting products, or ensuring resource-saving material cultivation and a commitment to regional supply chains. For the most part, work takes place regardless of location, wherever possible, with remote work being the standard. This requires communication, trust, and reliability. These so-called New Work concepts are intended to foster greater equality within the working environment.

> "We try to apply this regenerative effect to everything. So how can we work in such a way that it has a regenerative effect? Or what does that even mean? " — Anna Yona

The company is organised in focus-based teams, known as 'circles', each dedicated to specific strategic priorities. Numerous points of intersection between the circles make internal communication essential for effective teamwork. Ideas that emerge within the circles are carried upwards through an interplay between bottom-up and top-down processes.

> "And this is our group of people who come together to make strategic decisions, [they] are these Circle Leads together with two Company Leads that we have. This is where we define the roadmap, what we think the important strategic priorities will be in the next two years." — Anna Yona

Finance Design

For *Wildling Shoes*, the interaction between finance design and network design is rooted in their start-up funding. They founded their business with the help of a crowdfunding campaign based on a community of people who support their purpose. Crowdfunding allowed *Wildling Shoes* to maintain their independence and minimise risks and costs when entering the market. The prefinance model, based on pre-sales, allowed *Wildling Shoes* to generate revenue before having to pay all their production invoices. This approach to finance design allows *Wildling Shoes* to remain financially independent from external capital and to align their decision-making solely with their values and purpose.

Profits are reinvested into the business and used to pay salaries. In their decision-making, it is crucial for *Wildling Shoes* to align every business decision with their purpose:

> "So, we don't operate in such a way that we somehow always look for the cheapest way, but we look for the best way. And if it's more expensive, then that's a very meaningful investment that happens during the year, so to speak." — Anna Yona

Recommendations for Adopting a Re:generative Network Design

1) Re:generative Network Design is Based on a Re:generative Product

For *Wildling Shoes*, adopting a re:generative network design is rooted in offering a meaningful and regenerative product:

> "It really is a meaningful, necessary product, because otherwise all the raw materials that go into it are wasted and all the energy is wasted." — Anna Yona

Therefore, adopting a re:generative network design requires an honest reflection on whether the specific product is truly necessary.

2) Driven by Intrinsic Conviction – What About Your Intrinsic Conviction?

The pursuit of a regenerative purpose is the primary driver for *Wildling Shoes* in their relationship with their stakeholders, while financial goals are of secondary relevance:

> "We don't run the company according to financial targets. So of course, we have a financial plan, and we know how the structure has to work so that we can manage our expenses and costs financially. But we don't have financial targets in the sense that we want to somehow, I don't know, have a 15% increase in turnover." — Anna Yona

This intrinsic motivation is woven into every aspect of the company, from the founding vision to inspiring customers to buy and empowering employees to find purpose in their work. Nothing is done for its own sake; ideally, everything is connected to the purpose of the business.

> "We could produce a much cheaper shoe if we didn't produce it on an equal footing with our partners, as we are currently trying to do." — Anna Yona

3) Enabling Authentic Connections

Wildling Shoes goes beyond typical footwear. Its direct channels (e.g. online size consultations, showrooms) make an authentic connection possible in the first place, thereby enhancing the quality of every interaction. Through partner selection based on shared values and personal connections, the company has built truly meaningful relationships, striving together to develop the use and processing of regenerative materials in regional supply chains.

Inspiring Redesign Beyond the Business

Wildling Shoes prioritises being a role model for collaboration and deep partnerships, offering an alternative to more commodified, short-term, and competition-focused approaches. Anna Yona emphasises that the interaction between all design traits – governance, ownership, finance and network – is crucial. All traits are deeply intertwined in the inner transformation of a business. However, network design holds special importance, as it shapes *Wildling Shoes'* direct relationships with internal and external stakeholders. It also reflects their commitment to being part of a broader ecosystem of businesses, policymakers, activists, individuals, and scientists working together to transform the economic system towards regeneration.

> "Well, we also want this change from within, the transformation from within, of the economic system and this 'Who can we move all this together with?' Well, that would be my big dream somehow; to say we are really doing this very, very much in collaboration with many other actors in society." — Anna Yona

As a medium-sized company, *Wildling Shoes* still faces the challenge of maintaining its position on the market. They therefore highlight the need for stronger support within a broader network and deeper collaboration, such as lobbying for regulations that would level the playing field. This includes efforts to prevent circular products from being at a price disadvantage by driving consumer pressure to change the practices of less sustainable competitors or advocating for investment in models like *Wildling Shoes*. As one of the initiators of the Unlearn Business Lab, *Wildling Shoes* actively engages in creating and strengthening such alliances for systemic economic change.

References

Interview

With Anna Yona, CEO Wildling Shoes, Interview, (21.06.2023, 0:58h).

Homepage

Wildling Shoes (2025a): https://www.wildling.shoes/en/pages/der-wildling-ansatz, [Accessed 5 March 2025].
Wildling Shoes (2025b): https://www.wildling.shoes/pages/keine-perfektion, [Accessed 5 March 2025].

Wildling Shoes (2025c): https://www.wildling.shoes/en/blogs/news/wildlinge-war me-fusse-und-nordwolle, [Accessed 5 March 2025].

Wildling Shoes (2025d): https://www.wildling.shoes/en/blogs/news/hanfliebe, [Accessed 5 March 2025].

Wildling Shoes (2025e): https://www.wildling.shoes/en/blogs/news/so-wird-ein-sc huh-draus, [Accessed 5 March 2025].

Wildling Shoes (2025f): https://www.wildling.shoes/pages/hanf, [Accessed 10 April 2025].

Wildling Shoes (2024): https://www.wildling.shoes/blogs/news/eine-stabile-bezieh ung-der-aufbau-des-wildling-repair-centers, [Accessed 5 March2025].

Other Sources

B Lab (2025): Was ist eine B Corp?, https://www.bcorporation.de/b-corp-zertifizier ung/was-ist-eine-b-corp/, [Accessed 5 March 2025].

European Environment Agency (2025): Risk of PFAS for human health in Europe, https://www.eea.europa.eu/en/european-zero-pollution-dashboards/indicato rs/risk-of-pfas-in-humans, [Accessed 28 February 2025].

Kaufmann, Kayla (2022): Photo – Figure 2 Repair Centre.

Schlieder, Frank (2022): "Was ist regeneratives wirtschaften, Anna Yona?", in: Fabrik für Immer, Purpose und Krisenresilienz, Podcastfolge puk 03/10, 27.02.2022.

UBL (2025): https://www.unlearnbusinesslab.com/vision, [Accessed 5 March 2025].

Governance Design

Case Study: Wigwam

Ines Bauer

Purpose: We conceive and design effective communication for a just and self-determined life for all on a healthy planet
Design Trait: Governance
Innovative Practice: Self-Organisation-Based Governance Design

Key Facts

Wigwam eG is a communication agency based in Berlin that conceives and designs effective communication for a just and self-determined life for all on a healthy planet. To achieve this goal, the company advises and supports actors from civil society, politics, culture, education and business with a social focus. As both a cooperative and a democratic laboratory, it operates and works in a self-organised manner.

Seat: Berlin
Established: 2009
Founders: Sandra Diana Trögl, Ole Seidenberg, Daniel Kruse
Ownership: Registered Cooperative
Legal Form: Registered Cooperative
Employees: 28
Webpage: https://wigwam.im/

Purpose, Business Model & Objectives

Purpose: "We conceive and design effective communication for a just and self-determined life for all on a healthy planet."

Wigwam eG is a communication agency based in Berlin, consisting of around 30 team members. It operates as a worker cooperative with a self-organised governance design. *Wigwam*'s purpose is shaped by a strong commitment to distributive and regenerative principles. Its mission extends beyond designing and creating impactful communication that supports a fair and self-determined life for all on a healthy planet; it also aims to promote the well-being of its members, which is reinforced by its chosen legal structure and ownership design. Furthermore, at *Wigwam*, social goals often take precedence over financial ones, with a focus on fair compensation and supporting flexible, self-managed working methods. Rather than seeking growth or hiring to increase revenue, the cooperative focuses on working effectively with the current team.

Since 2016, *Wigwam* has operated as a cooperative, meaning the business is owned equally by all its members, who share responsibility for its success. Unlike many traditional businesses, *Wigwam* does not rely on external investors. Instead, it is primarily funded through the projects it undertakes. Members also contribute a cooperative share, but it provides only limited financial benefits to the business. *Wigwam*'s membership is divided into two categories: active members and investing members. Active members are those who have permanent employment contracts with the cooperative and therefore have voting rights. This means they have a direct say in the decisions that shape the future of the business. Investing members do not have voting rights, and consequently, their role is more limited.

Insights into the Self-Organisation-Based Governance Design

Wigwam's governance structure is distinctive for its innovative combination of self-organisation, the cooperative legal form, and the day-to-day work of their agency, all working in harmony (see figure 1). This structure is supported by a unique salary model, known as the wish salary, along with other key aspects such as flexible time management, role rotation, and their approach to leadership and goal-setting, all of which embody the principles of what *Wigwam* describes as *New Work*.

The term *New Work* was coined in the 1980s by the social philosopher Frithjof Bergmann to describe the reorganisation of work towards meaningful and individually designed work. Today, the term is used to describe structural changes in the world of work (Hackl et al. 2017). At the company level, it can be concretised through the following fields of action, among others *Individuality*, such as participation in company processes and decisions; *Leadership*, through the development of a democratic leadership culture in which managers tend to take on the role of moderators; *Agility*, through fast decision-making processes in flat hierarchies, open learning and a positive error culture; *Flexibility*, in terms of the type and location of work, such as job rotation, flexible working hours and remote working (Hackl et al. 2017: 72–77).

Figure 1: Wigwam's Governance Structure

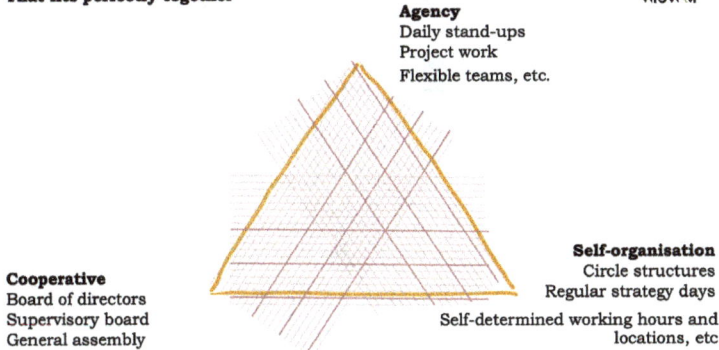

Source: Modified design based on Wigwam 2020.

The members of *Wigwam* collectively lead and own the company following cooperative principles which are structured as follows: The organisation has a board composed of four members responsible for managing the business. In accordance with cooperative structure, a supervisory board oversees the board's activities. The members democratically elect both the board and the supervisory board during general assemblies, which are held at regular intervals at least once a year.

Figure 2: Wigwam's Organisational Chart

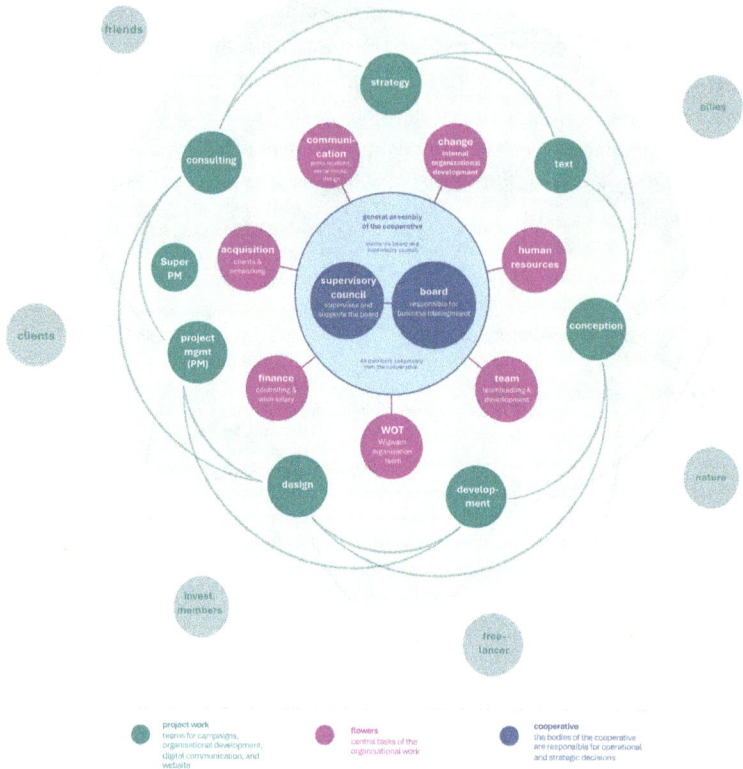

Source: Modified design based on Wigwam 2024b.

Wigwam is organised into various circles, such as finance, acquisition, human resources, organisational development, team development, and communication circles. Decision-making processes are designed to allow individuals within these circles to make decisions independently. To guide individuals and enhance their comfort during decision-making, a budget is also created. Circles or individuals can make independent decisions within this budget. If the budget is exceeded, others from the team or the board are consulted to ensure the decision has broader support. Collective decisions are particularly important when it comes to company management, strategy, or profit distribution. For organisation-wide decisions,

Wigwam often adopts a resistance inquiry method. When a group is working on a specific project and asks for objections or concerns, minimal or no resistance from the broader team is seen as a green light to proceed with the work. This method allows for decisions to be implemented without requiring full consensus, ensuring that progress is not hindered by the need for complete alignment. Such an approach not only speeds up decision-making but also empowers individuals to take initiative, knowing that their ideas can move forward as long as they do not encounter significant opposition.

Role rotation occurs regularly within the cooperative. This process happens through self-organisation, where roles can be reassigned. Regular elections for the board and supervisory board ensure that many members get the opportunity to serve in these positions, fostering a deeper understanding and appreciation of the responsibilities involved. Individuals elected to the board are chosen based on the trust of other members, who believe in their ability to drive or implement certain initiatives. *Wigwam* encourages its members to engage in areas where they feel confident and interested. In the self-organised setting, members can also switch to different areas if their skills can be better utilised elsewhere.

As part of their approach of self-organisation, *Wigwam* uses a variety of meeting formats designed to deepen discussions, achieve team-wide collaboration and ensure transparency regarding the organisation's financial matters. These include daily stand-up meetings, which provide quick updates on ongoing projects and tasks, ensuring that everyone is on the same page. These brief, focused meetings are a key part of *Wigwam*'s agile approach to work, allowing the team to stay connected and aligned on a day-to-day basis. In addition to daily stand-ups, *Wigwam* holds carefully structured monthly meetings called "Rundlauf" that provide a comprehensive overview of the cooperative's financial status, project progress reports, and organisational performance metrics. These meetings are an important part of *Wigwam*'s governance structure, offering a regular opportunity for reflection, assessment, and strategic planning. By keeping everyone informed about the cooperative's financial health and other critical aspects of the business, these meetings help to maintain transparency and accountability within the business and pave the way for the wish salary model.

Strategy days are another important meeting format used by *Wigwam*. These are dedicated to making collective decisions about clients, projects, and organisational structures. Strategy days provide a space for in-depth discussion and planning, allowing the team to consider the bigger picture and make decisions that will shape the future of the cooperative.

All these meetings and sessions also serve as an opportunity for members to bring forward new ideas, discuss challenges, and collaborate on solutions. *Wigwam* also holds monthly "Hörnchen" rounds, which are informal, mixed-group meetings (meaning they mix people from various circles), where members can share personal needs, concerns, and experiences. These rounds are a part of *Wigwam*'s commitment to foster a supportive and inclusive environment, where members feel heard and valued. The informal nature of these meetings encourages open and honest communication, helping to build strong relationships within the team and ensuring that everyone's needs are considered.

Due to the self-organisation, there are few hierarchies and no traditional leadership roles at *Wigwam*. Leadership naturally emerges when individuals take the initiative and are ready to drive change. It is crucial that those who take on leadership roles receive support from the rest of the team and are not hindered by unnecessary barriers. This approach to leadership ensures that initiatives are driven by those who are most passionate and capable.

Self-organisation also allows for flexible time management, tasks, and work locations. Members have a great deal of autonomy in structuring and executing their tasks, including in choosing the projects they work on. To manage the distribution of tasks among the members, while personal preferences are considered, there is also a task distribution system, which is based on three components: competence, motivation, and time. Competence refers to whether a person has the necessary skills to handle a specific task. Where this is lacking, support can be sought from other members. Motivation assesses whether the person is genuinely interested in and excited about the task. Lastly, whether the member has sufficient time is also considered. Ideally, all three components should align, but it is sufficient if at least two are met.

Wigwam offers highly flexible working hours but recognises the value of clear availability for the team's benefit, ensuring overlap and seamless communication. This creates a healthy balance, allowing everyone the freedom to work in the way that suits them best. Some individuals are more productive in the mornings, while others may need uninterrupted focus time to work effectively.

In line with its commitment to self-organisation and cooperative principles, *Wigwam* has introduced an innovative salary model known as the wish salary. This model is a defining feature of their governance structure and reflects their dedication to transparency, fairness, and inclusivity.

According to Lotte Harlan, Member of *Wigwam*'s Management Board,

> "We came from a salary model like this: Junior, Senior, and Managing Director. So, there were three levels, and nothing in between. And the reason it didn't quite work was because, in the end, there were too many special agreements. For example, Lotte gets a Junior salary, but we pay for her phone because she calls clients, or we pay for the public transport ticket. [...] Then it became chaotic. Some had this salary, others had that, and somehow many were dissatisfied."

After a long process of considering different salary models, the company came up with the wish salary. Every employee at *Wigwam*, from the executive board to the cleaning staff, participates in the model. After completing their probation period, each team member is invited to join this unique salary system.

The wish salary model empowers team members to independently state their salary wishes based on personal circumstances, without the need to justify their requests to others. There is no upper limit on the amount one can request, fostering a sense of autonomy and respect for individual needs. However, this flexibility is balanced by a strong organisational culture of transparency and frequent communication. All members are fully aware of the cooperative's overall budget and have access to view each other's salaries, ensuring that everyone makes responsible and fair salary requests that align with the organisation's financial reality.

To further promote fairness, a minimum salary is set. This safeguard prevents self-exploitation and ensures that even those who might otherwise undervalue their work are compensated fairly. The introduction of the wish salary model in 2016 coincided with *Wigwam*'s transition into a cooperative, symbolising a shift away from traditional salary negotiation models that often rely heavily on individual bargaining power. Instead, the wish salary model is rooted in the cooperative's values of self-organisation and mutual accountability.

How the Self-Organisation-Based Governance Design Enables Regenerative and Distributive Dynamics

One potential factor that supports *Wigwam*'s distributive purpose is its positive company culture. The culture promotes looking out for one another, even though it is acknowledged that this does not always work perfectly. Additionally, the desire to implement change is viewed positively within the business, and there is an awareness of how changes in one area can affect the broader team. As Lotte Harlan explains,

> "We are constantly evolving. So, I can definitely say that we are always optimising. Currently, there are four of us on the board. In the beginning, there were six, then five. When we realised that we don't need as many people or that adjustments would make more sense at that moment, and so we adapted accordingly. I would say we're pretty good at that."

The flexibility in work design and time management mentioned earlier at *Wigwam* is also seen as a potential that allows everyone the freedom to choose their working conditions. Lotte Harlan explains,

> "I know, for example, that someone once said — he's almost never in the office, he programs — and he said: 'I can very well appreciate that *Wigwam* doesn't try to persuade me to come to the office, although it would probably

be good for others now and then. But I actually can't work there at all.' And […] parents also really appreciate that they can be flexible, adjust things, or work from home when their child is at home."

The business also aims to encourage everyone to work on projects they are passionate about. To support this, information about incoming project requests is shared openly and early. Every request is visible, and team members are encouraged to respond. For example, a designer might express interest by saying they have always wanted to work on the *Berlin Against Nazis* project, by adding a brief comment to the shared document. This approach helps teams form naturally based on interest and motivation.

The broad participation of all team members is another significant strength. From the moment someone joins the team, they are given a voice—not only in board elections but also in influencing the strategic direction of the business. This means individuals can propose ideas and are encouraged to do so. If others agree, the idea can be presented to the entire business through various meeting formats, potentially even changing the business' direction. This high level of empowerment and support, even within a relatively small team of around 30 members, plays a crucial role in fostering innovation and ensuring that each individual recognises their contribution to the cooperative's success. Another notable potential at *Wigwam* is the high level of transparency, particularly in financial matters, which encourages the self-responsibility. This openness enables all members to engage with and understand the business' finances at any time. By making financial information accessible and providing updates during the monthly "Rundlauf" meeting, *Wigwam* encourages members to learn more about financial management and even take on financial responsibilities, thereby fostering a deeper sense of ownership and involvement across the cooperative. Lotte Harlan notes, "[…] when we hire new people, and I say, we are completely transparent, even regarding finances. Everyone always says: yes. But afterwards, not always, but often, the reaction is: yeah, okay, but I didn't realise we were *this* transparent."

Challenges Arising from Designing Governance around Self-Organisation

Wigwam faces several challenges, particularly those that personally affect its members. The freedoms inherent in self-organisation, which empower members to make autonomous decisions, can sometimes lead to individuals feeling isolated and overwhelmed in their decision-making. The pressure to meet expectations can amplify this feeling, creating the impression that everything must be managed alone, even when support is needed.

Balancing individual and group needs in time management and task allocation presents another challenge. In a self-organised work environment, it is crucial to consider how one's actions fit within the broader team context and to consider the needs of other members.

Members also face personal challenges when setting their wish salaries, primarily due to the lack of experience and skills with such salary models. Salary positioning within the group can be difficult, as the salary wishes of others influence one's own expectations. Comparing oneself to others can trigger strong emotions, such as insecurity when feeling inferior or discomfort when feeling overly demanding, which complicates the decision-making process around salary. Lotte Harlan also notes that it is particularly challenging to convey to new members that salary negotiation is not required and that freely determining one's salary is encouraged. This challenge stems from the fact that most people come from hierarchical organisations where salary negotiation is the norm.

To address these challenges, *Wigwam* emphasises regular exchange rounds, agreements, and mutual support among members. For instance, specific exchange formats have been established to assist in setting desired salaries. Additionally, *Wigwam*'s positive corporate culture plays a crucial role, as it is important to look out for one another and maintain open communication.

Interactions with Other Design Traits

Network Design

The governance approaches implemented, along with the cooperative ownership design, positively influence *Wigwam*'s relationships with its external stakeholders. According to Harlan, *Wigwam*'s governance practices and legal structure contribute to being perceived as authentic and credible. This perception is especially noticeable among clients, many of whom become interested in *Wigwam*'s governance structure and legal form, often leading to collaboration.

The cooperative's network extends beyond its immediate members, encompassing a diverse group of freelancers, partner agencies, friends, former employees, and clients. This network is not just a collection of business contacts; it is a community of like-minded individuals and organisations that share *Wigwam*'s values and vision for a better world. Business partners often include non-governmental organisations (NGOs) and foundations, which align closely with *Wigwam*'s mission. These partnerships are crucial for the cooperative, as they enable *Wigwam* to extend its reach and impact, collaborating on projects that have the potential to bring about meaningful social and ecological change. *Wigwam*'s emphasis on collaboration is also reflected in their approach to networking, exemplified by their regular organisation of a networking event called *reCampaign*, which serves as a platform for discussing relevant topics and fostering connections among participants with similar goals.

Ownership Design

The success of the self-organised governance structure, including the wish salary system, is largely influenced by the cooperative ownership design. *Wigwam*'s ownership structure is highlighted as one of the greatest factors for successfully implementing this governance model. Lotte Harlan emphasises, "I would say that's the biggest factor". While *Wigwam* originally started as a limited liability company (German: GmbH), they later transitioned to becoming a cooperative. Lotte Harlan explains, "We also had to take a very pragmatic approach and buy the company from the GmbH, because that's just how things are in Germany". The cooperative structure ensures that everyone is both an employee and an employer, meaning all members participate in economic activities and share responsibility collectively. "Only by adding the democratic principles of the cooperative can the methods of self-organisation and New Work fully realise their positive impact on the organisation and the people within it" (*Wigwam*, 2020). This distribution of responsibilities enhances motivation and strengthens mutual trust among members.

Another advantage of the cooperative ownership design is the role rotation facilitated by regular board elections, which helps foster mutual understanding. Members, who have served on the board gain first-hand experience of the responsibilities and challenges involved, enabling them to better empathise with the decisions and actions taken by the board. This shared experience contributes to a stronger sense of solidarity and collective responsibility within the organisation.

Recommendations for Adopting a Self-Organisation-Based Governance Design

Lotte Harlan emphasises the importance of recognising that the wish salary model may not be directly replicable in other organisations, especially those lacking the specific conditions that contributed to its success at *Wigwam*. Three factors were crucial for the successful implementation. First, the strong interpersonal relationships within the team, as Lotte Harlan explained, "we all knew each other," which facilitated the open and honest communication necessary for discussing sensitive topics like salary transparency and redistribution. Second, the availability of extra financial resources was essential for the first introduction of the wish salary model. As Lotte Harlan noted, "I don't believe that redistributing money works if you only have the same amount, because that means I'm actively taking something away from you" and could lead to dissatisfaction or perceived losses among employees. Therefore, having additional funds allowed the model to be implemented fairly, ensuring that no team member felt disadvantaged. Finally, the supportive and collaborative structure of *Wigwam* provided a solid foundation for the wish salary model to function effectively, offering support and opportunities for exchange for anyone who is struggling or in need of assistance.

Another critical factor for the success of the self-organisation and such formats as the wish salary was the adoption of a cooperative ownership design, which naturally supported the principles of transparency, mutual accountability, and shared ownership. This structure is particularly conducive to fostering a fair and equitable workplace, making it a strong recommendation for businesses looking to implement similar models.

Inspiring Redesign Beyond the Business

It is essential to have models that demonstrate how cooperatives can be more than just groups of people working together. They can be stable and successful businesses that deliver quality work, offer fair wages, and effectively navigate everyday challenges with the support of a well-functioning governance model. While cooperatives have a long history, it's crucial to show that this model can also flourish in modern settings, proving that alternative approaches are viable and can achieve success. Considering their salary model, Lotte Harlan emphasises, "[...] there always needs to be role models that show it's possible. And even though I would say our salary model isn't perfect, I believe it's important to see that things can be done differently". Examples like *Wigwam* are important for encouraging others to explore and adopt new ways of designing businesses and doing business. These examples can demystify cooperatives, self-organisation, innovative salary models and leadership models, aiming to inspire and educate others about these alternative approaches to business and governance. To support others interested in their governance design, *Wigwam* offers consultation and workshops, while also sharing key insights and experiences on their public blog.

References

Interview with

Lotte Harlan, Member of the Management Board (11/03/2024, 01:39h).

Homepage

Wigwam (2024a): https://wigwam.im/en/, [Accessed 9 April 2025].

Other Sources

Hackl, B; Wagner, M.; Attmer, L.; Baumann, D. (2017). New Work: Auf dem Weg zur neuen Arbeitswelt. Management-Impulse, Praxisbeispiele, Studien, Wiesbaden.

Wigwam (2020): New Work? Genossenschaft!, https://wigwam.im/blog/new-work -genossenschaft/, [Accessed 22 April 2024].

Wigwam (2021): Mal wieder über Geld reden: ein FAQ zu unserem Wunschgehalt, https://wigwam.im/blog/mal-wieder-ueber-geld-reden-ein-faq-zu-unser em-wunschgehalt/, [Accessed 22 April 2024].

Wigwam (2023): Satzung der Wigwam eG, https://wigwam.im/wp-content/upload s/230731_WigwamEG_Satzung.pdf?x97915, [Accessed 22 April 2024].

Wigwam (2024b): Haltung, https://wigwam.im/haltung/, [Accessed 27 January 2025].

Note: Shortly before the publication of this book, Wigwam announced its dissolution at the end of 2025. The reasons include reduced project budgets, increased price competition from large advertising agencies and the rapid transformation driven by AI. More information is available at: https://wigwam.im/

Case Study: Mein Grundeinkommen

Ines Bauer

Purpose: "We want a fair and crisis-proof world in which everyone can live a self-determined life" by raffling unconditional basic income and promoting education, science, and research on the unconditional basic income and its financing.
Design Trait: Governance
Innovative Practice: Holacracy-Based Governance Design

Key Facts

Mein Grundeinkommen is a Berlin based not-for-profit organisation that crowdfunds and raffles off unconditional basic incomes (UBI). They started giving away UBIs in 2014. As of today, more than 1,900 UBIs have been paid out. More than 3.8 million people have signed up to be able to participate in their raffles. More than 200,000 people support the organisation with their donations every month.

Established: 2014 in Berlin
Founder: Michael Bohmeyer
Ownership: Not-for-profit registered association
Legal form: Not-for-profit registered association
Employees: 38 (2025)
Webpage: https://www.mein-grundeinkommen.de/infos/in-english

Purpose, Business Model & Objectives

Purpose: "We want a fair and crisis-proof world in which everyone can live a self-determined life" by raffling unconditional basic income and promoting education, science, and research on the unconditional basic income and its financing.

Mein Grundeinkommen is an organisation based in Berlin dedicated to promoting the concept of unconditional basic income while simultaneously advancing research on its effects. Through crowdfunding, the organisation collects funds and distributes them as an unconditional basic income to individuals selected through a raffle. The organisation's primary goal is to study the impact of basic income on people's lives and to raise awareness of this concept within society. Operating as a registered not-for-profit association, *Mein Grundeinkommen's* purpose is legally binding, ensuring that all activities align with its mission to maintain not-for-profit status. The organisation is entirely funded by donations and relies on a network of researchers, institutes, universities, and individuals who share an interest in the concept of unconditional basic income.

Figure 1: The Raffle in which the Lucky Winners of The Unconditional Basic Income are Selected

Source: Melber 2021.

Insights into the Holacracy-Based Governance Design

For several years, *Mein Grundeinkommen* has been internally organised using the principles of holacracy. Developed by Brian Robertson in 2016, holacracy replaces traditional hierarchical structures with a system that distributes decision-making authority across various circles and roles. Each circle is a self-organised team responsible for specific tasks, operating within the broader framework of the organisation (here: *Mein Grundeinkommen*), which is referred to as the Super-Circle. The teams, known as Sub-Circles (e.g. Human Resource or software development), are granted autonomy in their decision-making, yet their actions influence other parts of the organisation, necessitating coordination and communication. To facilitate communication between these circles, holacracy employs two key roles: the Lead Link and the Representative Link. The Lead Link ensures that the Super-Circle's needs and priorities are reflected in the Sub-Circle's activities, while the Representative Link ensures that the Sub-Circle's work is visible and well-integrated within the broader organisation. This double linking helps maintain alignment across the organisation while preserving the autonomy of individual teams. Figure 1 shows holacratic structures with an example of the circles, as they exist at *Mein Grundeinkommen*. Maximilian Hoffmann, software developer at Mein Grundeinkommen, notes that the circles are not static but rather change dynamically over time.

Figure 2: Exemplary Representation of the Holacratic Structures at Mein Grundeinkommen

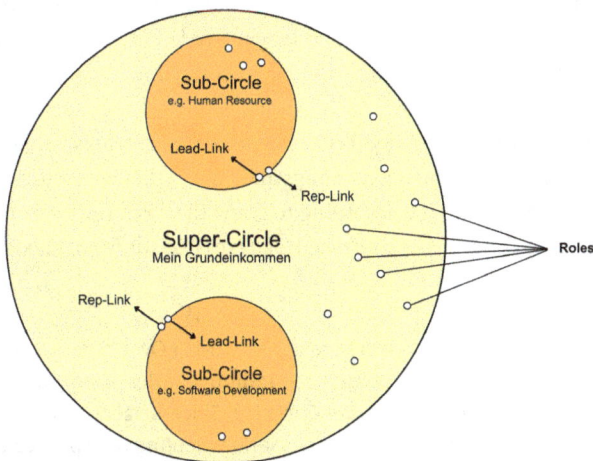

Source: Modified design based on Robertson 2016: 47.

The internal organisational structure is further influenced by *Mein Grundeinkommen*'s status as an association, with a board regularly elected by the organisation's members. The elected board chair, a single individual, has the authority to appoint additional board members. This selection process is at the discretion of the chair. The board must follow instructions from the general assembly of members, allowing for democratic leadership.

To overcome the board's bureaucratic workload and distribute responsibility more evenly, *Mein Grundeinkommen* has introduced the concept of Special Representatives. These individuals are granted legal authority to make decisions in specific areas, acting independently within their domain. This approach helps distribute the workload and efficient decision-making without overburdening the board, aligning well with the decentralised holacracy model.

One of the most distinctive features of *Mein Grundeinkommen*'s governance structure is its role distribution, which results in what is described as dynamic job design. This holacracy-shaped approach allows new roles to be created, assumed, and experimented with at any time, actively supported by the organisation's members. Within a circle, tasks are clearly defined, and the distribution of roles helps achieve the respective goals. Maximilian Hoffmann reports

"that responsibilities are not tied to a single person, such as a manager, but rather that we divide these responsibilities into several roles. These responsibilities can then be filled by different people, and one can also relinquish roles or take on new ones without having to resign or change companies."

Roles within the organisation emerge from existing tensions, needs, or through new hires and can also be relinquished if no longer needed or when a project is completed, illustrating the dynamic nature of role assignment.

In holacracy, additional roles such as Facilitator and Secretary, elected by the team, are needed. Facilitators organise and moderate meetings, while Secretaries provide technical support during meetings and ensure that holacratic rules are followed and decisions are made according to plan. The roles and their responsibilities are typically outlined in the so-called Holacracy Constitution. Maximilian Hoffmann emphasises,

"I started out primarily as a software developer [...] Over time, as often happens in Holacracy, I've taken on and tried out additional roles. For example, last year, I served as the Secretary of the Super Circle [...]. Since we also have the structure of an association, I was involved in the association meetings and particularly focused on taking minutes. Right now, our board stepped down at the end of the year, as many of them decided to move on to new companies or went on maternity leave. Therefore, a new board was elected at the end of last year, which opened up several new roles. I will likely be taking on the organisational development role at *Mein Grundeinkommen*."

He highlights:

"I'm constantly in such a dual role or even multiple roles, as is the case with all of us. On the one hand, I'm still continuing with software development and remain active in various circles, but on the other hand, I also have this second part of organisational development coming up soon, as well as other roles, such as the Secretary role."

Another innovative aspect of *Mein Grundeinkommen's* governance structure is its needs-based salary model. This model assigns a transparent salary to each employee, considering their individual needs and life circumstances such as having children, repaying study loans, or pursuing particular hobbies. To realise this need-based salary approach, *Mein Grundeinkommen* uses four principles: the needs parameter, where team members indicate how much salary they require or wish to receive; the organisation parameter, which assesses the salary's fairness and feasibility within the organisation's financial and salary structures; the performance parameter, which determines an appropriate amount based on experience and working hours; and the ideals parameter, which considers non-monetary compensation, such as flexible working hours. Salary negotiations are conducted in team meetings to ensure transparency. Team members can always raise objections to adjustments. The salary system is being currently revised to better align with the association's legal form, as it may not comply with the not-for-profit status of the association based on the German law. The challenge is that salaries are financed through donations, making it difficult to justify allowing employees to set their own salaries. This raises concerns about transparency and compliance with not-for-profit regulations. Also, the company wants to more clearly define the objections and rules, making the basis for decisions more comprehensible for everyone.

Further innovative elements of the holacracy-based governance design are autonomous decision-making, purpose-driven goal-setting and decentralised leadership. Decision-making within *Mein Grundeinkommen* is characterised by role autonomy, a core principle of holacracy. This empowers individuals to make decisions related to their specific roles without seeking approval from others, contrasting sharply with traditional hierarchical models where decisions are typically made by a small group of leaders. By distributing decision-making power throughout the organisation, *Mein Grundeinkommen* fosters a culture of empowerment and responsibility. To support these decision-making processes, the organisation provides budgets that can be used autonomously by individuals and teams, giving members the confidence to make decisions within their scope without needing to consult others.

Furthermore, there are two main types of meetings: Tactical Meetings and Governance Meetings. Tactical Meetings focus on operational decisions, while Governance Meetings address structural issues such as role definitions and responsibilities. In line with the principles of holacracy, *Mein Grundeinkommen* employs integrative decision-making, ensuring decisions align with assigned roles and objective requirements. Decisions are based on consent, not consensus. While consensus requires the agreement of all involved parties for a proposed course of action, consent means that not everyone needs to agree. Instead, a decision can be blocked if a role holder presents a fact-based objection. This allows decisions to move forward even if not all participants agree and makes the decision process faster and more efficient.

Goal setting at *Mein Grundeinkommen* is largely driven by the organisation's purpose, with its social mission legally tied to the association. In most cases, especially for larger and long-term goals, decisions are made collectively within the team. To assist in this process, goals are defined within the framework of impact matrices and regularly monitored, based on the Organisation for Economic Cooperation and Development's OECD sustainability goals. The goal-setting process is divided into five key parts: inputs (determining resources needed), activities (outlining project implementation), outputs (tangible results generated), outcomes (assessing impact of outputs), and goal review (ensuring alignment with overarching objectives). This structured approach ensures projects not only produce concrete results but also achieve their intended impact in line with broader objectives.

Leadership at *Mein Grundeinkommen* is decentralised and not governed by hierarchy, operating in a role-based system. So, "there are different roles, and the individuals within their roles can make decisions independently". However, despite holacracy, leadership by individuals is necessary in certain situations not to make decisions for others, but to take on responsibility and manage specific tasks. Maximilian Hoffmann explains that leadership

"always requires energy, and it's always a matter of weighing things up. There are people who may have more energy, and others who have less energy, or are more inclined to take the lead, while others are less inclined to do so."

This results in a dynamic leadership style shaped by situational factors, supported by leadership workshops offered by *Mein Grundeinkommen*.

How the Holacracy-Based Governance Design Enables Regenerative and Distributive Dynamics

The dynamic roles and distribution of responsibilities within holacracy enable several regenerative and distributive dynamics compared to traditional companies. Responsibilities are distributed across multiple roles held by different individuals, allowing employees to easily take on new responsibilities or tasks or relinquish roles with relative ease. This flexibility benefits employees, as the duration of a role can be shortened if resources are no longer available, and responsibilities are fulfilled more effectively with increased time, resources, and capacity. These practices unlock a fairer distribution of the tasks to be done based on time needs and individual resources of every member. The potential for individuals to assume roles such as Facilitator or Secretary, is also noteworthy, enhancing their understanding of holacracy's functionality.

An additional benefit is the holacratic constitution, which documents the essential rules, structures and processes of the holacracy "operating system" for the leadership and management of the organisation. It forms the foundation of an organisation that wants to use holacracy. Roles are documented and recorded outside the constitution. For this end, Mein Grundeinkommen employs the digital software Holaspirit, although this is merely one possible method of documenting holacratic roles. Thereby, individuals who take on a role know the extent to which they can make autonomous decisions and what responsibilities they must fulfil. This clarity helps to avoid conflicts or misunderstandings and allows the constitution to be flexible and adaptable to new circumstances.

A further significant potential lies in the transparency achieved through the implementation of governance structures, extending beyond decision-making processes to encompass salary structures and related decisions. In practice, monthly club meetings, which are informal gatherings rather than formal general assemblies, allow each circle to present updates on current activities, changes being implemented, future directions, and progress. By making these elements visible and understandable to all members of the organisation, a culture of trust and accountability is fostered, where employees feel more informed and engaged in the company's operations.

The greatest potential, according to Maximilian Hoffmann, lies in the high level of autonomy and freedom that members of *Mein Grundeinkommen* enjoy. Maximilian Hoffmann emphasises, "I have never felt so free in a company before." Every individual is free to decide which roles they want to take on or create and in which areas of the organisation they wish to participate. The high degree of autonomy also impacts decision-making processes, as decisions made independently by individuals can be faster and more efficient. Maximilian Hoffmann explains, "when I am active in my domain, for example in software development, I can make decisions independently as long as they are within my domain, without needing to consult extensively with others."

This goes along with inclusiveness and possibilities of participation, meaning "you have the opportunity to take part in everything, ultimately to become part of the circles". This strongly supports *Mein Grundeinkommen's* internal focus on distributive fairness.

Challenges Arising from Designing Governance around Holacracy

During the initial implementation of holacracy, the following challenges emerged:

The perception of leadership within the organisation presented significant challenges. Many people, accustomed to hierarchical systems and receiving instructions, viewed Lead Links as de facto leaders. However, these roles are not intended to give orders and do not have directive authority.

Coordinating between roles is also challenging, as different roles often have divergent goals, potentially leading to conflicts. Even in a task-divided environment, ensuring that the goals of various roles align remains a challenge, making close coordination among team members essential.

One of the most significant challenges for *Mein Grundeinkommen* arises from the conflicts between holacracy as an organisational structure and the legal form of an association. The difficulty lies in reconciling these two structures, which operate on different principles. The association functions as a democratic construct, with the general assembly acting as the central body that elects the board and leads the community. Alongside this democratic level, the holacratic structure emphasises self-organisation and involves less collective management. This results in an ongoing negotiation process at *Mein Grundeinkommen* regarding the balance between collective and autonomous decision-making. These conflicts are also evident in the legal responsibilities that rest with the board, leading to discrepancies within the organisation. As a first step towards resolving these issues, *Mein Grundeinkommen* introduced Special Representatives, as mentioned earlier, who bring the personal level into the association context and can better distribute responsibilities.

Related to this is the challenge of missing collective decision-making processes within self-organisation. Holacracy lacks a clear method for making collective decisions, with the consent method often perceived as inadequate for strategic and planning decisions. Maximilian Hoffmann explains,

"Consent means that someone makes a proposal, others can raise objections, and those objections must somehow be integrated. However, this process can theoretically take months, depending on how difficult it is to reach an agreement. That's why consent can sometimes seem quick, because at some point people might stop raising objections, either because they're tired of the process, find it too difficult, or want to avoid conflict. In such cases, things might move faster, but certain interests and perspectives may no longer be heard because people are discouraged from participating."

He emphasises,

"what I see here is a bit of the difference between democratic decision-making and individual autonomous decision-making. You could say that holacracy is somewhat based on the idea that if everyone looks out for themselves, then everyone is taken care of. But that's only true to a certain extent. It's similar to how markets work—when everyone acts in their own interest, they try to get the best outcome for themselves. However, what's missing in this approach is the level of community and collective responsibility."

Consequently, structural problems can result in responsibility being shifted to individuals due to the absence of a collective decision process within holacracy.

Employees also face personal challenges, especially when it comes to making decisions. Integrative decision-making processes require individuals to be willing to engage in conflict Maximilian Hoffmann tells,

"a consent-based decision is usually centred on individuals. I make a proposal, and then we check if anyone in the group has objections. If someone does, there's an immediate conflict between two people—not necessarily involving everyone. This means that holacracy requires a certain willingness to engage in conflict. Some people are less comfortable with conflict, and that's perfectly fine. However, I believe this system tends to favour those who are more willing to engage in conflict, which may also include people who enjoy competition, are outspoken, or are extroverted. It's important to be mindful that this dynamic doesn't end up shaping the entire organisational culture."

Interactions with Other Design Traits

Network Design

The self-organised and decentralised structures at *Mein Grundeinkommen* positively impact its network and the relationships with business partners. Maximilian Hoffmann highlights that business partners recognise that the individuals they interact with have decision-making authority and competence within the organisation, eliminating the need to refer to higher management levels. This enables faster decision-making, a process to which many people are unaccustomed. Maximilian Hoffmann explains:

> "when we organised the Congress of Society[1] last year, if a decision needed to be made, people were more used to saying, 'Okay, good idea, good suggestion. I'll discuss it with my supervisor or manager.' But that doesn't happen with us. If the person involved shares the same perspective and we reach a similar conclusion, the decision is simply made on the spot. I think these are small moments where holacracy or self-organisation has a noticeable impact on the relationships we have with others."

Ownership Design

Talking about ownership in the legal form of a not-for-profit registered association under German law requires some clarification. The association as a whole can be regarded as the owner, for example of money raised through crowdfunding, but not the individual members of the association. It is important to emphasise that the funds must be used for the charitable purpose of the association as stated in the articles of association.

The governance structures and their successful implementation at *Mein Grundeinkommen* are closely linked to the organisation's legal form, as it determines participation opportunities, decision-making authority, and the allocation of responsibility. Hoffman emphasises that "the ownership structure of organisations is extremely important". The choice of ownership structure forms the foundation for decision-making processes within the organisation. In critical moments, the right ownership structure ensures that important decisions are not left to a single individual in a leadership role who might not act in the best interest of the company.

For other organisations looking to adopt similar governance approaches, Maximilian Hoffmann recommends carefully considering the ownership structure to prevent decision-making from being concentrated in the hands of a few. The ownership structure has also impacted *Mein Grundeinkommen*'s salary system, as it may conflict with the organisation's not-for-profit status. Since the organisation is entirely funded by donations, and maintaining its not-for-profit status requires responsible use of these donations, salary increases have to consider that according to the tax office, administrative expenses for not-for-profit organisations must re-

---

1   The "Kongress der Gesellschaft" (Congress of Society) by *Mein Grundeinkommen* is an annual event that first took place in 2023. It brings together experts from politics, economics, and society to discuss social justice, income distribution, and Unconditional Basic Income. The goal is to promote public debate on social security and explore practical solutions.

main below 50% of income and there must be no disproportionality in salaries (i.e. no disproportion between remuneration and work performance).

Recommendations for Adopting a Holacracy-Based Governance Design

According to Maximilian Hoffmann, the key success factor for implementing innovative governance approaches is how ownership structures are organised within the organisation, as these structures ultimately determine who has the power and authority to make important decisions. In traditional organisational forms, such as a GmbH[2], ownership stakes often give certain individuals the ability to veto decisions or override the collective will of the organisation. This concentration of power can undermine the effectiveness of innovative governance approaches like holacracy, which rely on the decentralisation of decision-making. This means owners or CEOs can overrule decisions due to their ownership rights, regardless of any supposedly flat or self-organised structure. In such cases, self-organisation can become merely an illusion if the owner has ultimate veto power.

To avoid these issues, Maximilian Hoffmann advises organisations to consider alternative ownership structures that align with their governance model. For example, cooperative models or not-for-profit companies offer more democratic and equitable decision-making processes, where power is distributed more evenly among members. By aligning ownership structures with governance models, organisations can ensure that decision-making processes are truly collaborative and that the principles of self-organisation and decentralisation are upheld.

To support employees, especially through personal challenges arising from decision-making processes at *Mein Grundeinkommen*, the organisation offers tools such as non-violent communication[3], coaching, and workshops on interpersonal interactions, and mediation sessions. The implementation of partnership agreements, which define cultural aspects and behaviour within the organisation, along with the previously mentioned support structures, helps to improve interpersonal relationships and contributes to successful interactions.

---

2   GmbH stands for Gesellschaft mit beschränkter Haftung, meaning "company with limited liability." It is a common legal business structure in German-speaking countries, similar to a Limited Liability Company (LLC) in the U.S. or a private limited company (Ltd.) in the UK.

3   Nonviolent Communication (NVC) is a communication method developed by Marshall Rosenberg that encourages empathetic dialogue by focusing on observations, feelings, needs, and requests, with the goal of fostering understanding and reducing conflict.

Inspiring Redesign Beyond the Business

Through its purpose in particular, *Mein Grundeinkommen* aims to build a more just and equitably distributed society by introducing a universal basic income. Maximilian Hoffmann emphasises that the

> "idea of attraction rather than pressure [...] is most effective [...], meaning to inspire people with an idea and draw them towards it, rather than imposing an idea on them and telling them, 'This is what you should do.'"

The organisation's strategy is based on convincing people through positive examples and voluntary participation rather than imposing ideas. This approach is reflected in the successful implementation of lotteries and pilot studies, demonstrating that alternative systems are possible and beneficial. The ultimate goal is to garner broad support to achieve political majorities for its implementation. Not only does *Mein Grundeinkommen* express a commitment to a distributive approach, but it also embodies this through its governance design. This is achieved by fostering a high degree of autonomy, providing extensive participation opportunities for its members, ensuring transparency, and striving to implement an innovative salary model that compensates employees based on their needs. In doing so, *Mein Grundeinkommen* serves as a role model, contributing to the transformation of the economic model.

References

Interview

with Maximilian Hoffmann, Software Developer at Mein Grundeinkommen e.V., (28/02/2024, 01:34h).

Homepage

Mein Grundeinkommen (2016): So ist es, bei Mein Grundeinkommen zu arbeiten, https://www.mein-grundeinkommen.de/magazin/so-ist-es-bei-mein-grundeinkommen-zu-arbeiten, [Accessed 25 April 2024].
Mein Grundeinkommen (2024): https://www.mein-grundeinkommen.de/infos/in-english, [Accessed 28 April 2024].

Other Sources

Holacracy Constitution (2024): MeinGrundeinkommen: Holokratische-Verfassung, https://github.com/MeinGrundeinkommen/Holokratische-Verfassung/blob/master/Holokratische-Verfassung-MGE.md, [Accessed 12 Dezember 2024].

Melber, Fabian (2021): Photo – The raffle in which the lucky winners of the unconditional basic income are selected.

Robertson, B. (2016): Holacracy: Ein revolutionäres Management-System für eine volatile Welt, München.

Rosenberg, Marshall B. (2010): Gewaltfreie Kommunikation – Eine Sprache des Lebens, Paderborn.

Ownership Design

Case Study: FoodHub Munich

Laura Reinstorf

Purpose: Bringing producers and consumers closer together through the first cooperatively organised supermarket in Munich
Design Trait: Ownership
Innovative Practice: Cooperative Ownership Design

Key Facts

The *FoodHub* is the first solidarity supermarket in Munich, offering fair, fresh, regional and predominantly organic food in cooperative ownership. Every member is co-helper and co-owner.

Established: 2020
Location: Munich, Germany
Founder: Kristin Mansmann, Quentin Orain and Karl Schweisfurth
Ownership: Registered Cooperative (e.G.)
Legal Form: Registered Cooperative (e.G.)
Members of Cooperative: approx. 2000 (in 2024)
Webpage: https://foodhub-muenchen.de/

Purpose, Business Model & Objectives

Purpose: "Bringing producers and consumers closer together through the first cooperatively organised supermarket in Munich"

Vision: "Make social and ecological change suitable for everyday use and as simple as possible"

The *FoodHub München Market e.G.* was established following the "Biodiversity and Natural Beauty" referendum in Bavaria in 2019, driven by the vision of fostering closer connections between producers and consumers. In July 2021, this initiative materialised into a supermarket in Munich, modelled after established cooperative supermarkets such as the Park Slope Food Coop in New York and Coop La Louve in Paris.

Figure 1: Welcome at FoodHub Munich

Source: FoodHub Munich 2021.

The *FoodHub* is collectively owned and managed by its cooperative members, with a small team of employees supporting daily operations. Its mission is to economically promote and support its members while placing a strong emphasis on ecological sustainability and social responsibility. The primary objective of the cooperative is to facilitate social and ecological transformation in a way that integrates seamlessly into daily life while maintaining simplicity. The organisation is dedicated to exclusively and directly pursuing not-for-profit goals. Its operational model is founded on three core principles: co-ownership, participation, and transparency.

The cooperative envisions creating a viable alternative to the existing German food retail market, which is dominated by four major players – Rewe, Edeka, Lidl, and Aldi – that collectively control over 80% of the market share and largely dictate consumer choices. By redefining traditional notions of ownership, the *FoodHub* empowers its members to actively participate in shaping the food landscape, an influence that is unattainable within the framework of conventional supermarket chains.

Insights into the Cooperative Ownership Design

The ownership base of *FoodHub Munich* is primarily composed of local customers and community members, reflecting the cooperative's strong ties to the local area. This design fosters a sense of shared purpose and mutual benefit among those who directly engage with the cooperative's services. While the focus remains on local engagement, the cooperative's structure allows for potential expansion, including people from surrounding regions or those with a vested interest in the cooperative's mission. This localised ownership model ensures that the cooperative remains grounded in the needs and values of its community, while also allowing for the flexibility to attract new members who share its vision.

The bodies of the cooperative are the Executive Board, the Supervisory Board and the General Meeting. The Executive Board manages the cooperative on its own responsibility and conducts the cooperative's business. It consists of a minimum of three and a maximum of five members with a term of office of three years. Every six months, the Management Board is obliged to report to the Supervisory Board on the general business development, compliance with the promotional purpose, the cooperative's total liabilities and the annual corporate planning. The Supervisory Board also consists of a minimum of three and a maximum of five members, who are elected individually by the General Meeting. Each candidate is elected through a separate election and must receive a simple majority of all valid votes cast to secure a position. The term of office is four years, and the central duty is to monitor the management by the Executive Board and to obtain information on all opportunities for the cooperative.

In the General Meeting, the members exercise their rights in the affairs of the cooperative. Each member has one vote, which may be used at the annual ordinary general meeting within the first nine months after the end of the financial year or in the course of extraordinary general meetings.

The ownership structure of the cooperative is designed to balance individual freedom with collective stability. Each individual is allowed to sell their shares or cancel their membership. The cooperative is not seen as a compulsory community and should not be treated as one. However, there is a 2-year notice period, so that the cooperative is not endangered by the possibility of too many people cancelling their memberships at once. With the 2-year notice, they get the chance to find new members to replace the ones that cancelled their membership.

How Cooperative Ownership Design Enables Regenerative and Distributive Dynamics

The cooperative ownership design of the *FoodHub Munich* enables regenerative and distributive dynamics through three main aspects:

Co-Ownership

Individuals, partnerships, and legal entities under private and public law are eligible to become members of the cooperative by signing a membership declaration and obtaining approval from the board. Membership requires a one-time fee of €180, although a reduced social rate of €36 is available for students and individuals with lower incomes, granting them co-entrepreneurial status within the organisation.

Figure 2: Interior View – FoodHub Munich

Source: FoodHub Munich 2021a.

The cooperative's legal structure embodies a model in which a broad collective can jointly operate a business. This framework is governed by clear, legally defined regulations on organisational processes, while ensuring that the ownership of the enterprise ultimately resides with its customers.

By becoming a member of the cooperative, you assume the role of a co-entrepreneur. Additionally, if you wish to purchase groceries from the supermarket, there is an obligation to contribute three hours of work per month. This principle emphasises that, in addition to shared ownership, every member contributes their time. The underlying idea is that part of the cost is offset through this cooperative effort, resulting in food prices that are approximately 20% lower than in organic markets or the same products in traditional supermarkets.

Participation in the Decision-Making

The *FoodHub* offers two levels of participation for its members. The first level is standard for cooperative structures. Once a year, the general meeting convenes to inform members about the outcomes of the previous year and to make decisions, including the election of the Supervisory Board. The Supervisory Board, in turn, elects the Executive Board. The general meeting also provides members with opportunities to propose motions or amend the articles of association, among other governance-related matters. In this regard, the general meeting serves as the official governing body, or the "sovereign".

In addition to this formal governance structure, the *FoodHub* has implemented several participatory mechanisms. One key instrument is the opportunity for members to influence product selection and participate in the daily operations of the cooperative. For example, the "wish book" allows members to suggest products they would like to see in the store. This process ensures that decisions regarding the product range are not made solely by the board, but that each member has a voice. Whether the desired products remain in the range depends on ongoing demand, reflecting a dynamic and member-driven approach to inventory management.

The *FoodHub* also fosters active member participation through various working groups covering areas such as product selection, communication, events, and IT. Members volunteer in these groups, and an instrument has been created to elect two or three members from each working group. These representatives meet once a month in the "Speaker Circle," where they can present their questions. These working groups provide members with a platform to engage directly with the cooperative's processes and decision-making.

One example of such a discussion was whether the cooperative should exclusively offer organic products or establish specific criteria for selecting non-organic items. Another debate focused on the direction of the *FoodHub*'s communication strategy: Should the emphasis be on price, or should it prioritise the quality and regionality of the products? These discussions reflect the cooperative's commitment to incorporating its members' perspectives into its operations and values.

Participation in the working groups varies. For example, the product range working group has around 40 participants, though not all of them attend every meeting. On average, about ten people join each meeting. There are also several communication tasks that need attention, which is why there are quite a few members in that group as well. The *FoodHub* is active on social media, handles press work, and prints flyers, all of which require design and coordination.

> "But as I said, sometimes they are there and sometimes they are not. So, on average, there are maybe 5 to 10 active members per working group, but there are more in total. It changes from time to time, sometimes someone leaves and then someone else comes back and so on, that's how it goes for people. Sometimes you have more time and sometimes less." – Karl Schweisfurth, Co-Founder

Within this framework of working groups, fundamental questions are discussed, while always considering economic indicators.

Transparency

Another advantage of the cooperative structure is the high level of transparency. In addition to the legally required annual general meeting, the *FoodHub* organises other events at shorter intervals to keep its members informed and up to date.

A key aspect of this transparency is the clear pricing in the market. A standard 30% markup is applied to every product, ensuring that prices are always transparent to members when shopping. This approach also counters the issue of price dumping, which is commonly practiced in many traditional supermarkets.

The *FoodHub* distinguishes itself from traditional supermarkets, where industrial products are typically prioritised due to their low mark-up, with the aim of offering them at the lowest possible price. In contrast, regional or organic products often carry a much higher mark-up in traditional supermarkets, which is where they generate their profits. The *FoodHub*, however, applies the same pricing structure to all products, meaning that particularly high-quality items are offered at more affordable prices. This approach aligns with the philosophy of the Slow Food Coop, one of *FoodHub*'s role models from New York, which refers to such products as "Good Food." The goal is not to provide cheap industrially produced goods but rather to make high-quality products from regional, organic agriculture and artisanal production accessible and affordable. The pricing policy is determined by the farmer, who independently sets the prices for their products. This approach is highly distinctive, as it shifts the responsibility of pricing from centralised market forces to individual producers. By directly engaging in pricing decisions, farmers must consider both the purchasing power of consumers and market demand, fostering a more dynamic and responsive pricing model. This model not only empowers farmers but also encourages a closer connection between producers and consumers, potentially leading to greater transparency and trust within the marketplace.

> The *FoodHub* typically does not engage in price negotiations but instead adds a standard 30% mark-up. From there, it is up to the supplier – whether a farmer, baker, or other producer – to determine if the product sells or if the price-to-performance ratio needs adjustment. The *FoodHub* provides feedback to farmers about how their products are perceived and sold, allowing them to assess whether the pricing is justified or if changes are necessary. However, the final decision always rests with the farmer. Essentially, the *FoodHub* serves as a platform for selling products and facilitates market access for the farmers.

Challenges Arising from Designing Cooperative Ownership

Scepticism Towards Memberships

A core challenge for businesses based on membership models, like the *FoodHub*, is that people often hesitate to become members before they can start shopping, as opposed to traditional supermarkets. The primary barrier is not the membership fee itself but rather a general reluctance to commit to membership, combined with the initial deterrent effect of the required working hours.

This can sometimes pose an obstacle, as customers cannot simply shop – they must first become members and contribute their working hours. However, the *Food-Hub* has established flexible regulations to accommodate exceptions. For instance, members over the age of 70 are not required to work, and single parents are exempt from working during the first few years. Additionally, parents with children can still shop without working if needed. The cooperative is generally willing to find arrangements for those who truly cannot manage the required work hours. While not everyone can be exempted from working, the *FoodHub* is committed to finding solutions for cases of genuine hardship.

Membership Fluctuation

Another challenge in member acquisition is member fluctuation. As people move away or relocate, they may no longer have the time or ability to shop and work in the store, even if they remain official members. As a result, many members transition from active to inactive status. While many continue their membership to support the cooperative's mission, they no longer have the capacity to actively participate or contribute to the day-to-day operations. This ongoing need to recruit new members can be extremely time-consuming and resource intensive.

To attract new members, the *FoodHub* implements a multifaceted outreach strategy, including in-person events such as open days, where visitors can explore the cooperative, make purchases, and gain a deeper understanding of its operations. Additionally, regular virtual information sessions and an active presence on social media platforms enhance engagement with potential members. Press coverage further contributes to public awareness, with notable publications just as the *Süddeutsche Zeitung* and *Bayerischer Rundfunk* reporting on the *FoodHub*'s milestones. Both outlets are among the most prominent media sources in Germany, with the Süddeutsche Zeitung being one of the country's leading newspapers and Bayerischer Rundfunk serving as a major regional public broadcaster. Their coverage lends credibility and visibility to the *FoodHub*, reaching both local and national audiences.

However, the most effective method for gaining new members is through word of mouth. The key is to maintain a positive image, foster a good atmosphere, and ensure that people enjoy their experience – this, in turn, encourages them to spread the word. As Karl Schweisfurth emphasises, "the whole thing has to be fun."

Lowering Barriers to Membership: Addressing Time and Energy Constraints

After the initial excitement and positive response following the opening of the *FoodHub*, the cooperative now faces the challenge of transitioning from novelty to the realities of everyday operations. In order to remain functional and sustainable, the initial enthusiasm and popularity must be transformed into a long-term, viable structure.

The current geopolitical climate, marked by crises and states of emergency, also plays a significant role. It not only shapes the work of organisations but also influences the daily lives of many individuals. This situation can be advantageous for organisations that are pursuing new and innovative concepts, as there is increasing societal demand for such approaches. However, many people are becoming more anxious and often lack the mental space to engage with new models and ideas. To truly understand these concepts, individuals need time and energy to familiarise themselves with them, as these models are not yet commonplace.

Interactions with Other Design Traits

Network Design

The cooperative form and business model make *FoodHub Munich* naturally a part of a broader community and movement of similar cooperatives based in other cities. The networks with which these interactions are formed can be divided into two categories.

First, there are supermarkets with similar concepts already established in other cities, whose expertise the *FoodHub Munich* can now leverage. The cooperative is transparent about its influences, acknowledging that it has drawn inspiration from successful models:

> "Yes, it's not our idea, we stole the idea. We do it just like them because they are successful. And all these basic principles have been adopted, we didn't invent them." – Karl Schweisfurth

FoodHub Munich, in particular, collaborated closely with LaLouve, a food cooperative in Paris, receiving significant support from the founders and employees there in setting up and founding the cooperative. Building on this, *FoodHub Munich* now also plays an advisory role as efforts are underway in other German cities to establish similar cooperatives.

Second, there are strong connections with suppliers and other parts of the supply chain. The relationship with farmers and food producers is crucial, as they not only supply products but also provide support in a collaborative sense:

> "The suppliers, the farmers and food producers are important. Yes, they are also supporters in a certain sense, who sometimes help you. So, you help each other. They sometimes offer cheaper products, and we also make sure that we sell the products that they might be selling badly, that we promote them." – Karl Schweisfurth

The cooperative structure of the *FoodHub* enables its members to respond flexibly and individually to different business relationships, allowing for temporary adaptations when necessary. These partnerships are grounded in shared values, fostering creative freedom and mutual support.

Recommendations for Establishing a Cooperative Ownership Design

Build Strong Community Ties through Deep Partnerships

Relationships and networks play a crucial role in the success of *FoodHub* Munich. Community building is central to the cooperative's operations, as it forms the foundation upon which all other steps are built. This includes not only addressing practical matters such as selecting a suitable location for the store, defining the articles of association, and identifying cooperating farmers, but also ensuring that a strong community of members is formed. These members, who share the values and goals of the cooperative, are essential to its success, as turnover directly depends on the number of members, and vice versa.

Equally important is the exchange between organisations that pursue similar ideas, processes, and values. This networking allows *FoodHub Munich* to share its knowledge and experience with others, as well as to receive support and advice from like-minded initiatives. The cooperative frequently advises and collaborates with other initiatives that are working toward similar goals.

In addition to relationships within the cooperative and its network, it is crucial to maintain strong connections with local organisations, including NGOs. Networking with these groups is vital to establishing a supportive community and ensuring that the cooperative is recommended to others. Moreover, maintaining contact with local authorities, such as the city of Munich, is key to gaining support. However, the willingness of local authorities to support alternative economic models can vary greatly depending on the city and the individuals in positions of power. For instance, while Berlin has provided substantial support for similar initiatives, the support in Munich has been less forthcoming.

Suppliers, particularly farmers and food producers, are also an important part of the *FoodHub*'s ecosystem. They are not only critical suppliers of goods but also play a supportive role in the cooperative's success. There is a mutual exchange of support, where suppliers may offer discounted products, and the *FoodHub* ensures that these products, which might not be selling well, are promoted effectively. *FoodHub* works with about 70 to 80 direct suppliers, while the remaining products come from wholesalers and smaller suppliers. This network of suppliers is essential for the cooperative's ability to offer diverse and high-quality products to its members.

Ensure Entrepreneurial Courage and Leadership to Drive Success

Another key factor contributing to the success of *FoodHub* Munich is entrepreneurial courage. For a cooperative to thrive, there needs to be at least one individual whose vision inspires others to join the initiative. This individual acts as a driving force, demonstrating the entrepreneurial courage necessary to turn an idea into reality. While the concept itself may be compelling, the success of the *FoodHub* ultimately depends on the people behind it—those who are willing to take the initiative, make decisions, and adopt an entrepreneurial approach to managing the cooperative.

This entrepreneurial spirit not only allows for the implementation of the concept but also attracts and motivates others. By demonstrating a clear vision and the drive to bring about change, those involved in the cooperative can engage potential new members and supporters, fostering growth and expanding the cooperative's reach. Thus, the combination of entrepreneurial thinking and the ability to inspire others plays a central role in the *FoodHub*'s ability to succeed and evolve.

Cultivate Enjoyment to Strengthen Engagement

Despite the ideological principles and values that drive the cooperative, it is ultimately essential that everyone involved enjoys the process. This enjoyment is crucial for the success and sustainability of the initiative. This advice is not only important for the founders and initiators but also for the members within the community. A positive and enjoyable atmosphere is key to maintaining motivation and engagement.

A good atmosphere within the cooperative fosters a sense of comfort and belonging among members, making them more likely to share their positive experiences with others. Word-of-mouth recommendations are a powerful tool in attracting new members and spreading the cooperative's values and mission. Therefore, creating and maintaining a supportive and enjoyable environment is fundamental to both the internal dynamics of the cooperative and its growth.

Inspiring Redesign Beyond the Business

The *FoodHub* model is grounded in a pragmatic approach, recognising the challenge of competing with large corporations that have vast advertising budgets and the ability to shape consumer behaviour on a daily basis. Despite this, the *FoodHub* believes that change can still be achieved, even if in small ways. The key, the company argues, is to empower individuals by demonstrating that they have the ability to take matters into their own hands and effect change. This sense of empowerment is not only motivating for the cooperative's members but also serves as inspiration for other initiatives in different sectors to adopt similar approaches to transformation.

While the *FoodHub* does not envision surpassing traditional supermarkets like Edeka in the near future, it sees its work as part of a broader shift toward changing the ecological and agricultural systems. Its model, which has attracted attention from students and researchers, serves as a case study for alternative ways of organising consumer markets. This interest, particularly from academic institutions like the Ludwig Maximilian University of Munich, reflects a growing recognition of the potential for such alternative systems to contribute to broader societal and environmental change.

References

Interview

with Karl Schweisfurth, Co-Founder (04/11/2022, 0:50h).

Homepage

FoodHub Munich (2025): https://foodhub-muenchen.de, [Accessed 7 April 2025].

Other Sources

FoodHub Munich (2021): Photo – Welcome at FoodHub Munich.
FoodHub Munich (2021a): Photo – Interior View – FoodHub Munich.
FoodHub (2020): Articles of Association, https://foodhub-muenchen.de/wp-content/uploads/2023/02/FoodHub-Muenchen-Market-eG_Satzung-1.pdf, [Accessed 21 January 2026].

Case Study: Robinhood.store Berlin

Laura Reinstorf

Purpose: Establishing a new economic model to promote a fair global distribution of wealth.
Design Trade: Ownership
Innovative Practice: Redistributive Ownership Design

Key Facts

The *robinhood.store* in Berlin is a community-driven organic supermarket with over 1,000 members, where all surplus revenue is fully allocated to combating global poverty and climate change. Between 2021 and 2022, a total of €10,275 was redistributed toward these causes.

> **Established:** 2020
> **Location:** Berlin, Germany
> **Founder:** Mattis Steib, Jurek Katz, Noah Barthel
> **Ownership:** Civil Law Partnership (GbR)
> **Legal Form:** Civil Law Partnership (GbR)
> **Members:** more than 1000
> **Webpage:** https://www.robinhood.store/

Purpose, Business Model & Objectives

> Purpose: "Establishing a new economic model to promote a fair global distribution of wealth."

Robinhood.store is conceived as a pioneering model that integrates social responsibility into the core of its operations. Its primary objective is to generate a direct positive impact on disadvantaged communities and promote sustainable development by donating 100% of its profits to charitable organisations dedicated to combating extreme poverty and climate change.

In addition, the model employs a participatory membership system that not only offers price advantages to members but also actively involves them in decision-making processes. This dual pricing system – with different conditions for members and non-members – has been designed to ensure competitiveness against large organic supermarket chains while internalising ecological and social costs associated with food production.

In the long term, *robinhood.store* aims to establish a network of like-minded companies that follow similar ethical principles. The envisioned paradigm shift moves away from traditional profit maximisation toward a system that prioritises collective well-being and environmental sustainability.

Ultimately, *robinhood.store* is not just a supermarket; it is a movement aimed at inspiring individuals and organisations to rethink their roles within the economy and to actively participate in creating a more just and sustainable world. Through its innovative approach, it seeks to serve as a model for other enterprises, demonstrating that it is possible to operate successfully while prioritising social and ecological values over mere profit accumulation. Jurek Katz, Co-Founder of *robinhood.store*, explains:

> "Our current focus is on building a kind of umbrella organisation – a structure that enables the creation of its own ecosystem of enterprises which do not operate in the conventional capitalist sense. "

Insights into the Redistributive Ownership Design

Robinhood.store identifies itself as a "social participatory supermarket" that seeks to overcome capitalist structures by redistributing all profits to organisations that fight extreme poverty and climate change worldwide. The organisation not only aims to transform the local market but also to create long-term structures that predominantly benefit the Global South. In addition to the key business figures that are important, there are other decision-making dimensions, such as the resource consumption of products as well as moral and social issues.

Due to the peculiarities of the German legal system – namely, the incompatibility of nonprofit status with profit generation for subsequent donation – *robinhood.store* operates as a civil law partnership (GbR).

> "It is still very unclear whether we'll ever be able to enter a legal not-for-profit structure at all, even though we are definitely not-for-profit." – Jurek Katz

It is planned to reorganise in the future, possibly in collaboration with the *Purpose Foundation* or through the emerging legal form of steward-ownership, which would contractually exclude both saleability and private profit.

Within the organisation, the ownership concept is understood as "commons", while a cooperative structure is deliberately avoided. This decision results from legal requirements (e.g., for board elections) and the practical infeasibility of holding members liable.

Figure 1: Robinhood.store – Interior View

Source: Robinhood.store 2025.

Internally, *robinhood.store* adopts the principle of Holacracy, which emphasises the radical decentralisation of decision-making authority and the abandonment of traditional hierarchical structures. Through this participatory approach, both team members and general members can express concerns and influence strategic decisions – such as defining the organisation's purpose or determining leadership roles.

The prerequisite for initiating a decision lies in the demonstrable responsibility of the individual involved, who typically contributes more than three voluntary hours per month and has successfully completed the onboarding process. This approach enhances transparency and autonomy within the organisation while simultaneously fostering creativity and innovation.

In the organisation, roles are continuously evaluated based on their alignment with the collectively defined purpose. If at any point an individual in a specific role is perceived as no longer serving this purpose effectively, any team member has the opportunity to express concerns. Regularly designated spaces facilitate such discussions. Initial steps may involve raising issues informally, such as pointing out neglected priorities or areas requiring greater focus. However, if a critical aspect of the purpose remains unaddressed and necessary resources are not allocated accordingly, the individual in that role may ultimately be removed from their position.

While certain leadership-like roles exist within different organisational areas—for instance, in strategic direction and resource allocation within designated circles—these positions remain subject to collective oversight. The individual holding a role has autonomous decision-making authority within their scope; however, if their decisions are deemed misaligned with the organisation's purpose, they can be replaced. The focus is on modifying roles rather than overriding specific decisions, ensuring that leadership remains purpose-driven and adaptable.

Membership Model: The membership model enables active contributions to the shaping of the supermarket. In addition to operational tasks such as stocking shelves or handling the cash register, members have the opportunity to gain deeper insights into the organisation's management through various roles. This model not only incentivises participation but also creates a sense of ownership among members, who contribute to the store's mission and benefit from its success. The dual pricing strategy, which offers 15% off the full price for members compared to non-members, further emphasises the store's commitment to inclusivity while maintaining financial viability.

Robinhood.store aims to make all tasks accessible to members, allowing them to choose their own shifts. Most shifts involve managing daily operations, such as stocking shelves, operating the cargo bike, or handling cashier duties. More advanced responsibilities depend significantly on individual interests, skill sets, and ideas.

For members who can only commit limited time (less than three hours per month), primarily routine tasks are designated, whereas more intensive involvement leads to extended participation in decision-making. Whether contributing regularly in-store or deeply engaging in organisational work, all members collectively contribute to the growth of a movement that seeks to collaborate in addressing global challenges through shared economic efforts.

In the long term, the organisation aims to investigate and implement additional tools for collective decision-making, particularly concerning critical issues such as the allocation of donations. For instance, participatory mechanisms such as upvoting could be explored to facilitate decision-making regarding the distribution of a portion of donation funds and, in the future, investment funds.

The option to become more deeply involved in the work of *robinhood.store*, and thus participate in more significant decision-making, is open to everyone through an onboarding process. However, if a values-based alignment is not met, participation may be declined.

At present, *robinhood.store* consists of six individuals who are fully committed to the cause, alongside two part-time employees with more conventional roles and less involvement. The core team, comprising these six individuals, has gradually expanded over time. Prior to integrating new members, extensive discussions were held regarding the organisation's values and objectives. Currently, efforts are underway to formally document these principles and subsequently conduct a consensus-based review to verify that all members share the same values and goals. Should consensus not be achieved, the group will be restructured accordingly.

Figure 2: Robinhood.store Community

Source: Robinhood.store 2025.

Also, regular member council meetings, as held in the summer and fall of 2021, serve as a direct consultation process between members and the organisational team. Each council consisted of 10 randomly selected community members who met once to discuss questions, suggestions, requests, and concerns with representatives from the organisational team. The random selection of 10 members for each meeting was intended to ensure a broad range of perspectives. For every council meeting, a new group of 10 members was randomly selected to ensure a diverse range of perspectives. Although this specific initiative has been paused, it may be revived or replaced by a new approach in the future.

> **Focus on Redistribution**: Active participation in steering the organisation requires a commitment to its core values and objectives. A fundamental principle within this framework is the adherence to self-imposed financial limitations, ensuring that individuals do not exceed a fair share of global resources in terms of both income and wealth.
>
> The ownership structure is designed to prevent private capital accumulation. Instead of generating profits for individual shareholders, any surplus generated by the store is reinvested into the community or donated to organisations that address global poverty and climate change. As of January 2024, the *robinhood.store* allocates one-third of its donations to GiveDirectly, one-third to Cool Earth, and the remaining third to NGOs selected by the community. The selection of the first two NGOs was guided by the criteria established by organisations such as GiveWell and Effective Altruism, focusing on addressing the world's most urgent problems through the most measurably effective interventions. So far, no technical solution has been found which is why the community-selected third portion has not yet been technically implemented but is expected to be integrated into the online platform in the near future.

How the Redistributive Ownership Design Enables Regenerative and Distributive Dynamics

Increased Justice through Redistribution

The store's model embodies the economic theory of redistribution, which posits that wealth and resources should be allocated in a manner that reduces social inequalities. By redistributing profits to support social causes, *robinhood.store* aligns with the principles of distributive justice, which advocate for a fair distribution of resources based on need and contribution.

Moreover, the store emphasises the internalisation of external costs associated with production and consumption. External costs, such as environmental degradation and social inequities, are often not reflected in market prices, leading to market failures. By incorporating these costs into its pricing strategy, *robinhood.store* promotes a more equitable economic system that encourages consumers and producers to consider the broader social and environmental impacts of their choices.

The ownership structure of *robinhood.store* also challenges business models that prioritise profit maximisation over social welfare. By redistributing profits to combat poverty and climate change, the store embodies a commitment to social justice, advocating for the rights and dignity of all individuals, particularly those who are marginalised or disadvantaged. This focus on equity not only addresses immediate needs but also contributes to long-term systemic change.

Furthermore, the redistribution of resources through the ownership model aligns with sustainability goals. By directing profits towards social and environmental initiatives, *robinhood.store* contributes to the creation of sustainable systems that benefit both current and future generations. This long-term perspective is essential for addressing the root causes of inequality and injustice, promoting a holistic approach to economic development that considers social, environmental, and economic dimensions.

Creation of Sustainable Business Practices

The creation of sustainable business practices at *robinhood.store* encompasses a holistic approach that integrates environmental stewardship, social responsibility, and economic viability. This commitment is reflected in several key areas.

To begin with, the store emphasises sustainable sourcing by selecting products from environmentally friendly and fair suppliers, which not only reduces the carbon footprint but also strengthens local communities.

To achieve that, the *robinhood.store* has strategically accepted certain compromises. For instance, the retail outlet deliberately offers non-regional products, such as bananas, in order to remain competitive and attract a sufficiently large customer base. This approach helps the store incrementally facilitate societal transformation. Consequently, the organisation has deliberately phased its objectives, recognising that achieving significant market power is a prerequisite for effecting substantial changes, such as displacing bananas from conventional supermarkets in Germany. Without attaining a critical mass, such actions might merely result in a loss of customers rather than fostering a broader impact.

At the same time, *robinhood.store* acknowledges that there are inherent limits to its compromises. In cases where decisions involve trade-offs – such as accepting a temporary deterioration in environmental metrics in exchange for the potential to achieve significant long-term impacts – the organisation prioritises strategies that maximise overall effectiveness. This approach, although not universally accepted among stakeholders, has been consistently communicated as the foundational principle guiding the organisation's initiatives.

Another key aspect is waste reduction, where strategies are implemented to minimise food waste, such as donating unsold products to local food banks. Additionally, energy efficiency is promoted through the use of energy-efficient appliances and renewable energy sources, providing both ecological and economic benefits.

Another crucial aspect is active community engagement through workshops and educational programs to raise awareness of sustainable practices. Furthermore, social equity is prioritised by ensuring fair wages and safe working conditions for all employees and suppliers. The *robinhood.store* operates with a salary cap based on the level of wealth an individual can have globally without living at the expense of others. Preliminary calculations, which require further professional refinement, estimate this cap at €1,500 net per month, adjusted for purchasing power parity which is also the number that the *robinhood.store* uses.

Challenges Arising from Designing Ownership Around Redistribution

Inadequate Legal Forms

Innovative business models like that of *robinhood.store* face the challenge that existing legal structures in Germany and comparable European countries are primarily designed either for for-profit corporations or for not-for-profit organisations. This dichotomy makes it difficult to establish a hybrid model that integrates both objectives as well as their social and environmental missions.

> "What has definitely caused considerable difficulties along the way is precisely this separation between legal facts and internal practice. By now, I think we have made significant progress in this regard, though I would not call it perfect yet. It is likely that even at this stage, finding a legal form that genuinely corresponds to our approach would still lead to further improvement." – Jurek Katz

Navigating the legal landscape can also be complex and burdensome for innovative organisations. The lack of tailored legal forms can lead to confusion regarding compliance with regulations, tax obligations, and governance structures, making it difficult for these businesses to operate effectively and sustainably.

There is a growing recognition of the need for hybrid legal structures that can accommodate businesses with social and environmental missions. These models, such as benefit corporations or social enterprises, are designed to allow for profit generation while ensuring that social goals can still be prioritised. However, the absence of widespread legal recognition for such structures can hinder the growth and scalability of innovative enterprises.

The lack of recognition for hybrid legal forms also negatively affects financing, as investors tend to prefer classical, clearly defined corporate structures. This can stifle innovation and prevent these organisations from achieving their full potential.

Limited Experience and Data

Another challenge that must be highlighted is making informed decisions and developing effective strategies despite a lack of empirical evidence and practical knowledge in the specific operational context.

Organisations like *robinhood.store* often operate under new and unconventional business models that blend social impact with commercial activities. As these models are relatively novel, there is limited historical data or case studies available to guide decision -making, making it difficult to predict outcomes or assess best practices. This absence of standardised metrics for measuring social impact, sustainability, and community engagement complicates the evaluation of performance and effectiveness. Without established benchmarks, organisations may struggle to quantify their impact, making it challenging to communicate their value to stakeholders, including customers, investors, and partners.

In the face of limited data, *robinhood.store* must rely heavily on intuition, anecdotal evidence, or the personal experiences of team members when making decisions. While this can lead to innovative approaches, it also introduces a level of uncertainty and risk, as decisions may not be based on comprehensive analysis or empirical evidence.

To address these challenges posed by limited experience and data, organisations can benefit from collaboration with academic institutions, research organisations, and other social enterprises as the *robinhood.store* is planning on. By sharing knowledge, resources, and best practices, these collaborations can help build a more comprehensive understanding of effective strategies and approaches in the social enterprise sector. This way organisations like *robinhood.store* can adopt iterative learning processes, where they continuously test, evaluate, and refine their practices based on real-world experiences and feedback. This adaptive approach allows them to learn from successes and failures, gradually building a more informed and effective operational model.

Diverging Interests and Conflicts

The diversity of participants naturally leads to differing views regarding the organisation's priorities and goals. Especially regarding the core team, "There were many conversations about values and goals before new people were brought on board" (Jurek Katz). As unclear decision-making processes can result in tensions.

Organisations that aim to address complex social issues often bring together individuals from diverse backgrounds, experiences, and expertise. While this diversity can foster creativity and innovation, it can also lead to disagreements about priorities, methods, and goals. Different stakeholders may have varying views on what constitutes success or the best approach to achieving the organisation's mission.

Disagreements may stem from fundamental differences in values or beliefs among team members. For instance, some individuals may prioritise social equity, while others may focus on environmental sustainability or economic viability. These conflicting values can create tension and hinder collaboration, making it essential for organisations to establish a shared understanding of their core mission and values.

To this end, *robinhood.store* is developing a strategic blueprint to serve as a standardised framework that can be collaboratively reviewed and subsequently customised to meet individual or departmental requirements. This blueprint is anchored in a clearly articulated purpose, which defines the overarching objectives of the organisation. This clearly defined purpose has tangible operational implications – specifically, it informs decisions regarding recruitment practices, salary distribution, and prioritisation of tasks. This approach ensures that the organisation's strategic intentions are systematically translated into practical and measurable outcomes.

Interaction With Other Design Traits

Governance Design

Interactions with other design elements, or design traits within an organisation like the *robinhood.store* refer to the interconnectedness and mutual influence of various components that shape the organisation's structure, operations, and overall effectiveness.

The ownership structure directly impacts its governance model. In a collaborative environment like *robinhood.store*, where decisions are made collectively, the ownership model must support shared responsibility and accountability.

For example, one could argue that offering capitalist products still positions the organisation within a capitalist framework. At its current stage, operating within the retail sector, the organisation can primarily redistribute its profits through donations. However, in the long term, the aim is to expand this model into other economic sectors, including production. The *robinhood.store* envisions a transition towards a post-capitalist economy, recognising that such a transformation requires gradual development rather than immediate implementation. Each new project that operates through self-organisation in the interest of society rather than capital represents a step toward this objective. This interaction ensures that all stakeholders have a voice in governance, fostering a sense of belonging and commitment to the organisation's mission.

Robinhood.store's ability to build and maintain networks and partnerships is influenced by its governance and ownership structures. Collaborative governance models can facilitate the establishment of strong relationships with external stakeholders, including other organisations, community groups, and funders. These networks can provide valuable resources, knowledge, and support, enhancing the organisation's capacity to achieve its purpose. Additionally, the organisation's reputation and alignment with its purpose can attract like-minded partners, further strengthening its network.

The interplay between different design elements can drive innovation within the organisation. For example, insights gained from collaborative decision-making processes may lead to new approaches to achieving the organisation's purpose. Similarly, financial constraints may prompt creative problem-solving and resourcefulness.

For example, individuals purchase a 60€ ROBIN credit, which is distributed in twelve monthly instalments of 5€ to their membership card over the course of a year. This mechanism functions as a form of microcredit for the organisation, facilitating financial planning and enabling necessary investments.

Holacracy Principle: Internally, *robinhood.store* adopts the Holacracy model, which emphasises decentralised decision-making and the distribution of authority among all members. This approach contrasts sharply with hierarchical structures typical in conventional businesses, where decision-making power is concentrated at the top. In a Holacratic system, roles and responsibilities are clearly defined, but authority is distributed, allowing for more democratic participation in governance. This structure encourages collaboration and collective ownership, fostering a sense of shared purpose among members.

Collective Decision-Making: Decisions within *robinhood.store* are made collaboratively rather than through a top-down approach. This participatory model ensures that all stakeholders, including employees and members, have a voice in decision-making. This collective approach enhances engagement and aligns with the store's mission of promoting social equity and community involvement.

Recommendations for Adopting a Redistributive Ownership Design

The following recommendations can help organisations to effectively implement the model exemplified by *robinhood.store* and benefit from its principles of shared ownership, collaborative governance, and purpose-driven operations.

Launch Pilot Programmes to Test Distributive Ownership Design

Organisations should consider launching pilot programs to test the model in a controlled environment. This allows for experimentation and learning without the risks associated with a full-scale implementation. Feedback from these pilots can inform broader adoption strategies. Choose teams or departments that are already inclined towards collaboration and innovation to pilot the model. Their enthusiasm can serve as a catalyst for wider acceptance within the organisation.

Use Diverse Approaches to Engage Stakeholders in Decision-Making

During the process, engage all stakeholders, including employees, customers, and community members, in the decision-making process. This can be achieved through workshops, focus groups, and regular feedback sessions to ensure that diverse perspectives are considered. Foster a sense of community among stakeholders by creating forums for discussion and collaboration. This can enhance commitment to the organisation's purpose and values.

Empower Collaborative Leadership through Continuous Training

It is then important to provide continuous training programs focused on collaborative skills, such as facilitation, negotiation, and conflict resolution. This equips stakeholders with the tools needed to navigate the complexities of shared decision-making. Invest in leadership development that emphasises the importance of supportive and participatory leadership styles. Leaders should be trained to guide teams through the transition to a more collaborative model.

Cultivate a Culture of Experimentation and Growth

Lastly, it is also crucial to foster a culture that encourages experimentation and innovation. Allow teams to explore new ideas and approaches within the framework of the model, promoting a sense of ownership and creativity. Recognise and celebrate successes achieved through the model, while also learning from challenges and setbacks. This approach reinforces a growth mindset within the organisation.

Inspiring Redesign Beyond the Business

Building a Cooperative Ecosystem

The founders of *robinhood.store* envision the establishment of a broader ecosystem of businesses that share similar values and operational principles. By creating a network of socially responsible enterprises, the store aims to amplify its impact and promote systemic change within the economic landscape.

At the heart of this ecosystem is the idea of solidarity among local enterprises. By working together, these businesses can leverage their collective strengths to address common challenges, share resources, and enhance their impact on the community. This collaboration can take various forms, such as joint marketing efforts, shared supply chains, and cooperative purchasing agreements, which help reduce costs and increase efficiency.

The *robinhood.store* is sometimes criticised for not going further in proposing an alternative to retail and market-based models. It is correct that at present, the organisation operates within the retail sector and directs its profits toward donations. However, the long-term vision extends beyond this initial scope, aiming to expand these and similar principles into other sectors of the economy, such as production. The approach represents a roadmap toward a post-capitalist economy. Achieving this vision will not happen overnight, particularly when the ultimate destination must first be envisioned and created. Nonetheless, each new project that operates in a self-organised manner and prioritises the interests of humanity over those of capital marks a step closer to this goal.

This idea of a network of like-minded companies also emphasises the importance of inclusivity and participation. By involving community members in decision-making processes, *robinhood.store* ensures that the needs and perspectives of diverse stakeholders are considered. This participatory approach not only empowers individuals but also fosters a sense of ownership and commitment to the cooperative's goals.

Education and capacity building are essential components of this ecosystem. *Robinhood.store* provides training and resources to help local businesses adopt sustainable practices, improve their operations, and enhance their resilience. By equipping entrepreneurs with the necessary skills and knowledge, the ecosystem can thrive and adapt to changing economic conditions.

Furthermore, the cooperative model encourages transparency and accountability among its members. By sharing information about business practices, financial performance, and social impact, the ecosystem fosters trust and collaboration. This transparency helps to build a strong community of businesses that are aligned in their mission to promote sustainability and social equity.

In addition to supporting local businesses, the cooperative ecosystem also seeks to engage consumers in meaningful ways. By promoting local products and services, *robinhood.store* encourages community members to make conscious purchasing decisions that benefit the local economy. This not only strengthens the cooperative network but also cultivates a culture of sustainability and social responsibility among consumers.

Ultimately, building a cooperative ecosystem at *robinhood.store* aims to create a resilient and sustainable economic framework that prioritises community well-being, environmental stewardship, and social equity. By fostering collaboration, inclusivity, education, and transparency, this ecosystem serves as a model for other communities seeking to develop similar cooperative initiatives. Through these efforts, *robinhood.store* aspires to contribute to a broader transformation of the economic landscape, moving away from extractive retail models, and towards more equitable and sustainable alternatives.

References

Interview

with Jurek Katz, Co-Founder (28/10/2022, 00:54h).

Homepage

Robinhood.store (2025): Community-driven supermarkets fighting capitalism, https://www.robinhood.store, [Accessed 2nd April 2025].

Finance Design

Case Study: The Generation Forest

Niklas Tiesler

Purpose: Long-term oriented reforestation based on the concept of the Generation Forest
Design Trait: Finance
Innovative Practice: Long-term oriented Finance Design

Key Facts

The Generation Forest is a cooperative that enables its members to make a long-term, 'nature positive' investment in climate protection by reforesting and maintaining carbon-absorbing, biodiverse and productive permanent forests according to the *Generation Forest* principle (resilient, permanent mixed forests).

Established: 2016
Location: Hamburg, Panama (registered in Hamburg)
Executive Board members: Dr. Mathias Hein, Charline Joost
Ownership: Registered cooperative
Legal form: Registered cooperative
Members: 8316 (2025)
Webpage: https://thegenerationforest.com/en/

Purpose, Business Model & Objectives

Purpose: Long-term reforestation based on the concept of *the Generation Forest*

Vision: "The vision is that at some point we will reach a point where more is reforested than cut down. The vision is also that people will imitate what we do."

Iliana Armién, the founder of *The Generation Forest* and a Panamanian, witnessed in her childhood how her grandfather and other men cut down and burned the forest in front of her house, thereby killing many of the forest's animals to turn these areas into pastures for cattle. These images were so horrific for her that she vowed to reforest the entire area. She studied forestry and forest engineering and developed the concept of Generation Forests in collaboration with Andreas Eke from Hamburg, alongside key stakeholders such as indigenous communities, the Smithsonian Tropical Research Institute, and the United Nations Environment Programme.

In 1994, Iliana Armién and Andreas Eke founded the Panamanian forestry company Futuro Forestal to promote sustainable reforestation in Panama, using the concept of Generation Forests. In 2016, the two founders also established a cooperative, initially named Waldmenschen eG, comprising 13 members. In 2019, they rebranded it to reflect their concept: *The Generation Forest*. Futuro Forestal has been the cooperative's forestry partner in Panama since its founding in 2016. By the end of 2024, *The Generation Forest* had amassed a total equity of € 25,765,512.24 and boasted 8,075 cooperative members holding a total of 26,982 cooperative shares.

What sets *The Generation Forest* apart is that all approaches and the entire cooperative strategy are geared towards the long term. As Charline Joost, Executive Board member of the company, puts it: "The vision is that at some point we will reach a point where more is reforested than is cut down. The vision is also that people will imitate what we do." She wants the cooperative's work to bring about a change in the ecological and economic structures, "to return to the environment and economy in a hand-in-hand structure."

The primary objective of *The Generation Forest* is sustainable reforestation and the enhancement of biodiversity. Through reforestation, it aims to restore the flora and fauna that existed before the forests were cleared. The goal is to create permanent mixed forests where animals can resettle, naturally diversifying the ecosystem. For instance, birds or monkeys may carry mango tree seeds, further enhancing biodiversity. Additionally, this process restores and fertilises the soil while regulating the water balance. The growth of forests also enables certified and sustainable carbon dioxide sequestration. Beyond environmental benefits, *The Generation Forest* aims to provide economic value and promote social well-being for local communities in Panama through the expansion of forest areas.

> Generation forests integrate climate protection, biodiversity, and social perspectives. Through near-natural reforestation, resilient mixed forests are created that sequester CO_2, promote biodiversity, and offer sustainable solutions for both people and nature.

To achieve these objectives, *The Generation Forest* first jointly purchases or leases land in Panama through the cooperative. These areas are then reforested using a distinct type of forestry: the concept of Generation Forests. This concept incorporates a regenerative approach as a crucial element of *The Generation Forest*'s business model. Land is reforested in a way that increases biodiversity in both flora and fauna. Unlike other forestry companies, *The Generation Forest* relies on tropical rainforests with mixed tree species rather than monocultures. The repopulation and intermixing of species are intended outcomes of its approach.

More than 20 different types of trees native to Panama are planted. Tropical tree species grow faster and sequester more carbon dioxide than many other types of trees. Many of the trees planted are valuable hardwoods, which are harvested at the appropriate time; their timber is sold, and new trees are planted in their place. Since the trees grow at different rates, only individual trees are removed, allowing the forest to remain permanent. Due to the varied age structure of the trees in the permanent forest, *The Generation Forest* refers to it as a "generational forest".

Figure 1: Reforestation of Land Areas in Panama

Source: The Generation Forest 2025.

The reforested areas are managed for both agricultural and forestry purposes in line with the company's ecological, economic, and ethical standards. The resulting products from sustainable production are then marketed, primarily involving the sale of fair and sustainably sourced tropical hardwoods.

To make this possible, *The Generation Forest* issues cooperative shares. One cooperative share corresponds to 500 square meters of land and can be purchased for €1,633 in 2025. Of the cooperative capital, 55% is allocated to the reforestation and management of the forests, 20% to the purchase or leasing of land, and 25% to administrative activities, reporting, quality control, and marketing.

Insights into the Long-Term Oriented Finance Design

For *The Generation Forest*, an economically oriented cooperative, the finance design is of central importance. As Charline Joost explains:

> "The finance sector is our core. Our business model is based on a cash flow model. So, bringing together business and environmental protection does not work at all without the finance sector."

This highlights that the financial sector is both the foundation and the enabler of the cooperative's operations. However, in line with the cooperative's purpose, its financial structure is also geared towards the long term.

To work in accordance with its purpose, cooperative capital must first be available to invest in land acquisition, planting and forest management. This capital is generated through the sale of cooperative shares. A cooperative share can be purchased for €1,633 in 2025. A distinctive feature of *The Generation Forest* is that it continuously issues cooperative shares. Of this, €1,200 is the share capital, and €433 is the entry fee. The entry fee reflects the forecast increase in the value of the shares and is charged because future returns are distributed proportionally among all members. Prospective members are informed in advance about the cooperative's long-term orientation. This is reflected in both the long-lasting membership and the delayed payout of returns. The long-term orientation is evident throughout all areas of the organisation and plays a particularly decisive role in its financial model. Unlike typical plantations, which are fully harvested after a set period and thus generate returns that end the investment cycle, *The Generation Forest* aims to create permanent forests. This approach fundamentally distinguishes it from plantation-based models.

The reforestation of **permanent forests** is intended to generate long-term returns. The first areas of land were planted in 2019, and the trees require time to grow. In due course, some trees will be felled, and the valuable timber will be sold. Consequently, the first return distribution is projected for the year 2046 based on current calculations. After that, however, the forests will not be fully harvested. Instead, trees will be selectively removed, and new ones planted to maintain a permanent forest. Over time, trees will continue to be felled, and valuable wood will be sold periodically. Consequently, regular return distributions can be expected in the long term. According to *The Generation Forest*'s model, the cumulative distribution of a share by 2058 (i.e., 40 years after the start of the project in 2019) should exceed the current investment amount of €1,633. The expected return is 4.5%. However, future profits from cooperative shares depend largely on the development of wood prices. Several factors influence this, including tree volume growth, the shape of the trees, wood price trends, demand for tropical and precious woods, as well as the costs associated with forestry and the operations of the cooperative in Germany. *The Generation Forest*, therefore, represents a form of **"slow finance"**, a sustainable capital investment with no limited project duration. This approach involves long periods before potential returns are paid out, making the investment financially worthwhile only over an extended timeframe.

A long-term business strategy for *The Generation Forest* is fundamentally centred around cooperative members who prioritise regenerative and distributive practices over mere financial profit maximisation. It is crucial to engage with value-driven investors who exhibit lower financial pressure for immediate financial returns and are more inclined to advocate for sustainable objectives. These stakeholders value the tangible advancement of biodiversity over the pursuit of short-term financial gains. To effectively attract such investors, *The Generation Forest* must employ a values-oriented marketing approach that highlights its green success stories and ensures transparency in its operations. This strategy not only builds trust but also aligns the organisation's goals with the ethical considerations of its members.

Furthermore, a well-coordinated budget allocation that involves all employees in a 360-degree decision-making process is essential for the long-term viability of *The Generation Forest*. Given the uncertainties posed by factors such as potential natural disasters, financial predictability over an extended period is challenging. Therefore, enhancing organisational resilience is crucial. This encompasses not only the ecological resilience of forests but also the financial resilience achieved through the establishment of reserves and diverse financing options. By fostering both types of resilience, *The Generation Forest* can safeguard its mission and continue to make a positive contribution to the environment and society.

How the Long-Term-Oriented Finance Design Enables Regenerative and Distributive Dynamics

This long-term-oriented finance design enables several benefits, including value creation through the growth of biomass and accompanying ecosystem services, the creation of long-term employment opportunities, and reduced pressure to gain immediate financial returns.

Value Creation through the Growth of Biomass and Accompanying Ecosystem Services

The long-term-oriented finance design supports the gradual growth of biomass and the development of ecosystem services such as carbon dioxide sequestration and the enhancement of biodiversity. As Charline Joost explains:

> "We have now had a biomass audit carried out, which confirmed a total value of 39 million dollars for the area and the biomass on it. We had a member who works for a biomass calculation company make an extrapolation. And he confirmed that if we maintain what we have now reforested and nothing more is added, then in 34 years we would have a biomass value of 260 million dollars."

Such calculations give *The Generation Forest* confidence that its strategy is economically and ecologically worthwhile.

Creation of Long-Term Employment Opportunities

The Generation Forest's long-term financial design also enables social impact by creating access to stable employment for local communities, especially in the reforestation regions in Panama. This contributes to greater distributive justice by generating new job opportunities and ensuring fair wages. Employees also receive social insurance. In addition, *The Generation Forest* offers training programmes and long-term employment opportunities. In 2022, a total of 337 people from the local population were employed for *The Generation Forest*'s projects, including 92 individuals from indigenous communities. Charline Joost emphasised that by increasing the value of the forest, local communities also gain economic value. Furthermore, *The Generation Forest* is committed to social equity: there is no gender pay gap, and employee safety is prioritised, for example, through preventative measures against sexual assault. The organisation's social impact reaches beyond its employees, positively influencing broader community well-being.

Low Pressure from Members for a Quick Financial Return

The pressure from members to achieve quick or high financial returns is low due to *The Generation Forest*'s transparent communication and clear explanations of its long-term operational strategies. Investors often demonstrate a stronger interest in actively supporting regenerative and distributive approaches or CO_2 sequestration, rather than simply seeking substantial financial gains. This reflects a shift in priorities, with a greater emphasis on sustainable practices and social impact over short-term profit maximisation.

Challenges Arising from the Long-Term Oriented Finance Design

Dealing with and Preventing Fluctuation

Anyone can purchase cooperative shares at any time and thus become a member of *The Generation Forest*. Membership is regarded as a long-term investment, not a donation. This is why members are generally interested in holding onto the cooperative shares for an extended period. This is, of course, also important for the cooperative, as it enables long-term capital planning. Charline Joost explains:

> "when a member becomes a member and signs up his or her shares in the cooperative, we initially assume that there will be no major fluctuation and that the member will, for example, not drop out within the next four years. So, we expect that 80% or more of the members will stay forever."

While it is possible to divest cooperative shares, the strategy is not designed for members to do this frequently. Members can, if they so wish, either transfer or terminate their shares. Transfers can be completed more quickly than terminations. A member transfers shares to another or a new member for a price negotiated by both parties. Most of the time, the price is set between the previous and current prices. This can already result in a profit for the person divesting. *The Generation Forest* also helps mediate between the two parties. If a member terminates, the shares go back to the cooperative, and the departing member receives a settlement credit as soon as the minimum capital is no longer exceeded. If a person terminates their membership before *The Generation Forest* is in a positive financial position, they will not receive a refund. These strict rules also reflect *The Generation Forest*'s long-term approach and serve to support the organisation's purpose.

Balanced Growth Strategy

Since its founding, *The Generation Forest* has faced the strategic challenge of balancing investments between its reforestation projects in Panama and the development of its organisational structures in Germany. This balance is regulated through an overhead quota. Charline Joost explains that from the founding of *The Generation Forest* in 2016 until 2020, 85%-86% of the cooperative's capital was invested in the organisation's growth in Germany. Following a widely received media report that significantly increased public interest, the cooperative experienced substantial growth and was subsequently able to reduce this allocation to 16%. Currently, the quota is set at 25% for the organisation's growth in Germany and 75% for operational activities in Panama. Distributing the budget in a way that maintains this ratio in alignment with the cooperative's long-term strategy continues to pose a challenge for financial planning.

Negative External Factors

Negative environmental factors can repeatedly disrupt reforestation efforts in forest areas. For example, the Panamanian regions are still dealing with the effects of El Niño. In addition, the country faces extreme dry periods on the one hand and heavy rainfall on the other. Due to climate change, which *The Generation Forest* is trying to counteract through reforestation, these extreme weather phenomena will likely increase. This could delay both the project timeline and the distribution of returns. *The Generation Forest* and its forestry partners must therefore find ways to manage these events and their consequences. One approach is the selection of highly adaptable tree species—species that tolerate drought, require little water, and regenerate quickly after forest fires. *The Generation Forest* is also affected by broader social and economic challenges, such as wars, political uncertainties, and rising prices, all of which make people more hesitant to invest. Managing these external factors remains a significant challenge.

Transparency

The cooperative members invest their money in something that they themselves can hardly verify directly. Transparency is, therefore, essential when dealing with members. Although their return expectations are generally modest, members want to know that their money is being used in an ecologically, socially and economically meaningful way and that it is contributing to something tangible. As a board member, Charline Joost is aware that they are expected

> "to submit regular reports. We have a general meeting once a year where we answer questions, the annual financial statements are read out and defended, I would say, and approved, and then the board of directors is discharged, and the supervisory board is discharged. The members who come to the meeting are very interested and very committed. [...] In addition, we send our impact report to our members once a year by post. And I think that's another trust factor, our newsletter with actual pictures on site, with videos from the site. I think that's something that makes a big difference and is expected. If we didn't do that, I think they would start to think: 'They're doing something in Panama, do they really exist?' "

This also includes checking its own products and processes in Panama, as well as the data it publishes. In general, reporting is an important success factor for *The Generation Forest*. This also applies to both internal and external communication. The more people get involved and invest capital, the more effectively *The Generation Forest* can operate and fulfil its purpose.

Interactions with Other Design Traits

Ownership Design

The legal form of the cooperative serves the purpose of the organisation. It was chosen quite deliberately as it offers a particularly transparent and durable structure that is firmly regulated by the Auditing Association of German Transport, Service and Consumer Cooperatives in Hamburg. Unlike most associations, a cooperative is a commercial enterprise that can operate independently, managing its own forests and selling its own wood. Furthermore, the cooperative model enables *The Generation Forest* to continuously accept new members by issuing new shares, without requiring stakeholder approval for capital increases, as would be the case in a stock corporation. The General Assembly decides on the prices of the cooperative shares and adjusts them annually.

Network Design

In terms of its operational business, *The Generation Forest* as a cooperative is primarily responsible for strategy development, marketing, and attracting cooperative members and capital in Germany. For its activities in Panama, it operates through a wholly owned subsidiary called Waldmensch S.A. This structure simplifies business transactions such as land purchases, payments, and certifications. Waldmensch S.A. owns the land, manages forestry projects, hires employees, and procures equipment and transportation for forestry operations. The actual planting and reforestation work, as well as all other on-the-ground activities in Panama, are carried out by *The Generation Forest*'s forestry partner, Futuro Forestal. To further support its purpose of working for the common good in Panama and advancing distributive approaches, such as providing training for local communities or conducting research on the generation forest concept, *The Generation Forest* also established a foundation. This foundation is sponsored by Sinngeber gGmbH.

Figure 2: The Generation Forest's Business Model

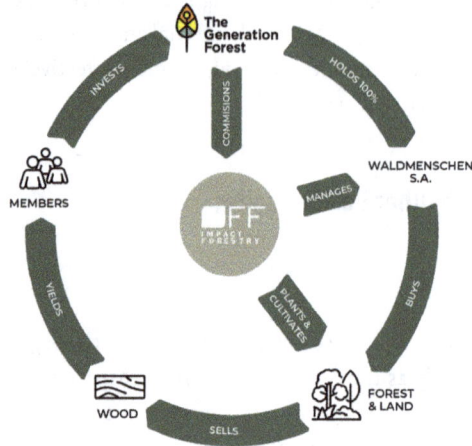

Source: The Generation Forest 2025a.

The Generation Forest has begun to establish a broader network that increasingly incorporates local communities into its strategies and operational approaches. The reforestation concept was originally conceived by a Panamanian, and *The Generation Forest* maintains regular communication with these communities. For instance, Charline Joost highlights that the Embera indigenous people have sought support from Iliana Armién, the founder of *The Generation Forest*, after their land had been entirely deforested. Drawing upon its expertise and resources, *The Generation Forest* facilitated a process that enabled the community to help itself, thereby fostering long-term sustainability, strengthening community cohesion, and supporting the preservation of Embera cultural practices. To deepen its commitment to social projects, *The Generation Forest* established *The Generation Forest Foundation* in 2023. This foundation is no longer administered by *The Generation Forest* in a fiduciary capacity but is now managed by Sinngeber gGmbH. Charline Joost explains that through this foundation, *The Generation Forest* was able to raise funds from cooperative members following a fire in Wala, a village adjacent to the cooperative's land. These funds to assist in the village's reconstruction. These funds were used to support the village's reconstruction and to establish a community school centre with Wi-Fi, benefiting the entire community.

Governance Design

The Generation Forest as a cooperative consists of three main bodies: the Board of Directors, the Supervisory Board and the General Assembly. The day-to-day business of the cooperative is managed by the Board of Directors. All matters of greater importance require the approval of the Supervisory Board, to which the Board of Directors is also obligated to report. The Supervisory Board, in turn, is appointed by the General Assembly, to which all cooperative members are invited. A cooperative member is any individual who holds at least one share in the cooperative. To ensure that *The Generation Forest*'s strategy serves the purpose of the cooperative in the long term, only elected ordinary members hold voting rights at the General Assembly. These voting rights are granted selectively to safeguard the mission of the cooperative. The remaining members are considered investing members. While their shares are legally equivalent to the shares of ordinary members, they do not have voting rights at the General Assembly. With this restriction, *The Generation Forest* protects itself from excessive influence by shareholders. The cooperative's founding team, along with some members of the Executive Board and the Supervisory Board are considered ordinary members and thus have voting rights. This also applies to certain individual members who have been selectively chosen based on their expertise. Investing members can apply to the Board to become full members by explaining why they are suitable for this role. If the Board approves, they may then be appointed. The cooperative nature of *The Generation Forest* is reflected not only in these governance structures but also in the principle that all members receive the same return per share, regardless of when they joined.

Given *The Generation Forest*'s awareness of its responsibility for using the cooperative capital in a purpose-driven way, all employees are involved in developing the financial strategy. Charline Joost explains:

> "It's a 360-degree process; all employees from all areas come together and work collaboratively to create the budget, for example. It's just super important and necessary that we are super well-positioned in the financial sector and are constantly working on it: 'Is that still right? Are we still on track? Do we need to revise something? Do we need to adapt a strategy?' That's the core, if I can put it that way."

Recommendations for Adopting a Long-Term Oriented Finance Design

Prioritise Stability and Resilience over Bursts of Growth

The Generation Forest was founded with a long-term focus, which has been maintained throughout its development. In the context of long-term financial strategy, it is essential to focus on enhancing resilience, both in production and financial management. Charline Joost advocates for a sustainable and modest growth strategy that prioritises stability over rapid expansion. Increased media presence and advertising can indeed drive growth by raising visibility and expanding market reach. However, Joost cautions against the temptation to make substantial organisational changes in response to a growth surge. She emphasises that it is vital to remain grounded and recognise that growth phases can be transient. A prudent approach involves acknowledging the cyclical nature of growth and preparing for potential downturns, ensuring that the organisation can navigate challenges without facing unpleasant consequences. In summary, a balanced, resilient, and humble approach to growth is vital for long-term success in financial design.

Inspiring Redesign Beyond the Business

The Generation Forest aims to drive transformation of the economic system through its strategy and the alignment of economic viability with the pursuit of regenerative and distributive approaches in order to "return to an environment and economy in a hand-in-hand structure" (Charline Joost).

Therefore, it is important for the company not to stand alone in its actions but to inspire other organisations to emulate what it is doing. On one hand, they want to be drivers of transformation, and on the other hand, they also want to offer a solution for green transformation. Charline Joost stated:

> "So green change, green transformation does not only mean imposing bans, but you can still continue to do your job. She wants to provide much more the opportunity of 'with us, you can become greener; look, you can already take the first steps with us', in order to make transformative actions easier and more accessible."

References

Interview

with Charline Joost, Executive Board Member (16/07/2024, 0:46h).

Homepage

The Generation Forest (2025): https://thegenerationforest.com/, [Accessed 7 April 2025].

The Generation Forest (2025a): Transparency builds trust, https://thegenerationforest.com/en/about-us/transparency, [Accessed 7 April 2025].

Other Sources:

The Generation Forest (2024): Annual financial statements, https://thegenerationf
orest.com/fileadmin/download/Externe_Pruefungen/Jahresabschluss_Berich
t_2024_The_Generation_Forest_eG_final_signed.pdf, [Accessed 7 September
2025].

The Generation Forest (2024): Articles of Association, https://thegenerationforest.c
om/fileadmin/download/Genossenschaft/TGF_125_SAT_Satzung_Englisch_in
teraktiv_01_2024.pdf, [Accessed 7 April 2025].

Case Study: Regionalwert Aktiengesellschaft Franken

Niklas Tiesler

Purpose: Transforming the structures of food supply chains towards regional, organic and fair production and processing from field to plate.
Design Trait: Finance
Innovative Practice: Citizen's Joint-Stock Finance Design

Key Facts

Regionalwert AG Franken issues citizen shares and invests the money in regional organic businesses: farms, food processing, retail and catering. Through joint marketing and logistics, regional organic food can be locally sourced and produced and processed under fair social conditions. *Regionalwert AG Franken* is part of Regionalwert Impuls GmbH, a German network with more than €20.5 million in share capital, over 6,200 shareholders and more than 250 partner companies (as of 2024).

Established: 2020
Location: Franconia
Executive Board members: Maria Zeußel, Dietrich Pax
Ownership: Citizens' joint-stock corporation
Legal form: Citizens' joint-stock corporation
Members: 200 (2025)
Webpage: https://www.regionalwert-franken.de/

Purpose, Business Model & Objectives

Purpose: As part of *Regionalwert AG* network, *Regionalwert AG Franken* follows the purpose of transforming the existing agro-industrial food system through a citizen joint-stock investment in regional organic farming. This enables farmers and citizens to work together towards an agriculture free from factory farming, bee mortality, nitrate pollution in groundwater, pesticide residues in food, and low wages in processing.

Regionalwert AG Franken was founded as a result of 'Forum 1.5', a discussion forum at the University of Bayreuth on how to achieve the 1.5°C climate target and is one of nine *Regionalwert AGs* in Germany, Austria and Luxembourg. The idea was to establish a joint-stock company to financially support regional and organic food production. Seventeen founding shareholders came together through this forum with a share capital of €80,000 and founded *Regionalwert AG Oberfranken* in 2020. During the founding process, they received support from Christian Hiß, the founder of the very first *Regionalwert AG* in Freiburg. After a while, they realised that shareholders were more likely to be found in the cities than in the countryside. Therefore, the initial founders decided to expand their sphere of influence to cover all of Franconia. The stock corporation grew and at the end of 2024, it had a share capital of €380,000 with 760 registered shares. In 2024, all nine *Regionalwert AGs* together had a share capital of over €20,5 million, more than 6,200 shareholders and over 250 partner companies.

The purpose of *Regionalwert AG* is to promote regional and sustainable economic activities in food production by supporting organic farms to transform the structures of food production. To serve this purpose, *Regionalwert AG* regularly issues citizen shares, for example in 2025 at €600 per share. The capital raised is then invested in social and ecological businesses in the respective region. In addition to financial support, *Regionalwert AG* also offers joint marketing, networking, and logistics to enable the local provision of regional, organic food while minimising greenhouse gas emissions through short transport routes. The promotion of organic farming is intended to contribute to the preservation of biodiversity and natural resources. *Regionalwert AG* also promotes the production and processing of organic food under fair social conditions and facilitates direct contact between producers, retailers and consumers. Accordingly, *Regionalwert AG* increases transparency in food production. The range of businesses that *Regionalwert AG* supports is broad and may include any stage from production and processing to the distribution of food, provided that the business meets the value standards of *Regionalwert AG*. Companies that do not meet these standards are not supported, thereby counteracting, for example, factory farming, nitrate pollution in groundwater, pesticide residues in food, species extinction, or unfair pay for employees.

Figure 1: Regionalwert Network

The Regionalwert Network

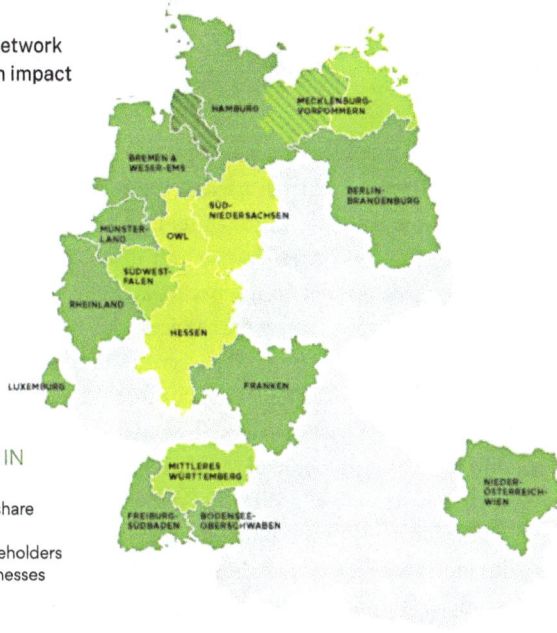

The Regionalwert Network grows and makes an impact

- founded
- in preparation
- interest

REGIONALWERT AG IN NUMBERS 2024
- over €20.5 million in share capital
- more than 6,200 shareholders
- over 250 partner businesses

Source: Regionalwert AG 2025a.

Insights into the Citizen's Joint-Stock Finance Design

For a joint-stock corporation such as *Regionalwert AG*, a financial design that aligns with the corporation's purpose and internal structures is of exceptional importance. Sound financial management is the fundamental enabling factor for the regenerative, distributive, and transformative impact of *Regionalwert AG*. This becomes particularly evident in its operating model, which is as follows:

> People acquire shares in the stock corporation, thereby increasing its share capital. In 2025, one Regionalwert share was priced at €500 and sold for €600, including a 20% agio. This agio is used to finance upfront costs, such as those associated with structural processes or notarial fees. The shares are registered and can be traded. The share capital is then used to financially support and invest in companies or projects. For the citizens of the respective region, in this case Franconia, *Regionalwert AG* offers a low-threshold investment opportunity through which they can actively participate in agricultural development and strengthen organic farming in their region. Consequently, the citizens have the opportunity to influence and benefit not only financially but also indirectly, by improving their regional food supply.

The companies supported by *Regionalwert AG* are selected using a specific tool called 'Regional Value Services', which is used to assess their social, ecological, economic, and transformative potential. Through its investments, *Regionalwert AG* promotes the pursuit of long-term regenerative and distributive approaches in the supported companies. Regenerative approaches are reflected in the company's support of projects that promote ecosystem services. For example, it promotes farming practices that protect the climate, conserve resources, and are characterised by repeatability. Only ecologically oriented farms are eligible for support.

At the same time, *Regionalwert AG* also pursues distributive approaches. While an Economy for the Common Good certificate is not currently required for funding, *Regionalwert AG* is strongly aligned with Common Good reporting. It has developed the 'regional value output' instrument to assess this, particularly in the agricultural sector. This tool is used to evaluate the societal value created by a company, considering, for example, fair wages for employees, the educational mission of the business, and other social criteria.

How the Citizen's Joint-Stock Finance Design Enables Regenerative and Distributive Dynamics

Financing Projects that Advance Regenerative, Distributive and Transformative Approaches – Projects that Otherwise Might Not Materialise

The defining feature of *Regionalwert AG's work* is that it enables and helps shape projects that would otherwise likely not be realised. Dietrich Pax, Executive Board Member, said:

"I always say, for me, the criterion is: if the bank had financed the company, then I don't really have to do it."

It is important to him to support projects and companies that would otherwise most likely not receive loans and therefore might never come into existence. Dietrich Pax noted companies in organic farming often find it particularly difficult to obtain bank loans, as profit expectations in this field are typically lower. As an example of *Regionalwert AG's* work, Dietrich Pax mentioned an organic farming association that approached them for financing to build a greenhouse. As a not-for-profit association, it faced significant obstacles in securing a loan from a bank. *Regionalwert AG* stepped in to finance the greenhouse, allowing the association to rent it, with the possibility of purchasing it in the future. While the financial return for *Regionalwert AG* is, of course, relevant in such investments, it is equally important for the organisation to promote regenerative approaches within the region. Regarding this financing, Dietrich Pax stated:

"This way it is feasible for people. And so far in winter there was only beetroot and an idea, and now there is beetroot, an idea and lamb's lettuce. And that is of course something that moves things forward. And that is exactly the kind of thing that we are now tackling."

Another example of *Regionalwert AG's* work is a catering company that supplies facilities such as kindergartens, hospitals and retirement homes with organic products. *Regionalwert AG* acquired a stake in this company because the caterer aimed to transition its food offering to organic and regional products. *Regionalwert AG* supported the company not only financially but also with expertise, networks and partners. Dietrich Pax states that this was a successful investment for *Regionalwert AG*, referring to both financial aspects and to the company's broader goals. The catering company's capital requirements were not particularly high, and it is expected to recoup the investment quickly through its sales. Additionally, the 3,000 and 5,000 people in facilities in the area around Coburg are now provided with regional, seasonal, and high-quality organic food. For Dietrich Pax, the provision of organic food, for example, through catering services, is a key lever advancing more regenerative approaches.

Strengthening Resilience

Regionalwert AG invests in a broadly diversified portfolio, with a maximum stake of 30% in any one company. When *Regionalwert AG* invests in a company, it increases the company's equity ratio. An investment of 25% to 30% is usually sufficient to increase the equity ratio to a level where the remaining capital requirement can be covered by a bank loan. In general, it is not intended to finance a project in full. This strategy offers several advantages for *Regionalwert AG*.

Firstly, it enables *Regionalwert AG* to invest in multiple companies through broad diversification and thus to contribute to the advancement of regenerative and distributive approaches. Secondly, it also protects against the risk of unsuccessful investments, as the capital is risk capital, and not all investments necessarily yield the intended returns. The corporation's share capital is limited, and only a maximum of two-thirds is intended for active investment. One-third of the share capital is as a reserve – for difficult times and as additional financing capacity. Dietrich Pax noted that such reserves proved particularly important during the Covid-19 pandemic. Nonetheless, a 30% stake in a company is sufficient to enable *Regionalwert AG* to become actively involved in that company.

Low Financial Return Pressure from Shareholders

The shareholders of *Regionalwert AG* should also benefit from the success of the companies and the profitable investments. *Regionalwert AG* therefore targets a return of 3%, which can then be distributed to the shareholders. However, many shareholders choose not to receive this return. It is more important to them that the capital is reinvested immediately in new regional, ecological projects. They wish to use their financial resources to promote the region and transform the structures of local food production. The shareholders are particularly interested in a long-term orientation, with many even viewing their investment as one made on behalf of future generations. Financial return expectations among *Regionalwert AG* shareholders are therefore significantly lower than those typically associated with other companies. Nevertheless, Dietrich Pax is aware of the responsibility that *Regionalwert AG* bears, stating:

> "The money that people give us, in the form of stocks, is money with which they express their will."

The shareholders' low expectations regarding financial return enable *Regionalwert AG* to align its strategy closely with its purpose. Still, both the Supervisory Board and the Executive Board remain accountable to the shareholders at the general meeting. They must explain their strategies and investments and ensure that developments are made transparent. As such, shareholders exercise a degree of oversight to ensure that *Regionalwert AG*'s actions remain consistent with its purpose.

Challenges Arising from the Citizen's Joint-Stock Finance Design

Decision-Making for Financially and Purpose-Centred Worthwhile Investments

Due to its limited financial resources, *Regionalwert AG* cannot invest in all the projects and companies it would like to. The projects it invests in are those that do not require a large amount of capital. Accordingly, each investment decision is made with great care, focusing on ventures that are both financially and purpose-centred worthwhile. To prevent the Executive Board from potentially acting alone, all investments over €2,000 must be approved by the Supervisory Board. Dietrich Pax expressed a strong desire to financially support many more projects and companies. He sees organic farming as an area with considerable potential for development, viewing it as the ideal path to serve the ecosystem and transform social structures towards more regenerative approaches. In particular, he wishes to see even more innovation and to provide further support. However, a major challenge lies in the fact that organic farming requires a substantial upfront investment. Major investments are necessary before cultivation can begin, and it takes time for crops to be harvested and revenue to be generated. *Regionalwert AG* currently lacks the financial capacity to make large-scale investments in this field. The company must therefore evaluate which investments are financially and purpose-centred worthwhile and feasible. Each case must be assessed individually to ensure that actions are both meaningful and economically sound.

Attracting New Shareholders

In addition to making smart and profitable investments with the available capital, *Regionalwert AG* urgently requires more share capital and, consequently, more share-holders. Attracting new shareholders remains a key challenge for *Regionalwert AG* and its financial design. Organic food production primarily takes place in rural regions; however, potential shareholders are more likely to be found in urban centres. Recognising this, *Regionalwert AG* expanded its sphere of influence to include the entire Franconian region. The low expected financial returns may deter profit-oriented potential shareholders. *Regionalwert AG*, as a citizens' joint-stock company, would therefore seek to appeal primarily to value-driven citizens who wish to support a long-term transformation of regional food production. It also aims to be as low threshold as possible in order to remain accessible to a broad base of the population. How to make the shareholding model more attractive to citizens is the subject of ongoing internal discussion. New incentive models such as offering practical benefits when purchasing products from businesses supported by *Regionalwert AG* are currently being explored.

Combining Regenerative and Financial Goals through Investments

External influences, such as climate change, can slow advancement of organic farming. For this reason, and due to the expected low returns, banks tend to avoid investing in this sector. *Regionalwert AG* aims to fill this gap, but its financial resources remain limited. At the same time, *Regionalwert AG* must act in a financially profitable manner. While its shareholders are primarily motivated by the desire to promote regional organic food production and do not expect high financial returns, the organisation must still ensure that its investments are economically viable. Good management of the company's capital is vital for the stock corporation's survival. If *Regionalwert AG* were to make poor investment decisions, lose capital, or even face insolvency, it would no longer be able to fulfil its purpose of supporting regenerative, distributive, and transformative projects.

Figure 2: Strengthening Regional, Organic Agriculture

Source: Regionalwert AG Franken 2025a.

A key part of *Regionalwert AG*'s transformative impact lies in its visible external impact which is communicated through success stories. Demonstrating both financial and regenerative success helps change social structures, support ecosystems, and inspire others. *Regionalwert AG* sees itself as a model, aiming to win new shareholders and encourage like-minded people and organisations to pursue similar initiatives. This explains why working economically and being financially profitable is essential to the purpose of *Regionalwert AG*. As the company is aware of this, it focuses on investments that require comparatively little capital but yield significant impact. Consequently, *Regionalwert AG* is currently concentrating on the processing of organic food rather than its production, where capital demands are higher. The aim is to achieve maximum effect with the available resources.

Interactions with Other Design Traits

Ownership and Governance Design

The highest governing body of *Regionalwert AG* is the Annual General Meeting of shareholders. At the Annual General Meeting, shareholders elect the Supervisory Board, which in turn appoints the Executive Board responsible for managing the stock corporation's operations. The Executive Board is elected for a term of two years and is tasked with the day-to-day leadership of the company. The Supervisory Board monitors the Executive Board and represents the interests of the shareholders. At present, the Executive Board consists of two members, while the Supervisory Board consists of six. All members serve on a voluntary basis. In addition to its oversight role, the Supervisory Board also actively supports the Executive Board in developing regional value chains and in distributing capital.

Investment decisions follow a clear process. The Executive Board develops strategic proposals for investments or equity participation in companies, which are then submitted to the Supervisory Board. These proposals are discussed collaboratively in Supervisory Board meetings. An investment can proceed only if the Supervisory Board approves it.

At the Annual General Meeting, the Executive Board and Supervisory Board report to the shareholders providing updates on the corporation's financial performance, investment activities, and overall business development. The Annual General Meeting is open to all shareholders. Anyone who acquires at least one share can become a shareholder of *Regionalwert AG*. While the company operates in the Franconian region, there are no geographic restrictions on share ownership—individuals from outside the region may also invest. Every shareholder has a voting right at the Annual General Meeting, with each share entitling the holder to one vote. To prevent concentrated influence and maintain democratic governance, *Regionalwert AG* has implemented a cap: no individual shareholder may hold more than 10% of the voting shares. This regulation ensures broad-based participation and protects the company's democratic and citizen-oriented character.

Network Design

Regionalwert AG deliberately seeks co-financing from banks in order to exert a transformative influence on them as well. Dietrich Pax said that from the moment they started, banks have increasingly been asking for ecological standards before they give out loans to local agricultural companies. This shows that *Regionalwert AG* is contributing to change. For companies, the investment of *Regionalwert AG* can also be beneficial for their image and marketing. During the investment period, *Regionalwert AG* also supports the project or company with expertise, advice, and access to its network.

Recommendations for Adopting a Citizen's Joint-Stock Finance Design

Design the Business and Strategy for Long-Term Success

Dietrich Pax recommends that, when founding a citizens' joint-stock company modelled on *Regionalwert AG*, the main priority should be securing capital during the start-up phase. If he were to found *Regionalwert AG Franken* again, he would have founded it for the entire Franconian region in order to cover the capital-rich urban area. In addition, he would only have founded *Regionalwert AG* if they had secured €300,000 to €400,000 in share capital, rather than the actual €80,000. He also recommends looking for cost reductions in the capital structure and administration, but at the same time striving for a continuous professionalisation of their own structures.

Inspiring Redesign Beyond the Business

Regionalwert AG has a strong commitment to contributing to transformative work. By investing in a company, *Regionalwert AG* also introduces ecological, social, and public welfare issues into the company. For example, it examines the proportion of ecologically produced products, the working conditions and wages of employees and partners, and whether the company also trains people or conducts other educational work.

Regionalwert AG aims not only to support companies and projects that already have high ecological and social standards and contribute to society but also those that wish to develop in this direction. To this end, the current status of the company in various areas is analysed at the start of the funding, and a strategy is developed to foster improvement in these areas.

During the funding period, *Regionalwert AG* supports the respective company not only financially but also with its expertise in transformation, the implementation of regenerative and distributive approaches, and its network. At the end of the funding period, an evaluation is conducted to determine what has changed in the company as a result of the investment. The evaluation questions examine whether an ecological transformation has been initiated or whether the company's social performance has improved.

Regionalwert AG supports not only projects that already produce or sell 100% organic products but also companies where the proportion is initially only 50%–60%, for example. In addition to the financial return, the aim of these subsidies is to promote development and increase the proportion of organic products to 90%. The goal is for the farm to receive an organic certification within three years. However, the intention is not only to drive a transformation in the respective farm in terms of ecology, but also in the social dimension, based on social criteria and by improving the farm's social service. Dietrich Pax stated that although some companies pay the money back to *Regionalwert AG* with interest and end their participation after the funding period ends, many wish to maintain contact with *Regionalwert AG* even after the funding period in order to continue advancing the development of their own structures.

References

Interview

with Dietrich Pax, Executive Board Member and Supervisory Board Member (01/07/2024, 1:01h).

Homepage

Regionalwert AG Franken (2025): Die nachhaltige Bürgeraktie für ganz Franken, https://www.regionalwert-franken.de/, [Accessed 7 April 2025].

Regionalwert AG Franken (2025a): Die Regionalwertidee, https://www.regionalwert-franken.de/regionalwert-ag/die-idee/, [Accessed 7 April 2025].

Regionalwert AG Freiburg und Südbaden (2025): Die nachhaltige Bürgeraktie für Freiburg und Südbaden, https://www.regionalwert-ag.de/, [Accessed 7 April 2025].

Other Sources

Regionalwert AG (2023): Annual Financial Statements, https://www.regionalwert-f
     ranken.de/fileadmin/user_upload/JHV2024/Seiten_aus_Regionalwert_JA_202
     3_mU.pdf, [Accessed 7 April 2025].
Regionalwert AG (2024): Annual Financial Statements, https://www.regionalwert-f
     ranken.de/fileadmin/user_upload/Texte/Hauptversammlung_24/Jahresabschl
     uss_2024_Ohne_Aktionaere.pdf, [Accessed 7 September 2025].

Summary

Summary and Critical Reflections

Annekatrin Meißner, Suleika Bort, Erinch Sahan

In this final chapter, we summarise the core insights from our case studies and explore whether—and how—these insights can inspire other organisations in their journey towards a stronger commitment to regenerative and distributive business practices. Yes, the cases discussed in this book vary regarding business models, goals, and legal structures. Yet, across this diversity, they share a common characteristic: the firms pursue social or ecological goals alongside meeting essential commercial outcomes. At the heart of this pursuit of regenerative and distributive dynamics are fundamental values and norms that guide the behaviour and actions of these firms. These values and norms reflect a "higher-order purpose that links to moral and ethical obligations" (George et al. 2023:1842).

Still, for these regenerative and distributive values and norms to be effectively embedded into business structures and processes, they must align with the organisational design traits. The focus here is to ensure that the regenerative and distributive purpose creates an organisation-wide responsibility by anchoring it within the different design traits. The case studies in this book focus on five specific design traits. First, we highlight innovative practices within each and examine the dynamics behind their contribution to an organisation's regenerative and/or distributive purpose. Second, we identify patterns across the design traits that can be observed and critically reflected upon, referencing also to Iris Marion Young's (2006) concept of global responsibility. Finally, we consider the importance of role models for regenerative and distributive business design.

Purpose Design

The Purpose Design case studies focus on how the specific regenerative and/or distributive purpose of the selected enterprises, *WEtell*, *Wildplastic* and *WoodenValley*, is embedded in and enabled by the overall business design. In all three cases, the design of ownership as "steward-ownership" can be seen as central to their purpose, while the legal model corresponds to the more traditional German spectrum of a limited liability company (GmbH) and a not-for-profit limited liability company (gGmbH). *WEtell* pursues the purpose of regenerative and distributive mobile communications, anchored by three types of shares (A-B-C shares). A-shares, for example, are owned by those who actively work in the company, ensuring that only insiders who understand the business make critical decisions. With a staff that has joined the company to pursue its core purpose, this ensures that *WEtell* always prioritises sustainable mobile networks. Linked to this is the financial model, which ensures that profits are reinvested in the business rather than distributed to shareholders. This gives *WEtell* the freedom to use its finances in service of its purpose. *Wildplastic* and *WoodenValley* share the same financial priority of reinvesting profits to advance their purpose.

The legal structure of *WoodenValley* as a not-for-profit limited liability company is an additional aspect that helps safeguard its purpose. At the same time, it assures partners that *WoodenValley* is not motivated by economic gain but by the commitment to advance its purpose of regenerative building, which in turn encourages deeper collaboration. *Wildplastic* which pursues the regenerative purpose of ridding the world of wild plastic, has adopted the stewardship ownership model of the golden share, where the Purpose Foundation holds 1% of the voting shares. While this may seem like a small percentage, the foundation carries significant power: the golden share grants it veto rights over any decisions that could divert the company from its purpose. This structure prevents profit-driven shifts and ensures that the company remains focused on its mission.

Network Design

Within the Network Design trait, several cases stood out, each illustrating different approaches to leveraging networks for impact. For example, the social enterprise *On Purpose* focuses on training and developing managers and leaders who seek to build purpose-driven rather than profit-driven organisations. A defining feature of *On Purpose* is its community-centred network design, which fosters a transformation toward purpose over profit. The organisation relies heavily on the commitment, ideas, and initiatives of its community members, embracing a bottom-up rather than top-down approach.

Furthermore, the network design based on the Economy of Love, used by *Sekem* and *EBDA*, is remarkable and can be characterised by a commitment to the holistic principles of regenerative and distributive development. These organisations have made the values on which their stakeholder relations are based visible in the Economy of Love Standard. This includes the important dimension of culture and the development of a credit system to reward farmers for organic and biodynamically grown food, as well as for their ecosystem services. This is significant given that this organic and biodynamic way of doing agriculture preserves biodiversity and stores

CO_2 due to its treatment of the soil, which helps to regenerate two of the already exceeded planetary boundaries (Biodiversity loss and Climate Change). The way *Sekem* and *EBDA* designed their network structures was based on the principle of fairness from the beginning, as the revenues from all sales of the CO_2 certificates were divided equally between all farmers. In addition, farmers receive additional income through their ecosystem services, allowing organic products to be priced more affordably. This also contributes to a more equitable distribution of, and expanded access to, healthy food.

For companies such as *Wildling Shoes*, *Sonnentor* and *Commown*, collaborations and strong partnerships with like-minded organisations play a crucial role in their success. *Wildling Shoes*, in particular, has cultivated a trust-based stakeholder network, fostering exceptionally loyal customer relationships that create interdependencies extending beyond finance. The company prioritises equal profit distribution and reinvests within its network to preserve financial independence, allowing it to stay aligned with its values. *Sonnentor*'s network is notable for its emphasis on direct communication and shared values, leading to enduring partnerships—many of which have lasted for years, if not decades. These relationships are built on mutual respect, fair cooperation, and reciprocity, including through fair wages instead of exploitation and investments in a shared future. Transparency and open dialogue further strengthen these collaborations. *Commown*, which is organised as a not-for-profit cooperative, is driven by the goal of making the electronics sector more sustainable and responsible by promoting a rental-based model instead of traditional sales. To achieve this, the company depends on trusted network partners who align with its mission.

Governance Design

The cases focused on the Governance Design trait highlight the crucial role of self-organisation and the high level of responsibility entrusted to each employee. The innovative practices within the framework of governance design aim at holacracy at *Mein Grundeinkommen* and self-organisation at *Wigwam*, both elements of New Work. For example, *Mein Grundeinkommen* is a not-for-profit organisation that crowdfunds and raffles off unconditional basic incomes. In order to achieve their purpose – 'We want a fair and crisis-proof world, in which everyone can lead a self-determined life' – a governance design that also enables a self-determined life within the organisation is an essential element to create internal and external coherence. One of the most distinctive aspects of *Mein Grundeinkommen*'s organisational design is its dynamic job structure, which enables employees to continuously create and experiment with new roles based on the organisation's evolving needs. The organisation operates under the concept of holacracy, a decentralised governance model that facilitates distributed decision-making. In this model, responsibility for decisions is not allocated to a single manager (as in hierarchical organisational structures) but is instead spread across several roles and people. This enables faster decision-making, which is also carried out by those holding the expertise. Combined with individual budget responsibility, these elements strengthen employees' self-efficacy and enhance their freedom to be co-creators.

Wigwam, a Berlin-based communications agency, follows a similar approach. The organisation stands out for its innovative governance structure, which uniquely blends self-organisation with a cooperative legal form. One of *Wigwam*'s most distinctive governance practices is its use of the resistance inquiry method for organisation-wide decisions. This model is based on the idea that when a team proposes a course of action and invites objections, minimal or no resistance from the broader group is taken as a green light to proceed. This method ensures efficient self-organisation and allows decisions to move forward quickly as long as they do not encounter significant opposition.

Both the *Wigwam* and *Mein Grundeinkommen* cases demonstrate how a dignity-based, human-centred approach to work—characterised by decision-making freedom, leadership through positive role models, and voluntary participation—can foster innovation and creativity while maintaining organisational effectiveness.

Ownership Design

Like *robinhood.store* in Berlin, *FoodHub* in Munich operates on the principles of co-operativism as a bio-supermarket. *Robinhood.store*'s innovative ownership structure makes it an outstanding case within the Ownership Design framework. The store is established as a civil law partnership (GbR) and pursues the purpose of achieving a fair distribution of prosperity worldwide. The store operates on a membership basis, where members receive discounts and actively participate in the community. This model fosters engagement, a sense of ownership, and long-term commitment among members. Its ownership structure is explicitly designed to prevent private capital accumulation. Instead of generating profits for individual shareholders, any surplus is redistributed globally – through donations to organisations addressing global poverty and climate change – or reinvested in the community.

Similarly, *FoodHub* as the first cooperatively organised supermarket in Munich is collectively owned and managed by its members, with a small team of employees handling daily operations. The purpose of the *FoodHub*, 'to bring producers and consumers closer together', is enabled by this cooperative structure. A defining feature of this model is its emphasis on co-ownership, participatory decision-making, and a high level of transparency, ensuring that members have a direct influence on the organisation's direction and values. Anyone can purchase a cooperative share of the supermarket. This share brings obligations, such as working 3 hours a month, as well as rights, including a say in what products are sold. The overall aim is to create a regional organic supply structure.

Finance Design

Figure 1: From Degenerative & Divisive to Regenerative & Distributive Business Design

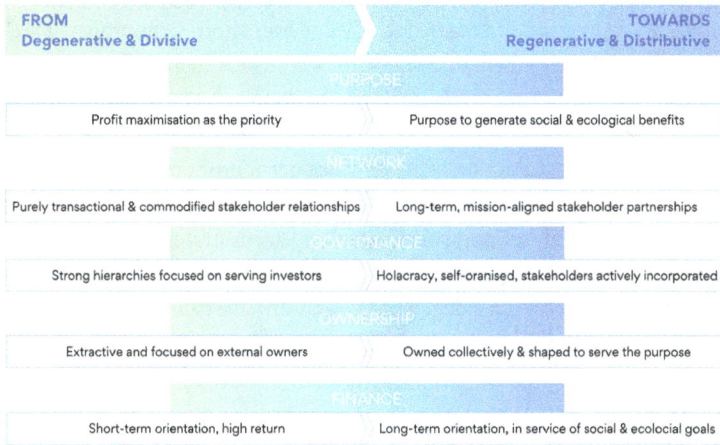

FROM Degenerative & Divisive	TOWARDS Regenerative & Distributive
PURPOSE	
Profit maximisation as the priority	Purpose to generate social & ecological benefits
NETWORK	
Purely transactional & commodified stakeholder relationships	Long-term, mission-aligned stakeholder partnerships
GOVERNANCE	
Strong hierarchies focused on serving investors	Holacracy, self-oranised, stakeholders actively incorporated
OWNERSHIP	
Extractive and focused on external owners	Owned collectively & shaped to serve the purpose
FINANCE	
Short-term orientation, high return	Long-term orientation, in service of social & ecolocial goals

Source: Own illustration.

Its citizen-led joint-stock cooperative structure makes *Regionalwert AG Franken* a compelling example of designing the finance of a business to pursue a social and ecological purpose. *Regionalwert AG Franken* aims to 'change the structures of food supply chains towards regional, ecological and fair production and processing from field to fork'. It functions as a citizens' stock corporation in which any citizen can buy shares to support precisely this regenerative and distributive corporate goal. *Regionalwert AG Franken* invests two-thirds of its capital in regional regenerative and distributive projects that would otherwise have little chance of receiving funding through official bank loans, such as organic farms or a greenhouse for solidarity farming. *Regionalwert AG Franken* provides up to 30% of a project's funding to support as many projects in the region as possible and to help them establish equity capital, making them eligible for additional bank financing. Many local shareholders do not seek financial return on their investment; instead, they prefer that *Regionalwert AG Franken* reinvests their money in further projects in their region. This form of financing enables regenerative agricultural projects to be implemented in the region and transforms local food production.

Similarly, *The Generation Forest*, structured as a cooperative, has developed a financial model based on a long-term investment horizon. This makes it another exemplary case within the finance design framework. The purpose of *The Generation Forest* is long-term reforestation. It enables the creation of mixed forests in Panama, with intact ecosystems, biodiversity, CO_2 sequestration, water regulation and restoration of soil fertility over a 20-year horizon. At the same time, it creates permanent jobs for local communities who maintain and preserve these forests. The patient capital approach generates expected returns of 4.5%, which consciously prioritises the organisation's regenerative value over short-term profits. *The Generation Forest*'s cooperative form of ownership, where new cooperative shares can be issued to anyone at any time, is the basis for this long-term form of investment.

In both cases, it is essential that shareholders adopt a long-term perspective on their investment rather than focusing on short-term profit maximisation. The examples of *Regionalwert AG Franken* and *The Generation Forest* illustrate how a long-term investment horizon can support sustainable long-term strategies while integrating ecological and social considerations into core business strategies. Figure 1 illustrates what it means to move from a degenerative and divisive to a regenerative and distributive business design.

Patterns and Critical Reflections

Founding a Business Based on a Regenerative and/or Distributive Purpose

The companies and organisations covered in the case studies were all founded on the basis of a regenerative and/or distributive purpose. A common feature is to have regenerative and distributive values deeply embedded in the convictions and commitments of the leaders, particularly the founders of organisations.

A founder's beliefs and values can leave a lasting imprint on a company, shaping its culture long after their departure. This is evident in the cases of *WEtell*, *Wildling Shoes*, *Sonnentor*, and *Sekem*. However, reinforcing and embedding these values structurally through the enterprise design is just as critical. For instance, strong member and employee engagement also plays a crucial role, as seen in *FoodHub* and *robinhood.store*, where members' dedication is essential to sustaining and running these organisations. It is the design of these enterprises that enables engagement to occur at this depth.

Shaping business design to deliberately reinforce the business's purpose is essential. This plays a central role in the development and establishment of innovative practices within the respective design traits, for example in the development of network design, as demonstrated by *On Purpose*, *Wildling Shoes*, *Commown*, *Sekem/Ebda* and *Sonnentor*. Moreover, it can inspire other company founders to follow this way of designing and doing business from the outset.

However, there might be limits to applying these models to other companies and organisations originally founded solely for-profit, with a focus on maximising returns to investors. We hope that the innovative practices of our case studies can exemplify how a shift within, for example, an organisation's ownership design or governance design toward a more self-organised form can serve as a first step in rethinking and reframing purpose. This, in turn, opens up possibilities for strengthening regenerative and distributive goals and unlocking strategies to pursue them with ever greater ambition.

Deep and Substantive Community Engagement

The case studies on network design focused on the community in and around the businesses, showing how this community makes this kind of business possible in the first place.

> Across all case studies, the presence of a community that supports the purpose of the business was central.

Having such a community also aligns with a long-term time horizon of investments, as seen in *The Generation Forest* and *Regionalwert AG*, or the community-owned supermarkets such as *FoodHub* in Munich or *robinhood.store* in Berlin.

Authenticity through Coherence between Purpose and Governance Design

Our case studies demonstrate that developing coherence between a business's regenerative and distributive purpose and its governance design enables a truly authentic approach.

For instance, the case study of *Mein Grundeinkommen* illustrates this: they do not only pursue the goal of a fairer distribution of time and money by raffling off a basic income but also adopt a self-organised governance design that enables the kind of freedom a basic income offers—not just for beneficiaries but also for their members.

Similarly, the case study of *Wildling Shoes* revealed that truly achieving their regenerative purpose depends on their internal governance design. By embracing self-organisation and holacracy, they create genuinely regenerative working conditions for their employees.

Supportive and Inclusive Processes for Moving to Self-Organised and Holacratic Governance

Effectively engaging employees and (where relevant) members of the business is essential when implementing a holacratic and/or self-organised governance design. Achieving this requires a focus on developing the necessary competences and skills. These were explored in the case studies of *Wigwam*, *Mein Grundeinkommen*, *robinhood.store*, *FoodHub*, *Wildling Shoes*, *WEtell* and *On Purpose*.

To avoid frustration with and the failure of new hierarchies and management structures, it is essential to allocate sufficient time and focus on engaging employees and members to understand their interests, motivations and capabilities. This was demonstrated in the case study of *Wildplastic*, which aimed to create flat hierarchies and a fair, efficient working environment but soon realised that such a transition would take time. They referred to the dangers of 'over-engineering', which slowed-down decision-making processes, as not everyone needed or wanted to be involved in every decision.

> Any changes to governance design require processes that support and empower teams, members and co-owners of an organisation (Breidenbach/Rollow 2019), as was the case with *WEtell*.

WEtell introduced a transparent wage system in October 2023 and gave this process the appropriate time and space. The founders encouraged a team of employees to co-create a new, fairer wage model. This group, which represented different parts of the company, worked through various options and gathered feedback from the entire staff to ensure the solution would be both competitive and transparent. The process was not just technical but allowed for emotional support as well. Discussing wages openly revealed how deeply money and fairness are connected, even for those who primarily view work through a values-driven lens. Ultimately, the team pro-posed three models, and after collective discussion and a company-wide vote where every employee had the right to veto, the new system was accepted unanimously.

There is a tendency across all case studies to implement or at least to experi-ment with some new and innovative governance models. These are partly referred to under the term "New Work". As covered in the introductory chapter, worldview and design are interrelated and strongly influence each other (Wahl 2022: 131). As Frederic Laloux (2016) points out, throughout history, the forms of organisation that have been invented were linked to the prevailing world view and consciousness. And whenever the view of the world has changed, new forms of organisations have been created.

According to Laloux (2016), a transition to a new form of organisation has emerged, which he calls integral, evolutionary organisations, drawing a compar-ison with living systems instead of machines. These emerging organisations are characterised by the following three breakthroughs that can already be observed (Laloux 2016: 54–55):

- **Self-leadership:** Just like complex systems in nature, evolutionary organisations function without the need for hierarchical order,
- **Wholeness**: In evolutionary organisations, all parts of the human self are rele-vant and brought to work (e.g. rational and emotional components); and
- **Evolutionary meaning:** Evolutionary organisations do not control their mem-bers, but allow them to participate in their own development, direction and meaning.

The case studies show a tendency towards the development of new forms of organi-sation across all the traits of enterprise design.

Design Traits Interact with, and Enable Each Other

Each case study contains an "Interaction with Other Design Traits" section. These illustrate the highly interactive nature of the relationship between different design traits, often with one design trait being central to enabling other traits. For instance, the case studies of *WEtell*, *WoodenValley* and *Wildplastic* demonstrate that the steward-ownership model of "Verantwortungseigentum" can be considered as a new and effective way of guaranteeing that an organisation's purpose is maintained over time.

In the case studies of *Commown*, the *FoodHub*, the *robinhood.store*, *The Generation Forest* and *Regionalwert AG Franken*, the interaction between the design traits of purpose, ownership, finance and network plays a crucial role, as each business's community enables its ownership and finance design and therefore its purpose.

Two of the case studies – *Wildling Shoes* and *Sonnentor* are family-owned. This provides them with financial independence, allowing other design elements to be woven into the business, especially into their network design.

These case studies reveal that it is possible to start with a transformation within one design trait, but to fully unlock regenerative and distributive dynamics, other design traits also need to be redesigned to reinforce the purpose.

Limited Legal Structure Options Restricting Regenerative and Distributive Dynamics

The case studies use different legal forms, including:

- limited liability company that incorporates a steward-ownership design (*WEtell*, *Wildplastic*, *OnPurpose*)
- not-for-profit limited liability company that incorporates steward-ownership design (*WoodenValley*)
- different cooperative models (*Commown*, *FoodHub*, *The Generation Forest*, *Wigwam*)
- not-for-profit, and for-profit associations (*Mein Grundeinkommen*, *EBDA*)
- civil joint-stock corporation (*Regionalwert AG Franken*)
- company under civil law (*robinhood.store*).

Yet across these, the case studies demonstrate a lack of options of legal structures in Germany, resulting in several obstacles for achieving regenerative and distributive dynamics. One main obstacle is demonstrated in the *robinhood.store* case study. Although they generate profit, which is reinvested and donated, there is no clear legal form that fully aligns with their approach. While the not-for-profit legal form cannot be adopted because it does not allow for profit-generation, the for-profit options also do not meet their needs. Another option is using the form of a company under civil law, which can work, but it does not fully align with their approach. The case of *Mein Grundeinkommen*, which uses the legal form of a not-for-profit association, exemplifies exactly this dilemma. Their legal structure forced them to suspend their needs-based salary model, and they are currently rethinking this concept.

Another challenge in the *robinhood.store* case study is the conflict between their holacracy and self-organisation model and the legal requirements of cooperatives and associations. As the forms require a management board, they complicate the implementation of a true holacratic design.

> Across the cases, there are multiple instances of legal structures not aligning with the regenerative and distributive purpose of the business, especially in relation to ownership and governance design. New and adapted legal structures are needed in Germany to overcome such challenges.

Innovating Beyond Conventional Business Thinking

A key characteristic of these case studies is their pursuit of unconventional ideas and solutions. Often, these ideas are considered impossible by mainstream businesses such as offering biodynamic food at an affordable price for all. The case of *Sekem/EBDA*, with the introduction of the whole credit system demonstrates how a regenerative business design serves both the environment and people by making biodynamic food accessible and affordable to all.

Similarly, *Commown* drives change across their industry through the establishment of a circular ecosystem. Instead of following the patterns of short-term incentives to sell new products (e.g. mobile phones), *Commown* established a rental model that enables using products "for as long as possible". This model contributes to transforming the entire incentive structure within their market and industry.

A third example is *Regionalwert AG Franken*, which uses patient and community-focused investment models to enable ecological and social projects that are often rejected under traditional investment approaches.

These examples illustrate that innovation is possible when businesses and entrepreneurs are willing to go beyond conventional business thinking.

Intertwining of Redesigning Business and Inner Development

Our case studies demonstrate that the inner development of organisations and businesses – towards anchoring their regenerative and distributive purpose within their design traits – is closely linked to the inner development of the founders and the community or cooperative members.

These inner development traits align with the **Inner Development Goals (IDG) Framework**, which focuses on five key categories: Being, Thinking, Relating, Collaborating, and Acting (IDG 2021). The way these individuals **think, relate, collaborate, and act** significantly differs from mainstream business practices, highlighting the importance of inner development in driving business transformation.

- Focus on **openness and learning mindset**: Willing to learn and discover new forms of regional production with fair and circular supply chains. For example, Anna Yona from *Wildling Shoes* shared how the organisation worked and experimented with new and unconventional materials such as washi tape or dog wool.
- A different way of thinking, focusing on **long-term orientation and visioning**: The time horizon embedded in the mindsets and values of those supporting the specific regenerative and distributive purpose can be critical. For example, it became clear that the financial design trait of *The Generation Forest* and *Regionalwert AG Franken* both depend on investors who take a patient approach to financial returns. Either as cooperative members or as shareholders, these investors view their investment as a contribution to intergenerational justice and to enabling fair and biologically dynamic food production in their respective regions.
- **Trust**: This value was mentioned in all network design case studies as one of the central elements for collaborating within their communities. The way trustful relationships are grounded differs from case to case, including practices like building partnerships based on personal connections, as seen in *Wildling Shoes*, or extending trust to all members, as *On Purpose* does.

These characteristics correspond to different sub-dimensions of the Inner Development Goals Framework which consists of the five categories: Being, Thinking, Relating, Collaborating, Acting (IDG 2021). They emphasise the importance and intertwining of the inner development of the people involved in redesigning a business towards regenerative and distributive dynamics.

Patterns of Responsibility

Iris Marion Young (2006) identifies four parameters of responsibility for assigning co-responsibility in changing global economic structures: power, privileged position, interest and collective ability.

Her concept of co-responsibility, which focuses on changing existing global structures, can also be applied to the internal design of companies and organisations. The key lies in combining external responsibility, namely the pursuit of a regenerative and distributive purpose, with internal responsibility – the regenerative and distributive design of internal structures such as financial structures, governance structures, network structures or ownership structures. This combination enables the creation of coherence both internally and externally, facilitating real change towards a regenerative and distributive economy.

Young's **criterion of power** relates to varying degrees of potential and actual possibility, such as access to resources and the ability to influence processes and their outcomes. At an internal level, our case studies show that redesigning businesses, e.g. through joint ownership structures or moves towards self-organisation, can lead to a more even distribution of power, thus enabling the adoption of more ambitious socially and ecologically focused strategies. However, our case studies also demonstrate that the power of conventional market players can hinder regenerative organisations from achieving their goals. *Wildplastic*, for instance, actively lobbies for broader policy change to level the playing field for businesses focused on driving social and ecological solutions. However, they face opposition from established, powerful and loud industry giants who benefit from the status quo.

Young's **criterion of privileged position is also relevant.** A notable feature across all case studies is that they originate from German-speaking countries. Given that these companies are located in the Global North and their supporters, including co-operative members, are also citizens of Global North countries, it can be assumed that the actors involved in these companies occupy a relatively privileged position within global structures. This position places greater moral responsibility on them to contribute to organised corrective efforts "because they are able to adapt to changed circumstances without suffering serious deprivation" (Young 2006: 128). Our case studies demonstrate that opportunities to contribute to regenerative and distributive businesses exist and can be created, especially for those in more privileged positions.

Finally, throughout the case studies, Young's **criterions of interest in transformation** and **collective ability** emerge as the most important parameters to unlock co-responsibility for redesigning businesses towards social and ecological goals. The high level of interest from the founders and the community members enables a collective capacity within a broad community of people, who become integral to the businesses' deep design. This insight can encourage organisations globally to commit to change, even if they initially appear powerless and unprivileged.[1]

---

1   You can find further examples of case studies based on Doughnut Design in other countries on the Doughnut Economics Action Lab website: https://doughnuteconomics.org/tools/dou ghnut-design-for-business-case-studies.

Final Considerations

The selected case studies go well beyond sustainable practices and provide valuable insights for founders, communities and businesses worldwide. They demonstrate the diverse possibilities of enterprise design that prioritise regenerative and distributive goals. In turn, they illustrate ways to contribute to a transformation towards an economy that meets the needs of all within the means of the living planet, while also operating as a profitable and innovative business. All our cases are situated in the zone of distributive and regenerative design, helping to move business towards a safe and just space in which humanity can develop and thrive. Figure 2 summarises our approach and puts it vis-à-vis with conventional degenerative and divisive business designs.

Figure 2: Regenerative and Distributive Design

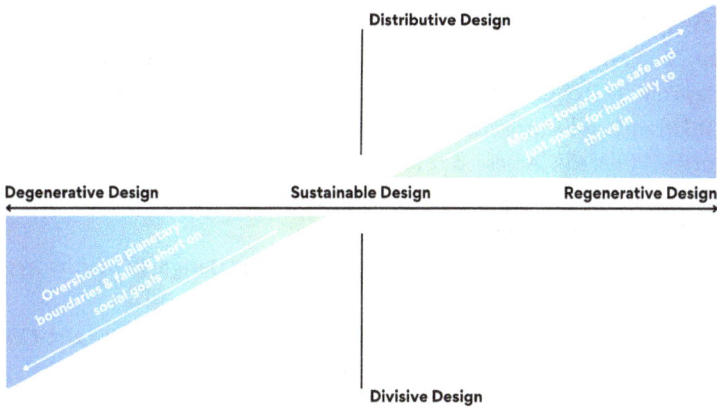

Source: own source based on Raworth 2017 and Mang/Reed 2012: 10.

In addition, we want to highlight that a distributive and regenerative design goes beyond a corporate sustainability, which is often understood as simply meeting the minimum legal and regulatory requirements, or as a way to do less harm. In contrast pursuing socially distributive and ecologically regenerative goals is about actively growing the benefits that can be generated through the business.

However, now more than ever, as climate change devastates communities and economic inequality continues to grow, it is crucial to leverage the influence of businesses to serve a purpose rooted in responsibility (George et al., 2023). The case studies presented in this book have succeeded in translating their values into various design traits and thus anchoring them structurally. We hope that our book serves as a guide for businesses towards a transformation in their deep design, so as to unlock the ambitious action needed to address the social and ecological crisis that we face.

References

Breidenbach, J., Rollow, B. (2019): New Work needs Inner Work. Ein Handbuch für Unternehmen auf dem Weg zur Selbstorganisation, 2. Auflage. München.

Doughnut Economics Action Lab (2025): Doughnut Design for business case studies, https://doughnuteconomics.org/tools/doughnut-design-for-business-case-studies, [Accessed 28 April 2025].

George, G., Haas, M. R., McGahan, A. M., Schillebeeckx, S. J., & Tracey, P. (2023): Purpose in the for-profit firm: A review and framework for management research. Journal of Management, 49(6), 1841–1869.

Jordan, T., Reams, J., Stålne, K., Greca, S., Henriksson, J. A., Björkman, T., & Dawson, T. (2021): Inner development goals: Background, method and the IDG framework, https://drive.google.com/file/d/13fcf9xmYrX9wrsh3PC3aeRDsorWsWCpA/edit, Accessed 12 March 2025].

Laloux, F. (2016): Reinventing organizations. Ein illustrierter Leitfaden sinnstiftender Formen der Zusammenarbeit. München.

Mang P., Reed B. (2012): Regenerative Development and Design, DOI: 10.1007/978-1-4614-5828-9_303.

Raworth, K. (2017): Doughnut Economics: Seven Ways to Think Like a 21st-Century Economist. London.

Wahl, D. C. (2022): Designing Regenerative Cultures. Axminster.

Young, I. M. (2006): Responsibility and global justice: A social connection model. Social Philosophy and Policy, 23(1), 102–130. https://doi.org/10.1017/S0265052506060043.

Author Information

Ines Bauer received her M.A. in International Cultural and Business Studies from the University of Passau, Germany, where she specialised in Sustainability Management and Intercultural Communication. She completed her master's thesis at the Institute of Applied Ethics in Business and Education. Following her studies, she gained professional experience in project management at a consultancy for climate protection and sustainability.

Jannes Kormann currently works as a project manager for digitalisation and organisational development in the further education and training sector. He graduated in business administration and gained experience in research and practice in social entrepreneurship and new work. He is Fellow of the On Purpose Community in Berlin, which connects individuals and companies to work together for a social and ecological transformation of the economy.

Laura Reinstorf drives inclusive entrepreneurship at Social Impact gGmbH through a transnational pilot project. With an academic background in International Cultural and Business Studies focusing on sustainability and business ethics, she is passionate about connecting global frameworks with local realities to foster sustainable initiatives.

Nelly Rahimy is a PhD student at the University of Passau, focusing on the intersection of corporate purpose and sustainability and works as a Research Assistant at the Institute of Applied Ethics in Business and Education. In this role, she made a substantial contribution to the publication of this book through both her research and her organisational support. She was also part of the third-party funded programme 'Passau – the Entrepreneurial Campus (PATEC)' and in this function coordinated the operational team. Moreover, she works as a start-up coach for sustainable enterprises and has supported ventures in Germany, Hungary, and Austria.

Niklas Tiesler graduated in Caritas Science and Values-based Management (M.A.) at the University of Passau with a focus on the sustainable financing of organisations. He works in the field of sustainable finance and investments at the 'Bank für Kirche und Diakonie', a German Christian bank.

Sarah Keil works as a Climate Protection Coordinator at the Energy Agency in Göppingen, Germany. She graduated with a Master's degree in International Cultural and Business Studies at the University of Passau, during which she focused on sustainability in the field of economics. She further worked as a student assistant at the Institute of Applied Ethics in Business and Education for one year. In this role, she supported the publishing of this book.

Sina Kehrwieder studied International Cultural and Business Studies as well as British Studies in Potsdam, Southampton, Berlin and Passau. Her academic interests focus on theatre, sustainable business and intercultural perspectives.

Index

GPSR Authorized Representative: Easy Access System Europe, Mustamäe tee
50, 10621 Tallinn, Estonia, gpsr.requests@easproject.com

www.ingramcontent.com/pod-product-compliance
Lightning Source LLC
Chambersburg PA
CBHW070104030426
42335CB00016B/2003